100 THINGS
LOUISVILLE FANS
SHOULD KNOW & DO
BEFORE THEY DIE

100 THINGS
LOUISVILLE FANS
SHOULD KNOW & DO
BEFORE THEY DIE

Mike Rutherford

TRIUMPH
BOOKS

Library of Congress Cataloging-in-Publication Data

Names: Rutherford, Mike
Title: 100 things Louisville fans should know & do before they die / Mike Rutherford.
Other titles: One hundred things Louisville fans should know and do before they die | A hundred things Louisville fans should know and do before they die
Description: Chicago, Illinois : Triumph Books LLC, [2017]
Identifiers: LCCN 2017021461 | ISBN 9781629374192
Subjects: LCSH: University of Louisville—Basketball—History. | Louisville Cardinals (Basketball)—History. | University of Louisville—Basketball—Miscellanea. | Louisville Cardinals (Basketball)—Miscellanea.
Classification: LCC GV885.43.U53 R87 2017 | DDC 796.323/630976944—dc23 LC record available at https://lccn.loc.gov/2017021461

This book is available in quantity at special discounts for your group or organization. For further information, contact:
Triumph Books LLC
814 North Franklin Street
Chicago, Illinois 60610
(312) 337-0747
www.triumphbooks.com

Printed in U.S.A.
ISBN: 978-1-62937-419-2
Design by Patricia Frey
Photos courtesy of AP Images unless otherwise indicated

To my wife, Mary, my family and friends, Tobiah Hopper's oversized undershirt, Otis George's pick against Washington, and everyone who has supported me and read my nonsense over the years.

Contents

Foreword

The thought of being a college coach, successful or not, didn't cross my mind much as a kid growing up in New York. The professional game dominates the basketball landscape in that part of the country, and as a result, my dream became pacing the sidelines inside Madison Square Garden as the head coach of the New York Knicks.

Every stop in my coaching career has been extremely special to me, including the two seasons I spent as the head coach of the Knicks. Having said that, there has been no stop more special than the University of Louisville. The people, the fans, and the enthusiasm throughout the entire athletic program are what make this place so unique.

Louisville is a different kind of basketball heaven than the one I grew up in. The city has been the top television market for college basketball for more than a decade. Despite not having a professional team, Louisville is also perennially ESPN's top television market for the NBA draft. Regardless of the opponent, more than 20,000 fans are going to pack the KFC Yum! Center each and every time the Cardinals take the court. That's special.

I think I love the game more today than I did in my 20s or 30s. That's not because of some age-inspired enlightenment; it's because of the players and the people I've been able to coach with and for at the University of Louisville. When you've been coaching for as long as I have and you still can't wait to get to work in the morning, that's only because of the people you have surrounded yourself with.

To call this job "work" would be an injustice; it's a privilege. It's a privilege because of the athletes who are so willing to put in the time and the effort to make themselves the best they can be.

It's a privilege because of the five-star people with whom I get to associate on a daily basis.

Louisville basketball was special before I arrived in 2001. What's been amazing about the years that have followed has been to see how special this place has become for all sports. I've been fortunate enough to be here while Jeff Walz has turned the women's basketball program into a national powerhouse. I've seen Dan McDonnell bring Louisville baseball to the brink of a national title and I've seen Ken Lolla do the same thing with men's soccer. I've also seen every other coach and program grow thanks to the leadership of our tremendous athletic director Tom Jurich, who has taken us from Conference USA to the Big East and now to the ACC.

The pages that follow will give you an opportunity to learn more about the people, events, and traditions that have helped make University of Louisville athletics so successful. That success extends from the hardwood to memorable victories in bowl games to All-Americans and Olympic champions.

I could not be more proud to have contributed to that legacy and I look forward to contributing more in the years to come.

Go Cards.

—Rick Pitino

Introduction

They say if a seed is planted early enough, then the roots will spread too deeply to ever be unearthed. Typically the saying is used in reference to a person's religion or some other core belief about why we're here and why we act the way that we do. In Kentucky, and Louisville in particular, it works just as well when the subject is basketball.

I can't tell you when precisely I "decided" to become a Louisville fan. My guess is that many of you reading this can't either. All I know is there are tapes of me asking, which team is "the good guys," very soon after the time I first learned to talk. All I know is there are videos of me in a U of L basketball uniform performing mock starting lineups at an age when psychologists say I couldn't form conscious memories. All I know is that for as long as I can recall, Cardinals sports have been something that I've cared about far more than I care about most things.

For all of us, the timing of our entrance into this world comes with some positives and negatives. As far as my Louisville basketball fandom is concerned, most would say I was born at the perfectly imperfect time. I missed the '80s. There's no way around it. My parents hadn't met one another when the Cards cut down the nets in 1980, and I was hardly a living, breathing being when they did it again six years later. That's something of a bummer.

On the flip side, I didn't have to suffer through the years of futility that the other Cardinals sports endured in the decades before my arrival. Instead, from Louisville's playing miserable opponents in front of small crowds inside a minor league base-ball stadium to producing major bowl victories and a Heisman Trophy winner, I was able to watch and appreciate every step of the Louisville football team's climb to national relevance. I was able to experience programs like Louisville baseball and men's soccer go from not even being worthy of a paragraph in the local paper to feared national powerhouses. And when the Cardinals finally got back to the top of the college basketball mountain in 2013, I was able to appreciate it in a different way than I would have if I had been spoiled by years and years of top-notch success.

Like many who are cut from the same cloth, I often associate years and life events with specific U of L sports memories. My first year at a new elementary school was the year Louisville beat Alabama in the Fiesta Bowl. My senior prom was the night before the Cards were stunned by Butler in the second round of the NCAA Tournament. The year I got engaged was "The Year of the Cardinal."

Several months after that engagement, on the day of my actual wedding, one of my best friends had a final question for me before I walked out the door and across the street to the church where I would say "I do."

"When were you more nervous: now or right before the [2013] national championship?"

Easy answer.

"Before the national championship game. I'm pretty confident she's going to say yes. I was not as confident that we were going to beat Michigan."

My wife grew up about an hour south of Louisville and was the rarest of Kentucky sports fans who never picked a side in the rivalry between the Wildcats and the Cardinals. That changed after she moved to Louisville for college. The seed doesn't always have to be planted early for the roots to spread deep. This place, and this athletic program, has a way of getting in your blood.

Included in the pages ahead are 100 stories, profiles, or suggestions pertaining to Louisville sports—some you're likely familiar with; others you almost certainly are not. Some are silly; some are serious. Some are told objectively, and others are told from my perspective. I hope you enjoy, and thank you so much for reading.

1 Darrell Griffith

During the first half of the 1970s, it became a well-known fact within the city of Louisville that the area's next great basketball player was going to be a young man by the name of Darrell Griffith.

Griffith's playground exploits had been talked about since before the time he was a teenager. Years later, he became a full-fledged star at local power Male High School, carrying the Bulldogs to the 1975 Kentucky state championship and blossoming into a player who was recruited by every major college program in the country along the way.

What attracted spectators most to Griffith's games wasn't his teams' margins of victory or how many points their best player scored, but the fact that every time this kid stepped on the court, people in the crowd felt like they were about to see something they'd never seen before.

In the December 21, 1975 edition of *The Louisville Courier-Journal*, then-local sportswriter Dave Kindred recounted a play he'd seen the 17-year-old Griffith make in a game earlier that year.

Griffith's command of his body cost him one basket in that game. He went up to catch a lob pass. In the air, he faked a shot, double-pumping. As he landed and started back up, referee Jim Ashmore called traveling when, in fact, Griffith had not taken a single step. He'd just done something mortals couldn't do, and the referee was fooled.

Similar tales became commonplace across the city of Louisville as the legend of Griffith continued to grow. When Darrell was ready in 1976 to make the announcement that Cardinals fans had been dreaming of hearing for the past several years, he decided to toss in a quote that would enhance his local celebrity: "I'm going to play basketball for the University of Louisville and I plan on winning several national championships for my city."

It was a brash declaration that seemed out of character for the blossoming superstar at the time. At Male, Griffith had always been more likely to let his play do the talking then engage an opponent in some trash talking. Now he was openly discussing leading Louisville to its first national title before he ever donned a Cardinals uniform.

There were those in the city who didn't like the arrogance, even if it came from a homegrown talent. Not counted among that group was Griffith's new head coach. "That's what he wanted to do and that's what he expected to do," said Denny Crum. "He was good enough to do that, so I wasn't upset about that. As a matter of fact, it pleased me. You're thinking in terms of winning and you kind of want that word to get out that he's promising it. And what I would say was, come along and help. Help us get there and do that."

Before he arrived on campus, Griffith had one last headline to make in order for his arrival to be met with as much pomp and circumstance as possible. During tryouts for the 1976 United States Olympic basketball team, to which Griffith was the only high school player invited, the future Cardinal recorded a standing vertical leap of 48 inches. The jump was the highest ever officially recorded at the time and was entered into the *Guinness Book of World Records*.

At Louisville, Griffith was the rare No. 1 recruit who not only lived up the hype but exceeded it. Despite being a freshman on a team loaded with veterans, Griffith emerged as Louisville's fourth-leading scorer in 1976–77, averaging 12.8 points on a Cardinals team that would finish 21–7. He then turned into a full-fledged star, leading Louisville in scoring as both a sophomore and a junior, and helping the team to a Metro Conference Tournament and regular-season championship. Griffith's high-flying style was also making him a household name outside of Louisville. Or rather, his "Dr. Dunkenstein" nickname was becoming a household name.

Although many assumed that Griffith's famous nickname was the product of the amount of national coverage he received in college, it actually predated his days as a Louisville Cardinal. "I grew up in the funkadelic Parliament era," Griffith told ESPN in 2003. "And, you know, George Clinton had a character called Dr. Funkenstein. And it kind of came from that. My brother and the homeboys in the neighborhood sort of tagged me with the nickname."

Heading into his senior season, Griffith had already secured a place for himself in the Louisville basketball record books, but his three Cardinals teams had combined to win just two games in the NCAA Tournament. There was only one year left for the Derby City's favorite son to make good on his teenage promise.

For the entirety of his senior season, Griffith played like a man with an entire city on his back. He set still-standing records for the most points in a season (825), for the highest-scoring average in a conference season (22.4 points), for the most field goals made (349) and attempted (631) in a season, and set a record for steals in a season (86), a mark that wasn't broken until 2012.

More important than any of that, at least to Griffith, was that he led Louisville to a 33–3 record and the program's first national championship. He scored 23 points in a memorable national title game that saw the Cardinals top UCLA 59–54 and afterward he was named the Final Four's Most Outstanding Player. It was a trophy the consensus first-team All-American could set on his mantle next to the 1980 Wooden and Sporting News Player of the Year awards.

Still, there was one award that Griff never minded admitting brought him more joy than all the others combined. "I could have won 10 NBA championships, and it still wouldn't have compared to winning that national championship," Griffith said. "Especially since that was the first one and it was my last chance to do what I'd promised to do. We got it done, and there was no better feeling in the world."

Griffith's No. 35 jersey was retired in a ceremony soon after the end of the 1980 season. He left U of L as the school's career scoring leader (2,333 points), single-season scoring leader, steals leader, and first recipient of a major National Player of the Year award. He finished his college career, having scored in double figures in 41 consecutive games and he helped Louisville to a combined record of 101–25 over his four seasons as a Cardinal.

Griffith was selected with second overall pick of the 1980 NBA Draft by the Utah Jazz. The Jazz also retired Griffith's No. 35 after a successful 11-year career that included being honored as the 1981 NBA Rookie of the Year and a career scoring average of 16.2 ppg.

Following his retirement from basketball in 1991, "Louisville's Living Legend" returned home to be with his family and venture into the business world. "Louisville's always going to be home, always," Griffith said. "The city made me what I am, and I'm forever glad that I was able to give back by bringing it that first national championship."

Denny Crum

If you tried to pitch it as a screenplay or a manuscript today, no one would buy the story of Denny Crum and Louisville. Executives would criticize it for being overly fanciful and unbelievable. They would write it off as a sequence of events that would never occur in the modern world. They'd probably be right.

A West Coast lifer who was groomed by the most legendary coach in college basketball to take over the most dominant dynasty the sport had ever seen, he passed on the opportunity in favor of sticking with a program from Kentucky that had never won a national title. He was man who had been the first to dare to poke and prod the state's superpower—and ultimately get his way. He was a man who felt so much loyalty to his program that even when he was given an exit that he deemed unceremonious and unfair he couldn't bring himself to coach anywhere else. Instead, he decided to retire and spend his free time giving back to the school and attending each and every home game.

Again, it's a story that has no place in the reality of the modern world.

Denzel Edwin "Denny" Crum was born in San Fernando, California, where he spent his early years dreaming of playing college basketball for the UCLA Bruins. Even though Crum developed into one of the most highly touted high school players in the Los Angeles area, John Wooden—who wasn't yet known as "the Wizard of Westwood"—passed on the opportunity to offer Crum a scholarship.

Disappointed but not deterred, Crum enrolled at Los Angeles Pierce College, where he put up gaudy numbers as a star guard on the school's basketball team. Near the end of his sophomore season, a stroke of luck helped Crum bring his dream home. "After my sophomore year, our school president, John Sheppard, helped me out," Crum told the *Los Angeles Daily News* in 2010. "He went to the same church as John Wooden, so he told him how badly I wanted to play there. He brought him to one of our games—we didn't even have our own gym, we played at Canoga Park High. I guess [Wooden] liked me because he invited me to their practice and training table and called to set me up with some tickets to watch the Bruins play over at the Pan Pacific Auditorium. I had offers from Washington and Arizona State, but I still wanted to go to UCLA.

"It was funny. We were at training table. I was there with Coach Wooden and [trainer] Ducky Drake and after the meal, Coach Wooden just says, 'Well, are you coming or not?' He didn't say anything about a scholarship covering this or that or anything else. And I just said, 'Yeah, I guess I am.'"

Playing on a pair of Bruins teams that were highly successful but unable to finish ahead of Cal in the Pacific Coast Conference, Crum was honored with the Irv Pohlmeyer Memorial Trophy for being UCLA's most outstanding first-year varsity player in 1956–57. A year later he received the Bruin Bench Award—given annually to the team's most improved player.

After graduation, Crum returned to Pierce and spent four seasons as the school's basketball coach. He then returned to UCLA, where he first served as the program's freshman team coach, and then later as Wooden's primary assistant coach and head recruiter. With Crum on staff, UCLA won seven national championships in eight seasons and compiled a total record of 221 wins to just 15 losses. Then in 1971, Crum left the greatest dynasty that college basketball has ever seen to take the head coaching job at Louisville. "I never had any doubt Denny would succeed as a coach," Wooden said in the fall of 2000. "Of any player I coached, Denny was probably the most cut out to be a coach."

In his first season as a Division I head coach, Crum guided Louisville to just its second Final Four appearance in program history. The opponent, naturally, was UCLA, and the Bruins easily dispatched the Cardinals in a 96–77 blowout and went on to win its sixth straight national title.

Crum had U of L in a much better place in 1975, when the Cardinals and Bruins once again met in the national semifinals. Despite being in control for the bulk of the game, a disastrous final minute of regulation and a missed free throw in the closing seconds of overtime ultimately doomed Louisville in a heartbreaking 75–74 defeat. After the game, Wooden stunned everyone by announcing that the national championship game two days later would be his last before retirement. Crum was immediately tabbed by the media as the next in line at UCLA, but he put an end to the speculation before it could gain too much momentum. "I hadn't yet accomplished what I wanted to at Louisville," Crum explained to *The New York Times* in 1986. "And when I was offered the UCLA job after Gene Bartow left a couple of years later, I decided that I loved Louisville and didn't want to leave. I think I probably could have done the job at UCLA better than anyone else. It's never easy following a legend, but because I knew the people and the situation there, I don't think I would've had the problems other people had.

"Through the years, I've learned to be patient. Coach Wooden had tremendous patience. When he said, 'Goodness gracious, sakes alive,' he was swearing at you. He was at the end of the line with you as a player. And as an assistant coach, I had my conflicts with him on the bench as to what to do and who to put in the game. But that was good instead of bad. There's no value to having a yes man as an assistant coach. You need opinion from your assistants."

Crum's belief in his own abilities and newfound affection for Louisville resulted in the Cardinals morphing into college basketball's newest superpower. Conversely, it would be 20 years after Wooden's retirement before UCLA won another national championship.

Louisville's first national title would come in 1980, when senior Darrell Griffith—the winner of the National Player of the Year award that bears Wooden's name—carried the Cards to a 59–54 toppling of (who else?) UCLA. U of L returned to the Final Four in 1982 and 1983 and then claimed its second NCAA Tournament championship with a 72–69 triumph against top-ranked Duke in 1986. When the 1980s came to a close, *Sports Illustrated* named Louisville as its "Team of the Decade" for college basketball.

Success continued for Crum in the 1990s, just not at the unprecedented level that his fan base was now accustomed to. Louisville routinely played its way into the second weekend of the tournament, but played in just one regional final under Crum after the '86 championship season.

With Louisville struggling to land blue chip talent and in the midst of what would be just the third losing season in Crum's 30 years as coach, things got ugly at the start of the 21st century. U of L athletic director Tom Jurich had done little to hide the fact that he believed the basketball program needed to go in a different direction, and Crum had made his own thoughts on the matter known. "You can't say you don't know if it can happen," Crum said on February 22, 2001, about the speculation that he would be fired if he refused to accept a buyout. "It can happen to anybody at any time. The justification for it is another issue. Whatever decision is made, then they'll have to live with it."

Two weeks later, Crum called a press conference to announce his retirement. His words said that he was ending his tenure at Louisville after 30 years because he wanted to. His sullen, almost resentful demeanor said otherwise.

As he stood before the Louisville media, Crum was the only active coach in college basketball who had already been inducted into the Naismith Memorial Basketball Hall of Fame, an honor he received in 1994. He was also one of just two active coaches who had won multiple national championships. None of this made the surprising changing of the guard any easier to stomach for those whose closets were lined with mostly red and black attire.

Never one to carry a grudge, any ill feelings from Crum about the way things ended dissolved soon after the start of Crum's retirement. He discovered a life outside of basketball, one dominated by fishing and a local radio show that he co-hosted with Joe B. Hall, the former Kentucky head coach whom Crum had ribbed incessantly about his refusal to play his teams in the early 1980s. He also continued to attend Cardinals home games (and away games when he could) and always received some of the loudest ovations of the night when he showed up on the big screen during a timeout.

In 2007 Louisville held a ceremony in which it named the court inside Freedom Hall "Denny Crum Court." It was a deserving honor for the man who had taken a program with limited history and won two national titles, reached six Final Fours, made 23 NCAA Tournament appearances, and won 675 total games in 30 seasons.

So how does Crum explain the story that would never be accepted even as a work of fiction in this day and age? How does he explain turning down the chance to assume Wooden's throne at UCLA or not leveraging his status as college basketball's most dominant coach into an NBA gig during the 1980s? "You can't spend 30 years at a place and not grow to love it or you'd have been gone long before," Crum said. "The fact that I loved it here and they seemed to want me here and it just seemed to go on for a long time, that's special. It's not a common thing in this business for coaches to stay at one place. There's only a few of us who get a chance to do that."

"What I never expected when I originally took the job here was the love I developed for this university and the people of this city. After a while, there was just no place else I wanted to be."

3 The Doctors of Dunk

Though most commonly associated with Louisville's 1979–80 national championship team, it's the 1976–77 Cardinals squad that actually holds the distinction of being the first "Doctors of Dunk."

The nickname doesn't have a particularly compelling origin story, unless you're talking to someone with a knack for embellishing facts. The first mention of it in print came on December 28, 1977, when Darrell "Dr. Dunkenstein" Griffith explained to a reporter from the Associated Press why the team had been sporting warm-up jackets with a dunking Cardinals logo on the back of them for that night's 113–85 trouncing of La Salle. "The fans gave us the nickname 'Doctors of Dunk' last year, so we want to give them something to get wild on," Griffith said. "I came up with the idea because I wanted something to go along with our image."

Despite big man Wiley Brown's preference for being known as the Doctors of Hustle," the "Doctors of Dunk" epithet wound up becoming one of the best-known sports brands of the 1980s. In fact, Griffith believes the sequence of events originated branding in college basketball. "We were the first team to brand," Griffith said. "You talk about Phi Slama Jama, you talk about the Fab Five. The first college team to be branded was the Doctors of Dunk. We didn't have a lot of games on ESPN back then so we didn't get the advantage of the press that Houston and Michigan had, but we were a road show."

The "road show" phenomenon that was Cardinals basketball in the late 1970s and '80s was a product of both previously unseen athleticism and ideal timing. In a move that most believed was a direct result of the dominance of UCLA center Lew Alcindor (later Kareem Abdul-Jabbar), the NCAA banned dunking from 1967 to 1976. Its return to the game reinvigorated the sport's fans and left them hungry for all the above-the-rim action they could get. It was perfect timing for both Griffith and Louisville to capitalize. "The dunk had been away from the game for a few years because of Kareem Abdul-Jabbar," Griffith said. "Dunking wasn't allowed. You couldn't dunk during my whole high school career. Then, before my freshman season at the University of Louisville, the NCAA reversed the rule. So it was showtime for me. Dunking just fit right into my game and right with our style of play at Louisville, and so that's how the nickname and the whole thing came about."

Griffith and his 48-inch vertical leap were well-known across the country long before he completed one of the most famous dunks in NCAA Tournament history. In the second half of the team's 1980 regional final victory over LSU, Griffith found himself all alone on a fast break and capitalized on the opportunity to perform. He leapt, windmilled the ball around his entire body, and then slammed home what CBS announcer Al McGuire referred to as the "around the world" dunk. "When he got that dunk, it was like someone threw a javelin in my heart," former LSU coach Dale Brown told *The Kansas City Star* in 2014. "We recruited Darrell Griffith, and when I first saw him, I thought I'd never have to ever meet an astronaut or a cosmonaut,. He was further out in space than they were."

While Griffith was the ringleader, the Doctors of Dunk brand never could have caught on without the help of others. That help came in the form of fellow high-flyers Rodney and Scooter McCray, who later passed the torch to guys such as Milt Wagner and Lancaster Gordon. "[Dunking] became our culture, and that's still our culture," Griffith said. "The game changes, but Louisville is still a team that likes to get out on the break and throw down on you. I like to think I had something to do with that."

4 Luke Hancock Shoots Louisville to the 2013 Title

The groans that echoed throughout the KFC Yum! Center in November 2012 weren't Luke Hancock's fault, but in hindsight, it's hard to blame the Louisville fans who were making them either.

Hancock, an unheralded recruit out of high school, made the decision to transfer from George Mason to Louisville following head coach Jim Larrañaga's move to Miami after the 2010–11 season. His respectable averages of 7.7 and 10.9 points per game in two seasons as a Patriot led most to believe that he could serve as a solid role player on a far more talented U of L team.

Expectations for Hancock remained reserved until the early part of the 2011–12 season that he was forced to sit out because of NCAA transfer rules. It was then that Rick Pitino made the conscious decision to raise the bar. "You guys don't get the chance to see him every day, but Luke Hancock is the best player on this team," Pitino said during a November press conference. "He's mentally the best player on this team and he's physically the best player on this team. He's unlike any player I've ever coached."

Similar comments followed for the next several months. Louisville fans well-versed in what they refer to as "Pitino-Speak" still allowed their head coach's comments to seep into their subconscious and drastically alter their expectations for Hancock's debut season as a Cardinal.

The Most Outstanding Player of the 2013 Final Four, Luke Hancock attempts a three-pointer in Louisville's victory against Wichita State. (*USA TODAY* Sports Images)

Even with the "Hancock hype" circulating throughout the city, Cardinals fans were surprised to hear that the junior transfer named as a co-captain before the season. He would share the honor with Peyton Siva, a three-year starter who most expected to be the team's lone leader in his final year at U of L.

The "Captain Luke Hancock" who was going to make Louisville fans forget all about the graduated sharpshooting duo of Kyle Kuric and Chris Smith did not show up when the season began He attempted 29 three-pointers in U of L's first four games and he made just four. He finally broke out of the slump with a 19-point performance against Missouri…and then failed to score a single point in the two games after.

Cardinals fans quickly took to the Internet to declare that Hancock "wasn't a Louisville-caliber player." There were also a handful of instances at home games where the "oooos" from the crowd weren't shows of support in the form of a first-name cheer. Hancock admitted that he was aware of the unrest but downplayed its significance and vowed to not change his game. He appeared more comfortable in a reserve role and provided a solid lift off the bench for a Cardinals team that began to hit its stride once the second half of conference play rolled around.

The first indication that Hancock could wind up having a significant impact on any 2013 postseason success that Louisville might have came during the Cardinals' first game of March. U of L found itself in a dogfight with a Syracuse team that had defeated the Cardinals at the Yum Center with a last-minute flurry a month earlier. Pitino's team had gone on to lose two more one-possession games in the succeeding three weeks, leading fans and analysts alike to wonder whether or not this was a team capable of performing when the lights were the brightest.

With Louisville and Syracuse deadlocked at 53 and less than a minute to play, the man Cardinals fans had wanted off the team just months earlier was the one with the ball in his hands. Hancock drilled a highly contested three-pointer from the left corner, his fourth three of the game, to put U of L up for good. "Cool Hand Luke," a nickname that would have been tossed around only ironically a few weeks earlier, was born.

Once the physical tools began to manifest, the leadership qualities emerged too. The latter was never more evident than when sophomore guard Kevin Ware broke his right leg during the first half of Louisville's Elite Eight showdown with Duke. While the rest of his teammates understandably turned away from one of the most gruesome injuries the sports world has ever seen live, Hancock instinctively sprinted into action, grabbing Ware's hand and saying a quick prayer. "Lord, watch over us and let Kevin be okay during this tough time. The Lord does everything for a reason, and He will get us through this," Hancock said.

Ware, who was attempting to fight off shock at the time, expressed days later just how much Hancock's actions allowed him to stay strong in front of the rest of his teammates. "I really, really want to thank Luke," Ware said at a press conference three days later. "Because Luke jumped right on the scene like the captain that he is and just said a prayer for me. When he was saying that prayer, what was going through my head was I'm either going to cry and my team is going to be devastated and we probably won't win this game, or I'm going to just try to say some words to get us through."

If Hancock isn't strong for Ware, then Ware probably isn't strong for his team. If Ware isn't strong for his team, then his team probably doesn't go on to drill Duke by 22.

All of this sets the stage for what Hancock did in the national championship game on April 8, 2013. With his team unable to keep Michigan from hitting anything and everything in the first half, it was again Hancock—the man still bogged down with his fair share of haters—who rose to the occasion. He drilled four three-pointers in the final three minutes of the first half, almost single-handedly trimming a 12-point deficit to just one at the break. Though Michigan put more of a premium on defending Hancock in the second half, he still found a way to kill the Wolverines, most notably using his patented pump fake to draw a fourth foul on big man Mitch McGary.

When all was said and done, Luke Hancock, the man who "wasn't good enough to play at Louisville," had matched a career high with 22 points and become the first nonstarter to ever be named the Most Outstanding Player of a Final Four. Making the night that much better was the fact that Hancock was able to play in front of his father. "I'm so excited for this team to be in this situation. It's been a long road," Hancock said after the game. "There's really no way to describe how I feel that my dad was here. It's hard to put into words. I'm so excited that he was here. It just means a lot." His father would ultimately lose his battle with cancer just months later.

5 Tom Jurich

It's not hard to make the case that every single aspect of University of Louisville athletics has been improved since the day Tom Jurich arrived as athletic director in October 1997. There are counterarguments to be made, sure, but the majority of those are both minor gripes and personal in nature. The reality is that Jurich has taken an athletics program once known solely for its men's basketball team and playing in eyesore stadiums and reinvented it as an across-the-board national power with some of the best facilities in the country. The easiest way to grasp Jurich's impact on U of L and the city of Louisville in general isn't to look up the numbers on the amount of games his teams have won or the amount of money his program has earned. The easiest way is simply to look around.

Before Jurich arrived, there was never any reason to go down to Floyd Street by the U of L campus; in fact, there was reason to actively avoid it. The only buildings to look at in the area were scarcely occupied and sketchy-looking storefronts, an equally sketchy looking Econo Lodge, and a railroad yard that was later determined to be environmentally toxic.

The Louisville football and baseball teams played their games inside an old minor league baseball stadium that perpetually appeared to be on the verge of collapse. The basketball teams played in a dated arena that was originally built in large part to host horse shows. Nobody could tell you where any of the other teams played, because nobody knew they existed.

This simply would not stand for Tom Jurich, a man who still describes himself as "a builder" with far more frequency (and reverence) than he does as "an athletic director." In fact, the dilapidated state of U of L's facilities and campus in general nearly convinced Jurich to turn down the school's job offer and remain at Colorado State. Instead, he opted to view the architectural situation at Louisville as a challenge and he went to work. "It was like having a broken leg," Jurich said of the situation during a 2013 interview with CBS. "You can't race with a cast on your leg. You had to get that fixed."

Today, all 21 U of L athletic programs have the best there is to offer. The basketball and volleyball teams play games inside the KFC Yum! Center, an arena that would make fans of most NBA franchises gush with jealousy. The football team plays inside a revamped Papa John's Cardinal Stadium, which will expand to 65,000 seats after the latest helping of construction that will enclose the venue and also add 1,000 club seats, 70 premium boxes, and 12 exclusive field-level suites. Louisville's soccer, baseball, softball, field hockey, and lacrosse teams also compete inside state-of-the-art facilities that stack up with any of their structural contemporaries across the United States.

Still, it's the victories won inside these facilities that speak at a more audible volume to the rest of the world. Under Jurich's watch, the men's basketball program has gone from being on probation and struggling through its final years under Denny Crum to a revitalized national power that claimed a national title in 2013. Much of that success was due to the high-profile hiring of Rick Pitino, a man whom Jurich still refers to as "Elvis." Pitino is equally fond of his boss. Together they have been the biggest constants in U of L athletics for the better part of two decades, and their current contracts are set to expire in the same year, 2023. "Tom Jurich is the best AD in the business," Pitino said. "He could tell me, 'I know it's dirty, I know it's murky, but you're going to have to swim across the Ohio River, even though you're not a great swimmer.' I'd say, 'Let me put a wet suit on at least,' and there I'd go. Obviously, Tom and I, we'll probably go out together some time in the future."

Football, which is often referred to around Louisville as "Jurich's baby," has made a complete metamorphosis from a national afterthought to a program that has finished in the top 10 three times since 2004 and produced a Heisman Trophy winner. Women's basketball has evolved from a competitive program that had never made a Sweet 16 to one that regularly ranks in the nation's top 10 and has twice played in the national championship game.

Perhaps the most staggering changes have come in the non-revenue sports. Louisville baseball had never played in an NCAA Tournament before Jurich arrived. Since then, they have advanced to the College World Series three times and are a near lock to host the Regionals and Super Regionals each summer. The men's soccer program had also never played in the NCAA Tournament or won a conference championship of any sort before Jurich's arrival. With his support, Louisville has consistently been one of the tournament's 16 national seeds, and advanced all the way to the national championship game in 2010. There have also never been better days for Louisville volleyball, field hockey, lacrosse, swimming, or track, all of which regularly find themselves in the top 25 for their respective sports.

That is a steep climb for a school that was on the verge of being kicked out of Conference USA when Jurich first accepted the job. "The biggest break this university got was Mike Slive not kicking it out of C-USA," Jurich said. "That's what the rest of the conference wanted…I think there were lawsuits and everything, trying to get Louisville out of the league. Mike had the ADs and all the presidents, they were all telling him one thing, and I think he was fed up too. I look back today and shudder. What if we had gone through that without a conference?"

They didn't have to, thanks mostly to Jurich, who performed more magic in 2012 when the latest helping of conference realignment threatened to leave Louisville on the outside looking in at the world of major D-I athletics. When Maryland left for the Big Ten, the ACC was looking at two potential suitors: Louisville and Connecticut. UConn was perceived by most to be the runaway favorite, but Jurich once again went to work, calling anyone he knew who might be able to impact the decision and stating his case.

When Louisville was officially announced as the new 15th member of the ACC, conference commissioner John Swofford showered Jurich with the bulk of his praise. "Louisville's had the foresight and good sense to recognize an outstanding leader and understand what that kind of leadership over an extended period of time can mean and have kept him there because Tom's had numerous opportunities to leave," Swofford said. "I think the fact that he has stayed and built something very special has to give him a great deal of satisfaction. Tom won't make it about him, and good ADs don't, but you can't help but understand that much of what has happened at the University of Louisville is due to his vision and his leadership and his energy."

The praise was warranted for the man who was selected as the 2007 Street & Smith's SportsBusiness Journal/SportsBusiness Daily Athletic Director of the Year. Jurich also became the award's first two-time finalist in 2013. Swofford was equally correct in his recognition that Jurich had been pursued by a number of high-profile institutions once word of his work had become common knowledge. There was Indiana at first and then later "dream jobs" like Texas, USC, Tennessee, and Florida. Each and every time, Jurich said no. "I don't look for other jobs," Jurich said during a radio interview on 93.9 The Ville in 2015 when Texas had reportedly come calling for a second time. "I don't want to be a candidate. I don't know how my name got in there. I'm not interested in moving and I don't want to move. I've always said that the grass is extremely green in Louisville and I feel comfortable saying this is the best job in college athletics. What is there not to like about my job?"

6 Rick Pitino

The exact point in the season escapes him, but Rick Pitino was in the middle of a practice with the team that would wind up being his second to win a national championship. Pitino was teaching his players a new offensive set, one which he thought would be of extreme importance in its next game. There was no dribbling, no shooting, no talking—only Pitino giving instructions and his players following suit. In the middle of one of his instructions, Pitino was interrupted by the familiar sound of a basketball clanging against a rim. Inexplicably, someone had broken the golden rule and taken a shot in the middle of a drill for which the only skilled required was listening. The culprit was a predictable one: eccentric shooting guard Russ Smith, the team's leading scorer and a player who would become a consensus first-team All-American a year later. "I just looked at him and said, 'Russ, what the hell are you doing?'" Pitino recalls. "He just stared at me and then he started dying laughing. And then I started laughing. Pretty soon everyone in the gym was laughing, and I'd completely forgotten the point I was trying to get across."

There was a time in the early 1990s when Ken "Jersey Red" Ford, a longtime Pitino friend and well-known sports fanatic in the Northeast, referred to Pitino as "the Exorcist." The reason was because the combustible young coach always seemed on the verge of blowing up and spewing venom the moment something happened that he didn't like. How would that Pitino have handled Smith firing up a shot in the middle of a lesson when he'd been specifically instructed not to? "I wouldn't have just thrown him out of practice, I probably would have kicked him off the team. Hell, I might have killed him. And I would have really missed out because Russ brought so much laughter into my life for those four years. He really made coaching enjoyable for me."

Pitino's Linda Blair era wasn't limited just to his time at Kentucky or with the New York Knicks. It also bled over into the early years of his run at Louisville, something anyone who played or worked under him during that time can attest to. To pinpoint the exact moment of Pitino's partial metamorphosis, we can turn to Peyton Siva, the star point guard who arrived at Louisville in the summer of 2009 and left after leading the Cardinals to a national title in 2013. The man Siva had committed to play for and the one who propelled Smith's nickname of "Russdiculous" to become a national craze were unrecognizable. "You never would have heard him call someone 'Russdiculous' before," Siva told ESPN.com in April 2013. "I'm sure he had guys just as crazy in his career, but he didn't have that sort of relationship with them."

It took time for a lot of Pitino's relationships to blossom over the course of his lengthy coaching career, including the one he has with the Louisville fan base. Since the day that Denny Crum announced his retirement and Pitino was pegged as his most likely replacement, some Louisville fans were uneasy with the relationship. The first issue was the rivalry, which was straightforward enough. When the pushback continued even after Pitino started bringing Louisville back to the level of success it had enjoyed two decades prior, the phenomenon became more difficult to explain.

When Pitino announced in 2011 that he did not plan to coach at U of L after his contract ran out in 2017, conversation in the Derby City immediately shifted to potential replacements. The common thought at the time amongst the fan base was that they wouldn't like to see the program go to a former Pitino assistant but instead make an entirely fresh start. When outsiders wondered why—given the head coach's large and successful list of protégés— Cardinals fans would want to see the direction of the program altered so dramatically, a sufficient answer was once again hard to come by. The most common response was this: things were always more about Rick than they were about Louisville. The success was great, but the head coach, just as he had at Kentucky, thought he was bigger than the program and would always think he was bigger than the program. Basically, Rick Pitino wasn't a Louisville guy.

Then, at some point after that, Rick Pitino became a Louisville guy, saying that, it doesn't mean anyone should expect to see Pitino donning a red sweater vest at Cardinals home games in 20 years á la Denny Crum. It also doesn't mean that he's any less of a New Yorker than he was in 2002 or 2010. It simply means that at some point Pitino's actions finally caught up with the "Louisville First" motto that he himself concocted in 2011.

At the beginning, it didn't seem as though "Louisville First" was a saying Pitino truly believed applied to himself. It was merely a brand, a pair of words he smashed together to help with recruiting and public perception. That changed. The best evidence of Pitino's transformation—aside from not murdering Smith for his practice transgressions—can be caught in the opening minutes of a recording of any Louisville game played after 2012. Just before the tip, Pitino can be seen walking down the sideline giving "knuckles" to each one of his players and fist-bumping each one of his staff members. During the first half of his tenure at U of L, it was impossible to imagine Pitino sauntering down to the business class section of the bench for anything less than a verbal dressing-down or a better view of the action on the court.

Again, things changed. So why? Outsiders will name being humbled by the off-the-court events of 2009 and 2010 as the foundation for Pitino's transformation, and it's certainly more likely than not that those ordeals played a role. The subsequent support he received from the city, the fans, and athletic director Tom Jurich in the wake of those events almost certainly played a part as well. Above all else, though, Pitino credits a group of players, one that slightly predates Siva and Smith and includes many who came after them, with the creation of "Louisville Rick."

NCAA basketball isn't the most wholesome environment America has to offer. Yet some of the final chapters of Pitino's coaching story included not just winning big, but winning big with players whose character he held in even higher regard than their talent. "I don't think I have had as much fun coaching any period of my life than these last few years," Pitino said in 2016. "That's mainly because of the attitudes of the young men we are coaching. I wake up every morning and I cannot wait to go to work, and that's a testament to those players because they make my job so rewarding. We've just been blessed with guys with high moral fiber, great work ethic, and a great desire to learn. When you've got that, it makes your job much easier and much more fun."

It doesn't take a linguist to notice the stark contrast between a Pitino press conference during the first half of his tenure at Louisville and the second half. The intensity and the desire to produce victories has always been a staple of any meeting between Pitino and members of the press, but at the beginning of his time at Louisville, it felt almost joyless. Eventually, some sense of cheer, or at least, fulfillment entered the equation. At some point, Pitino began to embody the stance that most Louisvillians try to take with regard to all aspects of life: work hard, love and respect the people around you, and make sure you're enjoying it all. "When I was inducted into the [National Collegiate Basketball] Hall of Fame, I referred to Louisville as a family," Pitino said. "I almost meant that literally, because some of my best friends in life are the people I work for and the people I work with at the University of Louisville. I've loved every place I've coached, but I don't mind saying that Louisville has the best people I've ever worked with and the best fans I've ever coached for."

The basketball world saw Pitino's induction into the Hall of Fame in 2013 as an honor for his gaudy win total, for being the first coach to take three different programs to the Final Four, and the first to win national titles at multiple schools. In Louisville, however, it was seen as the ultimate reward for a man who had miraculously become one of their own.

Louisville fans were excited when Pitino was hired in 2001 because it represented an assurance of better days for a program that was clearly headed in the wrong direction. The promise of winning was the only asset that could make the group overlook the fact that he had lifted their archrivals out of the depths caused by probation and back to the top of the college basketball world.

The love affair between the coach and his fans in the Derby City became more intense when it became more complex. Cardinals fans became Pitino fans the moment "Louisville" and "First" became words best embodied by the man who initially shoved them together—when he became a Louisville guy himself, not just a person who works with and for them. From day one of their relationship, Pitino and Louisville fans made little effort to hide their shared desire for getting back to the championship-winning ways of their respective pasts. It took getting on the same page for it to finally happen.

The Louisville-Kentucky Basketball Rivalry

The vast majority of people who debate the superiority or fierceness of a particular sports rivalry usually have at most one direct tie to the feud in question. This isn't the case with Rick Pitino, who coached both the Celtics and the Knicks, grew up as a die-hard Yankees fan surrounded by Mets supporters, and is the only man to see the Louisville-Kentucky basketball rivalry as the dominant figure for both sides. So how does the Battle for the Bluegrass stack up next to everything else he's seen? "It's hard to declare one rivalry 'better' than another because that all depends on what you value," Pitino said. "But this is the sickest. There's no question about it. People in this state just go nuts over this thing. And they don't just go nuts one day out of the year, they go nuts 365 days out of the year."

For all the accomplishments and championships that both Kentucky and Louisville have racked up over the years, there's little debate that the defining element of the duo's endless quarrel is disdain. Use of the word "hate" is excessive in almost any context, especially when we're talking about sports, but the Battle of the Bluegrass brings utilization of the word closer to the edge of appropriateness than any other. Without delving too much into the issues, there is a concrete disconnect between the city of Louisville and the state of Kentucky that the citizens of Jefferson County and the citizens of the other 119 counties both agree on. That disconnect might be best exemplified through the basketball rivalry.

The Cardinals rose to prominence thanks in large part to homegrown talent from the largely urban city of Louisville— players such as Westley Unseld and Darrell Griffith, who led U of L's high-flying "Doctors of Dunk" to the program's first national championship in 1980. The rest of the state still idolizes Wallace "Wah Wah" Jones, Jeff Sheppard, and "the Unforgettables," a group of four seniors—three of whom just happened to be Kentucky boys—who stuck with the Wildcats program through its probation years in the early '90s. The popularity of the group remained so high that one of the players, Corbin-born Richie Farmer, wound up being elected agriculture commissioner.

The easiest (and the most common) way for a Louisville fan to work a Big Blue Nation member into a tizzy is to insinuate that Adolph Rupp was a racist. Regardless of what Rupp's actual beliefs were, there's no question that for a period of time race played a huge factor in the strained relationship between the state's university and the university of its biggest city. Louisville fans still take pride in being just the second program to start five black players and make it to the Final Four. The first? The famous 1965–66 Texas Western squad that stunned Rupp's Wildcats in the national championship game.

The issue—at least as it was then—is well laid out in Pitino's chapter of Eddie Einhorn and Ron Rapoport's book *How March Became Madness*. "The one big problem we had in recruiting at Kentucky was a bitterness about race. Once, when we were trying to get Dwayne Morton, who was born in Louisville, I went to talk to his family and gave this big speech about why he should play for us [at Kentucky]. His grandmother was listening and she said, 'Coach Pitino, I'm a big fan of yours.' I smiled, thinking we were in, and then she said, 'But every time I see those boys go on the court and step on that man's name, we applaud in this household.' She meant Adolph Rupp—the arena was named for him by then—and that was when I really understood the opinion of African Americans locally about Kentucky. Rupp might have been a legendary coach, but he sure wasn't legendary in the African American community. The University of Louisville was viewed as the place where African Americans could excel, and Kentucky was a white-bread university. We lost Morton to Louisville."

People don't like what they can't understand, and these two sides certainly don't seem to understand each other. The result is cultural warfare in the form of a 40-minute college basketball game.

Time has tempered the racial aspect of the rivalry, but it's also given rise to a new one: John Calipari vs. Rick Pitino. Near the end of the 1990s, the Bluegrass Rivalry had simmered to about the lowest temperature possible. Denny Crum was nearing the end of his run, and his teams were no longer competing for national championships. Tubby Smith's were, but the successor to the fiery

Rick Pitino was too congenial for U of L fans to loathe unabashedly the way they had before. Everything changed in 2001, when Crum announced his retirement and Louisville athletic director Tom Jurich successfully convinced Pitino to return to the commonwealth and take over at Kentucky's biggest rival. "The rivalry never really entered into my mind," Jurich said of his thought process at the time. "I was simply focused on who I thought would do the best job and who I would enjoy working with the most. I thought that Coach Pitino was the best coach in the entire country then and I still think that today. I'm thankful every day that he chose to come here."

Less thankful were the denizens of Big Blue Nation, many of whom were already growing disillusioned with Smith and who couldn't process the decision Pitino had made. Pitino was the man who had not just lifted the Wildcats out of the depths of probation, but the man who also made Kentucky basketball one of the coolest programs in the country during the 1990s. In the minds of his former disciples, Pitino going to Louisville less than a decade after doing what he did at UK signified that he never really understood what the culture of Wildcats basketball is all about. He was never really one of them, a realization that simultaneously tainted an era of glory and gave rise to a great degree of anger.

Time has only backed up the assertion. When Pitino returned to Rupp Arena for the first time in 2001, he wasn't naive enough to believe he'd be received as a conquering hero. He knew the home fans would boo Louisville and might even throw a few jabs his way, but he expected that some, if not most, of them would remember the successes. He thought they'd remember that he was the same person who took the program they love from one of its lowest points to the sport's pinnacle. He thought they'd remember that his name is still hanging from the Rupp Arena rafters and that he was the man responsible for assembling the 1995–96 team that still ranks as one of the most dominant college basketball teams of all time. He thought that no rivalry, regardless of its combustibility, could fully cloud all that.

He thought wrong.

When he walked onto the Rupp Arena floor on December 29, 2001, Pitino was showered with boos and insults. When he looked into the crowd for the first time, he saw a sign that was directed at his wife. Though he's never said so publicly, those close to Pitino will tell you that particular game changed him. It signified the first time he fully understood that Kentucky-Louisville would always trump any single accomplishment, any single team, or any single individual.

Pitino embraced the hate and guided U of L back to national prominence, setting the stage for the full-on rivalry eruption that occurred in 2009 when a Kentucky program wounded by the brief Billy Gillispie disaster announced that it had hired John Calipari away from Memphis. Louisville fans already disliked Calipari from his days with the rival Tigers, and though no one is able to pinpoint exactly where their once amiable relationship went awry, Coach Cal and Pitino weren't the best of friends either.

From a narrative standpoint, it was perfect. Kentucky fans immediately fell in love with Calipari. He accomplished what Pitino had two decades prior, taking an injured program and restoring it to a perch on which its fan base believed they should perpetually exist. And he did it in less time. With the signing of a top-ranked recruiting class headlined by John Wall and DeMarcus Cousins, Calipari immediately took Kentucky from a program losing its grip on in-state superiority and made them the hot name in college basketball again. A year later, he had the Wildcats back in the Final Four for the first time since the season after Pitino left Lexington for the NBA. A year after that, he'd locked up the program's eighth national championship.

Calipari also delighted his fan base off the court, where he didn't hesitate to jump fully into the rivalry that fuels the state for 365 days a year. When Pitino came out with the slogan "Louisville First" in 2011, Calipari countered with a "Players First" tagline that stressed the importance of getting players into the NBA over program success. When Pitino wrote a book titled *Success Is a Choice*, Calipari countered with a book titled *Success Is the Only Option* and shrugged off the notion that the concept was in any way a reaction to his rival.

When he was asked why basketball in the state of Kentucky is so special, Calipari didn't hesitate to throw even more gas on the fire. "It's a unique thing," Calipari said. "There's no other state, none, that's as connected to their basketball program as this one. Because those other states have other programs. Michigan has Michigan State, California has UCLA, North Carolina has Duke. It's Kentucky throughout this whole state, and that's what makes us unique."

Pitino wasn't about to let the jab go unanswered, countering days later with: "There are four things I've learned in my 59 years about people: I ignore the jealous, I ignore the malicious, I ignore the ignorant, and I ignore the paranoid. If the shoe fits anyone, wear it."

Both head coaches have consistently maintained that their comments and branding techniques are in no way directed at the other, but there was more subtlety in the Soda Wars. It's a trend that will almost assuredly fluctuate, but never disappear completely, until one of them makes the decision to walk away from his program, and the rivalry, for good.

Even when that day comes, it will do little to change the landscape of the Commonwealth of Kentucky and the role that one basketball rivalry has in all of it. Business deals will still be done, elected officials will still be voted into office, and relationships will still be created and disintegrated all because of affiliations to red or to blue. It is over-the-top, it is inconceivably visceral, and it is 100 percent impossible to comprehend for anyone who hasn't lived in the middle of it, but those are all the things that make it Louisville-Kentucky.

The Dream Game

March 26, 1983. Even if you weren't alive at the time, if you are or have ever been a citizen of the Commonwealth of Kentucky, you're likely familiar with the date. If you still need something to jog your memory, three words will do the trick: "the Dream Game."

Louisville and Kentucky hadn't played each other in basketball since 1959, when Peck Hickman's unranked Cardinals knocked off Adolph Rupp's second-ranked Wildcats 76–61 in the Mideast Regional Semifinals. The victory paved the way for U of L's first trip to the Final Four and brought increased tension to the relationship between the state of Kentucky's two largest universities.

Since that meeting the Cardinals had won a national championship and become a major player on the national scene. Louisville fans craved an annual shot at "big brother," and the national media began openly questioning why the game wasn't being played. Rupp had long believed that no other program in the state was on UK's level and thus refused to play Louisville, Western Kentucky, or any other team that existed within the same border as the Wildcats. It was a policy that his successor, Joe B. Hall, also adopted.

Despite constant poking and prodding from brash Louisville coach Denny Crum, Hall consistently dismissed the notion of playing the Cardinals unless the two happened to meet in the postseason. After a close call the year before, that's precisely what happened in 1983, when U of L and UK each advanced to the Elite 8 in Knoxville. The buildup to the game was expectedly intense, and seemingly everyone picked a side. Everyone, that is, except Kentucky governor John Y. Brown, who had long been in favor of the two programs playing a series, and attended the game wearing a half-red/half-blue blazer.

No. 2 Louisville entered the game ranked 10 spots higher than Kentucky, but Crum couldn't pass up one last opportunity to needle Hall and UK over what he perceived to be a false sense of being the "bigger brother." "The pressure is on Kentucky," Crum said before the game. "Our record is better the last 10 years. They have a chance to carve into our success."

Perhaps the Louisville players felt differently about where the pressure lay before the game, as the Cardinals appeared to come out tight, misfiring on 16 of their first 20 field goal attempts. Kentucky used its opponents' futility on the offensive end to open up a 23–10 lead before U of L managed to whittle it down to 37–30 at halftime.

After Kentucky extended its lead to 11 early in the second half, Crum opted to switch up his defensive game plan. He called for Cardinals defenders to put more pressure on the Wildcats ball handlers, a move which led to five quick UK turnovers and a 12–2 Louisville run. The pressure from U of L's superior athletes kept coming, and so did the turnovers. With less than 10 minutes to play, the Cardinals had stunningly turned an 11-point deficit into a 58–50 lead.

Louisville's own sloppiness allowed Kentucky to get back into the game, and with 2:22 to play, the two teams were tied at 60. With no shot clock in place, Hall ordered his team to hold the ball and take the game's final shot. Kentucky guard Dirk Minniefield attempted to do just that, but his running layup with just under 15

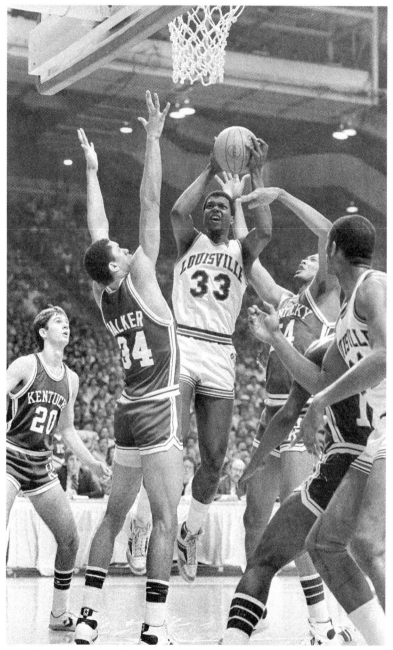

Charles Jones, who scored 12 points against the Wildcats, maneuvers around Kentucky's Kenny Walker in the Dream Game.

seconds to play was swatted away by U of L's Charles Jones. This started a fast break that ended with Lancaster Gordon banking in what appeared to be the game-winning shot with just eight seconds remaining. But the drama wasn't over just yet. Kentucky's Jim Master took the inbounds pass, raced down the floor, and buried a 14-foot jump shot in front of the UK bench to send the game into overtime and drive both fan bases to delirium.

The overtime period proved to be less scintillating...at least for one side. The two teams traded baskets before Louisville erupted for 14 straight points to punch their ticket to the Final Four and, perhaps more importantly, secure a monumental victory in what would eventually become college basketball's most contentious rivalry.

The Louisville win increased the pressure on all involved to create an annual game between the two Bluegrass powerhouses. Eventually, after a handful of government officials got involved, a deal was ironed out. To this day, many believe that Louisville and Kentucky still might not be playing one another had the team wearing blue prevailed on March 26, 1983. "I believe in my heart had we lost that game they wouldn't have played the next year," said Louisville star Scooter McCray. "They already had a few championships, they would have gone to the Final Four, and they would have beaten us head-to-head. Maybe the series would have started eventually, but they wouldn't have had anything to prove."

9 Lamar Jackson

To fully understand the way Lamar Jackson's 2016 season ended, you have to go back to the way it began. "Last year, I didn't like talking with the media. Like, not at all." This was the first line of the first answer that Jackson gave at the ACC's annual media day. At an event where the league's coaches and not top players typically answer questions in clichés and half-truths, the rising sophomore quarterback's words rang especially honest.

Given how quickly he was thrust into the spotlight, it's easy to forget that Jackson spent the 2015 football season as an 18-year-old true freshman who just months earlier had been wrapping up high school. After his breakout second-half performance in Louisville's season-opening loss to Auburn, the south Florida native went from a teenager who had only been a college student for a handful of weeks to both the current starting quarterback and the future face of U of L football. Put that way, understanding why Jackson didn't immediately embrace the spotlight becomes an easier task.

In the second week of the season, Jackson made the first start of his college career and struggled mightily. He turned over the ball three times and was ultimately replaced by sophomore Kyle Bolin in a 34–31 upset loss to visiting Houston. Jackson responded the way 18-year-olds sometime do in the face of adversity. He shied away from attention, he gave short, seemingly annoyed responses to questions, and he let his emotions get the best of him on social media after Bolin got the start for Louisville's showcase game against Clemson the following week.

Those first three weeks set the tone for an up-and-down freshman campaign from Jackson in which he didn't look fully complacent until the final game of the season. It was then that he had three weeks to catch his breath and prepare for a Music City Bowl in which he would go up against Texas A&M, a team known for having one of the best defensive lines in college football. But the Aggies had no answer for Jackson, who became just the third quarterback ever to rush and throw for more than 200 yards in a bowl game, joining college football legends Vince Young and Johnny Manziel.

Fast-forward seven months to a time when Jackson had been blessed with even more time to catch his breath and regain his footing. It showed. With microphones in his face at every turn during the ACC's annual season-kickoff event, Jackson sparkled. He gave well-thought-out answers to difficult questions, he was entertaining, he was pleasant, he was all the things you'd want the freshly anointed face of a program to be.

In the middle of his podium session at the event, Jackson was informed of the fact that he appeared to be much more comfortable in front of the media than he had at any point the year before. Jackson responded by addressing the statement and then asking the media member two more questions than had been posed to him. "I've been having a lot of training on my interviews. How am I doing? I'm doing good? All right. It's been fun. It's been a fun experience. At first I was like, 'Media Day, I don't want to do this, Coach.' But I'm growing up, so I have to do what I have to do. This is my responsibility."

That step would wind up being the first significant one on the path to what would wind up being the most sensational individual season in the history of Louisville football. When Jackson's name was called near the end of the Heisman Trophy ceremony in New York on December 11, 2016, every Louisville fan with their television tuned to ESPN knew they were experiencing one of the landmark moments in their favorite program's existence. Nobody had any idea at that time what Jackson's historic accomplishment would wind up producing for himself or for Cardinals football, but they figured it would be weighty and they figured it would be positive. They also knew it was cause for celebration.

At that kickoff event months earlier in the summer of 2016, Jackson admitted to everyone that he had spent the entirety of his freshman regular season playing the position of quarterback without knowing head coach Bobby Petrino's playbook. He admitted that he would stare down one receiver, and if that player wasn't open, he would simply take off and run. That strategy was good enough to carry the Cardinals to an 8–5 season, but it also produced an understandably erratic level of play that left Louisville fans troubled over the future of their program.

Twelve months later, the freshman who played the quarterback position off pure instinct was now the youngest player ever to win the most prestigious individual award in American sports. He was also the most famous college football player on the planet. Both distinctions were deserved.

Also the winner of the Walter Camp and Maxwell awards, given to college football's top overall performer, Jackson made history in 2016 by becoming the first FBS player ever to throw for at least 3,300 yards and rush for at least 1,500 more and the first to throw for at least 30 touchdowns and rush for at least 20 more. He set ACC and school records for touchdowns accounted for (51), total yards per game in a season (410.7), and points responsible for in a season (308). He also did it with flair, with grace, with swag, and with any other modern noun you can think of.

Speaking in the raw, genuine, and endearing manner that Louisville fans have become accustomed to—and donning a red velvet blazer with shiny black lapels that instantly became iconic in the Derby City—Jackson thanked everyone imaginable as he stood in front of the legends of college football past. He cut off his speech several times to pause and comment on the fact that he was still having trouble wrapping his mind around the moment he was experiencing. It was hard to blame him.

The pomp and circumstance of the Heisman Trophy ceremony make it nearly impossible to be unaware of the gravity of the award and the impact it can have on those who receive it and the programs they represent. For some Louisville fans, it took until that night for the reality to fully set in.

For Jackson, he'd been ready and expecting to bask in the brightest of lights since the moment his freshman season had ended. It's why he'd spent his entire spring focused solely on becoming a better passer and why he'd spent a large chunk of his summer focused on becoming a better public speaker. In order to take one day the biggest step, he had to start with the smallest. It was his responsibility.

10 Johnny Unitas

Long before he was ever at the center of the debate for the NFL's greatest quarterback, Johnny Unitas was a nervous, 6'1", 145-pound freshman showing up for his first day of football practice at the University of Louisville.

The third of four children born to Leon and Helen Unitas, Johnny grew up in Pittsburgh, where he showed great promise as both a quarterback and a halfback on the football team at St. Justin's High School. Although his lack of size led Unitas' dream school, Notre Dame, to take a pass after watching him play, the All-Catholic performer made enough of a name for himself to be offered a scholarship by the University of Pittsburgh. Months later,

Unitas' new dream of becoming a Panther was derailed when he failed the school's entrance exam.

Unitas wound up accepting a scholarship to the University of Louisville, which had a middling football program that wasn't even a part of the NCAA at the time. The coaching staff, which had pointed to quarterback as a position of need, had offered Unitas a scholarship without ever seeing him play. The program didn't have enough money to spend on travel or even phone calls, so Frank Camp and his assistants had corresponded with the Unitas family through letters. This had all come on the advice of two current Cardinals who had played against Unitas during their high school years in Pittsburgh.

Unitas' ability was apparent on his first day of college practice, but while the freshman had shown a remarkable arm and surprising athleticism for a player his size, Camp still wasn't about to send a 145-pound kid onto the field to go up against grown men twice his size. At least, not until the fifth game of the 1951 season. With his team trailing Saint Bonaventure 19–0 and his offense showing zero signs of life, Camp decided to give Unitas a shot. Unitas promptly completed 11 consecutive passes, three of which went for touchdowns, to give Louisville a 21–19 lead. Even though the Cardinals lost on a last-second field goal—the accuracy of which is still disputed to this day—Camp had stumbled upon both the future of his program and one of the greatest quarterbacks that football would ever see.

Under Unitas' guidance, the Cardinals ripped off four consecutive victories, including a stunning 35–28 upset of 19-point favorite Houston. Unitas made one of the signature plays of his early career in that game when he sidestepped two defenders before hitting Babe Ray for a 93-yard touchdown that put U of L ahead by two scores in the fourth quarter. The play still ranks as the second-longest passing touchdown in the history of Louisville football.

In the next morning's edition of *The Courier-Journal,* reporter Jimmy Brown summed up the feelings of most Cardinals football fans by writing: "If Coach Frank Camp is smart, he'll take Unitas, enclose him in a cellophane bag, and put him away with the Cardinals' uniforms for safekeeping over the winter." Thankfully for both Unitas' safety and Camp's peace of mind, Louisville's star quarterback grew a pair of inches and gained 40 pounds between the time he arrived on campus and the start of his sophomore season. Bulking up proved to be an absolute necessity for Unitas, who played behind an inexperienced and undersized offensive line that often left him running for his life. Unitas often credited his time at Louisville for the quick release that became one of his biggest assets at the professional level, once saying: "I knew if I didn't get rid of the ball quickly then I wouldn't be getting rid of it at all."

The supporting cast at Louisville got even thinner for Unitas after a new administration at the university decided that it was spending too much money on football and mandated that the program terminate 15 scholarships. The result was that after Unitas' freshman season, Camp and his staff weren't able to bring in another player on scholarship until 1954. With the Louisville program still not a member of the NCAA and suddenly even in worse shape than it had been when he arrived, Unitas, who had established something of a name for himself in the region by that point, pondered a transfer. He was offered an opportunity to transfer to Indiana, a school that had originally passed on his services, but ultimately opted to reward Camp and U of L for being the only ones willing to take a chance on him.

"We didn't win many games, so he didn't get a lot of notice in terms of wins and losses," former Cardinals teammate Reggie Bethea said in the book *Johnny Unitas: Mr. Quarterback.* "But he was known as a terrific football player. You knew he wanted to play pro football and he could have helped himself a lot in that regard by transferring to another program, but he didn't. His loyalty was to Louisville and Coach Camp, even though he had no chance of making All-American there."

When Unitas' sophomore season of 1952 rolled around, the few football fans who existed across the city of Louisville were liberally using the tagline "Unitas We Stand, Divided We Fall." At Old Manual Stadium, a high school field where the Cardinals played and typically drew about 3,000 fans per game, a sign was erected that read SEE UNITAS PASS. Not long after, a young prankster, who was never caught rubbed out the *P* from the last word.

Unitas led Louisville to victories in each of its first two games of 1952, including a 41–14 triumph against Florida State in which the quarterback completed 17 of 22 passes. The Cardinals' lack of depth and talent caught up with them as the season rolled on, however. U of L would win just once more and ended the season with a 55–26 walloping at the hands of Southern Mississippi. Still, the legend of Unitas grew as he wowed opposing coaches with his arm strength and earned their eternal respect by staying in games despite enduring some vicious beatings. It didn't help that the limited size of Louisville's roster meant that Unitas was also playing both ways as a safety.

As the number of seasoned players around Unitas continued to decrease, the Louisville star's injuries piled up. He was battered and bruised throughout a junior season that often saw the Cards trounced on their way to a 1–7 record. A week before his final collegiate season was set to start, Unitas suffered a hairline fracture of his ankle that should have kept him sidelined for the entire campaign. Worried that his dream of becoming a professional football player was slipping away as he toiled in virtual obscurity, Unitas instead convinced Camp to essentially let him play the season on one leg. Louisville went just 3–6, but its quarterback's status as a program legend was cemented.

Being an undersized quarterback from a bad football program that not many professional scouts had even heard of proved to be a tough sell for Unitas, who wasn't selected until the ninth round of the 1955 NFL Draft. He was released by the Pittsburgh Steelers before the start of the season, and the odds of him ever suiting up for an NFL team seemed slim until he was brought in by the Baltimore Colts just before the start of the 1956 campaign. When a door opened up early in the season after Baltimore's starting quarterback George Shaw suffered a broken leg, Unitas walked through it just as quickly as he had when Camp had inserted him into that game against St. Bonaventure six years earlier.

Though pedestrian by today's standards, Unitas wrapped up his Louisville career with 245 completions for 3,139 yards and 27 touchdowns. Many of his numbers stood as records for decades before the forward pass became a bigger part of the Cardinals football program, thanks to the likes of John Madeya, Ed Rubbert, Browning Nagle, Jeff Brohm, and Chris Redman.

Though he wore No. 19 as a professional, Unitas' No. 16 remains the only number that Louisville football has retired. A statue bearing his likeness sits prominently inside Papa John's Cardinal Stadium, and Louisville's players walk past it as they take the field before every game.

Freedom Hall

Completed in 1956 as part of the newly opened Kentucky Fair and Exposition Center, Freedom Hall was always destined to be a part of Louisville lore. For starters, the name Freedom Hall was chosen by a local student. The naming contest resulted in more than 6,500 submissions and was won by Charlotte Owens, a senior at DuPont Manual High School. In keeping with the city's love of equine, the building was designed so that it could host the nation's premier equestrian competition, the Kentucky State Fair World's Championship Horse Show. It was also set up to host the North American International Livestock Exposition each November.

Eventually, that same building would somehow evolve into one of the cathedrals of college basketball. Between 1958 and 1969, Freedom Hall hosted six Final Fours. Players such as Lew Alcindor, Oscar Robertson, Elgin Baylor, and Jerry West took its floor. Coaches such as John Wooden, Adolph Rupp, and Dean Smith paced its sidelines. Louisville made its first Final Four appearance there in 1959, Loyola of Chicago struck a huge blow in favor of integration there with its 1963 national title, and the building saw the first days of a dynasty when it played host to the first of UCLA's record seven consecutive national championships.

In the decades that followed, Freedom Hall became known less for its national role and more for the play of its primary team. Under the direction of Denny Crum, Louisville basketball blossomed into a national powerhouse inside the arena's walls. Somewhere around 16,000 fans regularly packed the place to see the nationally ranked Cardinals take on a slew of blue-blood opponents as they geared up for their next national championship run in March.

In 1984 Freedom Hall was refurbished. Among the moves made was a lowering of the playing floor that allowed maximum capacity to increase from 16,664 to 18,865 for home basketball games. The move helped spark a run during which the Cardinals ranked in the nation's top five in attendance for the final 25 years that they played their home games inside Freedom Hall.

Louisville's last game in Freedom Hall before moving into the KFC Yum! Center took place on March 6, 2010, as a record crowd of 20,138 watched the unranked Cardinals topple No. 1 Syracuse 78–68. Over the course of their 54 years playing inside the building, U of L amassed an overall record of 664–136, good for a winning percentage of 83 percent. Between 1956 and 2010, more than 12 million paying fans watched Louisville play basketball inside Freedom Hall.

12 What Did Freedom Hall Smell Like?

Strike up a conversation with any Louisville fan about their memories of Freedom Hall, and many of the topics you'd expect to hear about will be discussed. There were great games, fantastic teams, memorable plays, and new friends made over the years. But one thing that is guaranteed to come up that may shock someone who never set foot in those hallowed halls is the smell. What exactly was it? Nobody can say definitely, but everyone has his or her own very particular opinion. Here are some notable Louisvillians who spent a significant amount of time inside Freedom Hall giving their thoughts on the matter:

National college sports writer and former columnist for *The Courier-Journal* **Pat Forde**: "Freedom Hall had a baroque and bewildering bouquet, depending where you were. At the back entrance used by media, coaches, and players, it smelled like diesel from the idling team buses and other work vehicles. On the concourse it smelled like cinnamon almonds and spilled beer. And depending on the time of year, there was the occasional *eau de barnyard* floating through the place from the fairgrounds and horse stables outside."

Former Louisville basketball player Marques Maybin (1997–2001): "I have heard that smells are the most effective ways to trigger memories, however in this case every memory of Freedom Hall triggers the memory of a different smell. I feel like I would be doing a disservice to the historic debate of identifying the Hall's true smell if I lumped it into one category, however the relationship (yes, relationship) between my olfactory lobe and Freedom Hall must be separated at the very least by season. And I'm not going to use the 'it smelled better during my winning seasons as opposed to my rougher ones' cliché response.

"Without getting too analytical in what was supposed to be just a simple answer to a simple question, I felt like Freedom Hall smelled like a peanut and popcorn factory headed into the season almost like a complete staff of squirrels were preparing themselves for a long winter of hibernation and basketball. But as the season progressed and the expense of warming such a massive place increased, the smells of gasoline and machinery began to combine to give you more of a traditional fairgrounds smell.

"That brings us to springtime and the odd Louisville weather patterns that at times led to a moist, rainy smell. I would imagine this was mostly due to the melting of the ice underneath the basketball court—fun times. All these different smells existing in constant competition with each other give you the very complicated formula that answers the simple question of what Freedom Hall smelled like to me."

Longtime Louisville radio personality Terry Meiners: "My first job in the '70s was selling pop during Freedom Hall tractor pulls. Lugging racks of flat Pepsi through the upper decks filled my lungs with rancid diesel exhaust. Freedom Hall still smells like death by diesel. When I sneeze today, a wisp of diesel smoke shoots out of my nose."

Louisville radio play-by-play announcer Paul Rogers: "Caramel corn. And whenever there was a game after the big tractor pull, exhaust fumes would linger for a while. That was always a nice combination."

Former Louisville basketball player Robby Wine (1992–96): "Caramel popcorn, which was always my wife's [a former Louisville cheerleader] favorite. She laments that fact that the KFC Yum! Center doesn't have that same caramel popcorn. She really misses that smell at Freedom Hall. That wasn't the only smell that I remember, though. Here are some more.

"The cigarette smoke prior to the decision to install and enforce the use of new smoking rooms. There were some games before those rooms were installed where you could literally look up from the floor and see nothing but a thick cloud of smoke hanging above the scoreboard.

"There was a small musk of straw-and-dirt smell after horse shows sometimes. I used the word 'dirt' nicely because it wasn't really dirt after those shows that left the stench.

"There was the smell of stale beer, cigarette smoke, stale popcorn, hot dogs, cotton candy, and whiskey after concerts. We sometimes would have walk through or practices the day after a concert, and you could tell if there had been a country, rock, teenager boy band, rap, or R&B concert the night before based upon the smell test.

"The players and coaches entrance from the back garage door area would sometimes smell like Denny Crum's horse farm at his house. This was due to the horses being walked from time to time around that same area. Denny probably felt at home more than he realized. The smell of the dirt wasn't strong, but you could still sense it after truck pulls or monster truck events. The cleaning staff would clean as much up as possible, but you could still see and feel thin layers of it walking from locker room to the court under the stands in certain areas. I am sure that stuff was still settling down from the air for a long time after those events.

"I am sure that Yankee Candle could bottle all of this up into a nice aroma for all the die hard U of L fans who miss Freedom Hall."

Longtime Louisville TV/radio personality John Ramsey:
"It was part livestock, part caramel, part roasted nuts. Basically, it smelled like a cow who had eaten some nuts covered in caramel."

13 Kyle Kuric Saves Freedom Hall's Send-Off

On its surface, the 2009–10 season will always appear to be one of the more forgettable campaigns during Rick Pitino's tenure at Louisville. The Cardinals were coming off back-to-back regional final appearances, and the season before had won both the Big East's regular season and tournament championships, earning the NCAA Tournament's No. 1 overall seed as a result. Nothing came as easily for the 2009–10 group, which successfully balanced impressive victories with head-scratching defeats for four months before squeaking into the Big Dance as a No. 9 seed. When the draw was unveiled, U of L was immediately labeled as a trendy pick to upset top-seeded Duke in the second round. In keeping with the theme of the season, the Cardinals promptly laid an egg in their opening game, in which they were eliminated by California in a 77–62 defeat.

The reality is that when any Louisville fan thinks about the 2009–10 season, they're not going to immediately remember the NCAA Tournament loss or U of L's equally lackluster one-and-out performance in the Big East Tournament. That Cardinals team had already had its defining moment by the time both of those games were played.

On March 6, 2010, the Louisville basketball team played its 823rd and final game inside Freedom Hall. The building had opened to relatively little fanfare in 1956 and then watched a national powerhouse grow inside of it over the course of the next 54 years. While Cardinals fans were excited to see their team move into a new arena that people were already declaring more luxurious than most which hosted NBA teams, they were also understandably sad about being forced to say good-bye.

The event would have brought an inordinate amount of pomp and splendor regardless of the opponent or any other extenuating circumstances. The fact that it was, for more traditionally straight-forward reasons, easily the biggest game of Louisville's season only added to the spectacle. Louisville entered the game with a 19–11 overall record and a 10–7 mark in Big East play. The Cardinals were in desperate need of one more quality victory to put them-selves in the right side of the bubble for good before Selection Sunday arrived. Thankfully, their opponent on the final day of the regular season provided such an opportunity.

Winners in 28 of their first 30 games, the Syracuse Orange came to Louisville in early March as the No. 1 team in the country. They had been beaten just once since January 2, a stunning 66–60 home loss to this same enigmatic Cardinals team. Despite having won a national title in 2003, this was the first time Syracuse had been ranked No. 1 in an Associated Press Top 25 poll since the 1989–90 season. (The AP does not release a postseason poll.) Many believed Jim Boeheim had all the tools necessary to repeat the feat his team had accomplished seven years prior.

"Never before in my coaching career had I felt pressure like that," Rick Pitino recalled. "I couldn't sleep the night before. I woke up in the middle of the night and just thought, 'What if we lose?' All those fans would have been disappointed, all those legends that had traveled to come to the game would have been disappointed, and we might have been on the verge of not getting a bid to the NCAA Tournament. That was a new level of pressure for me."

Like a set of overbearing parents terrified of missing their golden child's recital performance, Louisville fans started showing up around Freedom Hall about three hours before the 2:00 PM tip. Among the group of early arrivals were former All-Americans and players from the 1980 and 1986 championship teams who signed autographs, posed for pictures, and even took time to capture some images for their own scrapbooks. When tip-off finally arrived, 20,135 fans had filed in to watch the Cards play in Freedom Hall one last time. It was the largest crowd to ever see a game in the 54-year history of the building, and all 20,135 of them got their money's worth.

The inescapable gravity of the moment had an adverse effect on both teams early on. Playing noticeably tight, the two teams combined to go 0-for-11 from the field over the course of the game's first three minutes. Senior guard Jerry Smith, a key contributor in each of his four seasons at Louisville, broke the tension by knocking down consecutive three-pointers to give the Cardinals an early advantage. Moments later, Smith nearly made the building collapse on its big day when he stole an errant Syracuse pass and then drove the length of the court for an emphatic one-handed slam dunk. Always known for his boundless enthusiasm, Smith followed the dunk with a solid, celebratory shove of fellow senior guard Edgar Sosa.

So caught up in the moment was Smith that after the game he couldn't recall whether he'd sprained his right thumb on the dunk or during the celebration. Ultimately, it didn't matter. What did matter was that Louisville was going to have to pull off the biggest win of its season without the services of its best three-point shooter and its third-leading scorer.

A back-and-forth opening 20 minutes resulted in Syracuse carrying a 35–30 lead into the locker room and Louisville fans terrified of walking out of their cathedral for the final time without a victory. "We wanted to win that game so bad," Sosa said. "Not just for ourselves, but definitely for the fans. Even when you're losing, they always show up and they always show you love. We knew we had to give them a going-away present."

With Smith sidelined and Louisville's offense in desperate need of a spark, Pitino turned to an unlikely source. Seldom-used sophomore guard Kyle Kuric came into the final game of the 2009–10 regular season boasting drab averages of 13.4 minutes and 3.5 points per game. The last time he had stepped foot on the Freedom Hall court in a game, he had played seven minutes and failed to record a single statistic in U of L's 70–60 loss to Georgetown. Still, this was the man Pitino selected to ignite his team in the most important half of its season.

What followed was one of the most remarkable, memorable, and improbable individual performances in the history of Louisville basketball. Over a span of 13 minutes and 41 seconds, Kuric ripped the net for four three-pointers against Syracuse's vaunted 2-3 zone, and rocked the rim with four violent dunks, each one sending the home crowd into a louder uproar than the one before. In 13 minutes and 41 seconds, Kuric had scored 22 points, a career high for the unheralded native of Evansville, Indiana. Over that same time span, Syracuse had only been able to amass 22 points as a team. The result of all this was a 78–68 Louisville victory and a mild court-storming from some of the Freedom Hall faithful. It was the first storming of the court in the building's history, according to some of its longtime patrons. "It couldn't have been any better," said hometown legend Darrell Griffith, the star of Louisville's first national championship team in 1980. "That was the perfect send-off."

After Louisville held its traditional postgame Senior Day ceremonies, the microphone was passed around from Denny Crum to Griffith and then to a number of former players who had all shown up to share their memories and pay their respects. The fans sat down in their seats for the first time all afternoon and stayed there long after the former players had finished talking. For many who had started attending games at Freedom Hall when they were young and had continued the tradition as their lives unfolded, it was almost as if they were scared to find out what would happen after they walked out of the building for the last time.

Finally, public address announcer Sean Moth had to take to the microphone and politely ask everyone to go home. And then he had to it again. And again. The throng got the message by the fourth announcement, and the familiar procession of smiling fans dressed in red commenced for the final time. The traditional post-game playing of "My Old Kentucky Home" by the U of L Pep Band accompanied the parade. Some sang along, some shed tears, and others just smiled the same goofy smile they'd been displaying all day.

14 Six Weeks of Glory for Louisville Football

The year 2013 will always be remembered in the city of Louisville as "the Year of the Cardinal," and for good reason. The men's basketball team claimed its third national championship, the women's basketball team advanced all the way to the national title game, the baseball team went to the College World Series, and the football team knocked off Florida in the Sugar Bowl to secure (at the time) its biggest win in program history.

It all started on the gridiron, where one of the most glorious six-week stretches in the history of Cardinals football actually began in the fall of 2012. After suffering stunning back-to-back losses to Syracuse and Connecticut, a Louisville football team that had just a week prior been 9–0 and claiming it deserved a shot at a national title now needed a win on the evening of November 29 to win its own conference and lock down its second ever appearance in a BCS bowl game.

In order to make that happen, U of L would have to go to New Jersey for a Thursday night road tilt against a Rutgers team it had trailed 49–0 at halftime during a regular-season finale in Piscataway almost exactly four years earlier. The situation wasn't quite as dire as it had been in 2008, but with the team trailing 14–3 and star quarterback Teddy Bridgewater on the bench hampered by both a severely sprained ankle and a broken left wrist, folks back in the Derby City weren't exactly gearing up to spend New Year's somewhere warm.

What took place in the final 30 minutes on that night will be exaggerated to the point where 30 years from now Bridgewater will have tossed the game-winning touchdown to DeVante Parker from his Hoveround. What actually transpired was extraordinary enough: a one-legged, one-armed quarterback entered the game, hobbled around the field, and made all the plays necessary to lead his team to a 20–17 victory and a conference championship. In terms of the most memorable individual performances in U of L sports history, Bridgewater's spot near the top was assured the second the game clock hit zero.

As it turned out, Louisville didn't leave any magic in Jersey. The Cardinals had appeared destined for a date in Miami against future ACC foe Florida State in the Orange Bowl before an absolute perfect storm of events allowed Northern Illinois to crash the BCS, sending Louisville to the Sugar Bowl instead. Looming there was a third-ranked Florida team that the vast majority of Cardinals fans readily admitted they wanted no part of. It was a widely held view that wasn't without merit. While U of L hadn't exactly sparkled against its 113th-ranked schedule (there were 120 FBS-playing college football programs at the time) in the country, the Gators were the nation's lone team to have defeated four squads ranked in

Wide receivers DeVante Parker and Damian Copeland celebrate Parker's second-quarter touchdown in the 2013 Sugar Bowl upset of Florida.

the top 12. They also possessed a defense that some were calling the best in the program's illustrious history and one of the best that college football had seen in the past decade.

The Cardinals, however, were eager to take on the Goliath where their head coach, Charlie Strong, had previously served as defensive coordinator. "What not a lot of people know is that ever since he got [to Louisville], Coach Strong was always talking about Florida," said Brandon Dunn, a defensive lineman on the 2012 team. "Every time he thought we were slacking off at practice, he would say, 'You think Florida's doing this right now?' We were all so sick of hearing about Florida. So when we saw Florida pop up during that selection show...I'll just say it, we knew we were gonna kill 'em."

If the players truly believed that, they were the only ones. In the weeks leading up to the game, most of the discussion about the Sugar Bowl surrounded the notion that it shouldn't be possible for the BCS system to produce a major bowl game that was as much of a mismatch as Florida vs. Louisville was. Nearly every prediction that was served up by a college football writer had the Gators prevailing by a wide margin. It was a sentiment that Florida players—who had faced Cincinnati, another Big East underdog, in the Sugar Bowl three years prior and demolished them by a final score of 51–24—held, too. "We're going to do the same thing to Louisville that we did to Cincinnati," Florida tight end Omarius Hines said on the night before the game. "We see them out here having a good time and just looking happy to be here. We're going to do the same thing to them. I just know we're gonna win."

The overall feeling surrounding the game remained the same all the way up until kickoff. All four members handling ESPN's pregame coverage of the bowl picked Florida to win handily with Kirk Herbstreit being the most resolute about his pick. "Teddy Bridgewater, Joe Montana, whoever you want to put back there, it doesn't matter," Herbstreit said. "Louisville has no shot."

The confidence of Louisville's detractors took a huge hit right off the bat. On the game's first offensive play, Cardinals safety Terrell Floyd intercepted a deflected pass from Florida quarterback Jeff Driskel and returned it 38 yards for a U of L touchdown. That score doubled after Louisville's first offensive possession, in which a locked-in Bridgewater would guide the Cardinals 83 yards down the field before running back Jeremy Wright punched in the game's second touchdown from the 1-yard line. Bridgewater, who completed 10 of his first 11 passes, would cement his status as a college football superstar by completing 20 of 32 throws for 266 yards and a pair of touchdowns against the vaunted Gators defense.

When the final whistle blew on the evening of January 2, something that even the most sanguine of Cardinals supporters wouldn't have dared to predict had just become a reality. A Louisville team that on paper needed just about every break imaginable to even keep the game close had absolutely dominated Florida for four quarters before walking out of the Superdome with a 33–23 victory that wasn't nearly as close as the final score indicated. It was the biggest upset in BCS history both in terms of point spread (the Gators were 14-point favorites) and the disparity in the rankings of the two teams involved (No. 3 and No. 21). There was some debate over whether or not it was the biggest win in Louisville's history, but there was little question that Florida was the best team a Cardinals squad had ever defeated.

"They kind of thought we were going to come in and lay down and give them the game," Floyd said after the game. "But Coach Strong always preaches that we're better than any team in the nation if we come out and play hard. Coach Strong believed in us, and our coaching staff believed in us, and we came in and believed in ourselves."

Six years earlier, U of L hit a similar apex when it knocked off ACC champ Wake Forest and claimed its first Orange Bowl title. The major difference then was that within 72 hours Cardinals fans would find out that head coach Bobby Petrino had worked the game with his bags packed for a move to Atlanta, where he had already accepted a position to become the new coach of the NFL's Falcons.

Those concerns were so three weeks ago this time around, as the whole of Card Nation had already sweated out Charlie Strong's brief flirtation with the University of Tennessee in early December. Though short-lived, the saga took a toll on the entire program. Most notable was the press conference following the Rutgers win during which Strong not only dodged questions about his future, but also took a few shots at the Cardinals fan base, including a recommendation that they be more like the fans of archrival Kentucky. Strong could have endorsed moving the Kentucky Derby to Indiana, and it would have gone over better.

Ultimately, Strong pledged his allegiance to the school that had finally given him his first shot as a head coach, saying during an emotional press conference: "You can buy a person a lot, but you can't buy his heart. His heart is where his enthusiasm is, where his loyalty is. My enthusiasm and heart are with the University of Louisville."

He was forgiven. The press conference was good, but resurrecting a program that some had believed to be irreparably damaged by previous head coach Steve Kragthorpe was still probably his ace in the hole.

Whatever their reasons, Louisville fans made the not-so-cheap trip to New Orleans in record numbers for the second time in eight months (the Cardinals basketball team had played in the Final Four there the previous March). Their presence was so great that Strong declared the fans the game's MVP during the postgame celebration. It was a perfect moment.

As sweet as the moment was, wild dreams—realistic or not—about the future always tend to be sweeter. U of L fans quickly turned their attention to the 18 returning starters who would guide the team to a 12–1 record a year later and the reverie of Strong staying for decades and turning Louisville football into a perennial powerhouse.

Those dreams were shattered in early 2014 when Strong announced he was leaving Louisville for Texas. Though the move devastated a large portion of the U of L fan base and turned out to be a poor career choice for Strong, both parties will still always have the memories of those beautiful six weeks in late 2012 and early 2013.

Learn the Words to Louisville's Two Fight Songs

The University of Louisville has two official school songs, which means there's no excuse for Cardinals fans to not know the words to at least one of them. And yet that's the case for many fans who attend games at the KFC Yum! Center and Papa John's Cardinal Stadium. Most can recognize the tunes, but far fewer can sing along with them.

The oldest U of L school song is "Fight! U of L." It was written in 1962 by Robert Griffith, who directed the U of L marching band from 1961 until it was temporarily disbanded in the fall of 1970.

Here are the lyrics to "Fight! U of L":

(Chorus)
Fight now for victory and show them
How we sure will win this game
Fight on you Card'nals and prove to them
That we deserve our fame. (End chorus)
Rah, Rah, Rah!

Roll up the score now and beat the foe
So we can give a yell
With a FIGHT! give them all you've got
For we are with you U of L.
(Repeat chorus)
(Chant)
C-A-R-D-S
(Faster) C-A-R-D-S, C-A-R-D-S

In 1978 Kentucky Governor Julian Carroll offered to help reestablish the U of L marching band under the direction of Randy Mitchell, and in the fall of 1979, the band resumed performing at home Cardinals football games. The band has performed at every Louisville home game since.

Noting that several high-profile programs across the country had multiple fight songs in order to keep their game atmospheres fresh, U of L athletic director Bill Olsen began exploring the possibility in the late 1980s of hiring a big-name composer to pen something fresh for Cardinals sports. That turned out to be unnecessary, as a U of L marching band graduate assistant named Al Greener put together a song called "All Hail, U of L," which instantly became a hit at home football and basketball games.

Here's "All Hail, U of L":

All hail to thee, our U of L
As we stand up for her fame.
All hail to thee our U of L
As we fight to win this game.
Sing praises for a victory,
We wish our heroes well.
All hail the Cardinal Spirit.
All hail our U of L!
GO CARDS!

Greener would go on to serve as the director of the University of Louisville Cardinal Pride Pep Band, which plays at all home basketball games.

Westley Unseld

Westley "Wes" Sissel Unseld was hanging out by himself during recess one afternoon when his school's fifth-grade teacher, Mrs. Dickerson, called for him to come talk to her. A reserved but obedient and gifted student, Unseld's initial reaction was one of concern. "I thought I'd done something wrong," Unseld told *The Washington Post* in 1988.

In actuality, Mrs. Dickerson was about to light the match that would ignite one of the city of Louisville's best-known basketball fires. "Somebody had decided to play a basketball game between the fifth and sixth grades," he said, "and she told me I was going to play. And after that game, I didn't touch a basketball again for three years."

After not making his junior high school's eighth grade team, Unseld figured he was finished with basketball. Then he grew. A lot. He attended Seneca High School in Louisville and was convinced to come out for the school's basketball team by freshman and junior varsity coach Carl Wright, the man who Unseld said first made him fall in love with the game. "Mr. Wright sort of look me under his wing," Unseld told *The Courier-Journal* in 1967. "He was 6'5" and big like me and he sort of beat me around in practice. He taught me a lot."

Although his coach would later admit that his star was listed at 6'8" purely in an effort to intimidate opponents, Unseld—who eventually conceded that he'd never been measured taller than 6'6"—would go on to guide Seneca to state championships in 1963 and 1964. At the end of his senior season, he became just the second African American to be named the state of Kentucky's Mr. Basketball. (The first had been his teammate, Mike Redd, the year before.)

Though it took place more than a half century ago, the recruitment of Unseld is still a much-debated issue in the Bluegrass State. What's known is that Unseld became the first African American to whom Adolph Rupp offered a scholarship to come play at the University of Kentucky. What's less clear is why Unseld ultimately chose to stay home and play his college ball at the University of Louisville.

Some say Unseld didn't want the attention that would have come with being a trailblazer. Others point to the fact that he was roundly booed while playing at the state tournament in Lexington. Pat Riley, then a member of the Kentucky basketball team who was attempting to help convince Unseld to come to Lexington, told *The New York Times* in 1994 that he knew Wes had received death threats.

Ultimately, Unseld chose to play for Peck Hickman and the already integrated Louisville Cardinals. Though he wasn't allowed to play on the varsity team because of the NCAA rules at the time, Unseld still made quite the impression on the U of L community during his first season on campus. He flourished in the classroom while majoring in both physical education and history and dominated on the basketball court, finishing his debut season averaging 35.8 points and 23.6 rebounds per game for Louisville's freshman team.

The next three years of Unseld's basketball career were fairly predictable. He scored 1,686 points in just 82 games (averaging 20.6 points per game) and grabbed 1,551 rebounds (averaging 18.9 rebounds per game), leading the Missouri Valley Conference in the category for all three seasons. Unseld led the Cardinals to the NIT in 1966 and the NCAA Tournament the following two years and was named a first-team All-American in both 1967 and 1968.

Although he arrived on U of L's campus leery of playing for a man who he had been warned was only taking African American players because he had to, Unseld left Louisville crediting Hickman for instilling in him the toughness that would go on to define his career. "I was told he wouldn't be the coach by the time I got to the varsity," Unseld recalled. "He was as different a person as I've ever met in my life. But I left, after playing for him, thinking he was the greatest person ever. To this day, he's one of the finest men I've ever been associated with."

Unseld left Louisville with a BS in health and physical education and history in 1968. He had even more appearances on the school's dean's list than he had All-American honors.

The next chapter of Unseld's story is better known to most. He was taken with the No. 2 overall pick in the 1968 NBA Draft and in 1969 became just the second player ever to be named the NBA's Rookie of the Year and its Most Valuable Player in the same season. His 13-year NBA career would feature five All-Star appearances and an NBA Finals Most Valuable Player award in 1978 when he guided the Washington Bullets (now Wizards) to their first and only world championship.

Unseld is one of just four Louisville players to have his number retired. He owns the school's all-time record for most points scored by a three-year player and for points in a single game (45).

In 2008 Unseld was honored as the University of Louisville's Alumnus of the Year, the highest honor bestowed on any graduate by the U of L Alumni Association. The award was given to Unseld as much for his off-the-court work as it was for the talent that landed him in the Naismith Memorial Basketball Hall of Fame in 1988.

In 1979 Unseld and his wife, Connie, also a Louisville graduate, founded Unseld's School under the philosophy "Every Child Can Learn." The coed private school located in southwest Baltimore offers a curriculum for children nine months to 14 years of age. It also provides programs that help its students in the areas of life skills, manners and etiquette, character education, outdoor education, sports, and drama.

17 Wiley Brown's Thumb

During his four-year career at Louisville, Wiley Brown scored 699 points, grabbed 407 rebounds, and served as a starting forward on U of L's 1980 national championship team and its 1982 Final Four team. After his time at Louisville, Brown enjoyed a successful career playing both professional basketball and football and has spent the past decade coaching college basketball.

Still, none of these statistics or accomplishments are the first thing that pop into any Louisville fan's mind the moment they hear the name Wiley Brown. When Brown was four years old, the Sylvester, Georgia, native accidentally cut his right thumb with a knife. The cut was never treated properly, which caused it to become infected, ultimately forcing doctors to amputate it above the first joint.

Despite the impairment, Brown taught himself to be left-handed and developed into an athlete skilled enough to be named Georgia's High School Player of the Year for both basketball and football. He turned down major football scholarships in order to play basketball at Louisville for Denny Crum, who already had a special plan to make Brown an even better player.

After consulting with world-renowned Louisville-based hand surgeons Drs. Joseph Kutz and Harold Kleinert following Brown's freshman season, Crum had U of L trainer Jerry May create a prosthesis that would essentially give Brown two working thumbs. Brown, who had spent the past 15 years perfecting life without the use of his right thumb, was hesitant at first but was ultimately given little choice by his head coach.

How much of a role the artificial thumb played in Brown's development as a player is still a fact that's debated by all parties involved. What isn't debatable is that every one of Brown's statistical averages improved dramatically, and that he went from a freshman reserve who played just 13 minutes per game to a full-time starter who rarely played fewer than 30 minutes.

Still, Brown wasn't a fan of the newfound notoriety that the artificial thumb brought him. He was even less of a fan of the fact that every now and then during a game or a practice the thumb would fly off his hand like a projectile, horrifying onlookers and sending his teammates into an uproar. Brown's pleas fell on deaf ears, as Crum was a staunch believer in the notion that the prosthetic was making his big man a better player—even if he was still instructing his other players to try and direct their passes to Brown's left side.

On the morning of March 24, 1980, Louisville was mere hours away from playing in its first national championship game. Brown, and his fake thumb, were a large part of the reason why. Brown had played an especially large role in the Cardinals' Sweet 16 win against Texas A&M, in which he had scored seven of his team's final 10 points in regulation, helping U of L claw back from a late deficit, force overtime, and eventually eliminate the Aggies with a 66–55 win.

Everything was going perfectly for Louisville. The Cardinals had looked like the vastly superior team in their Elite Eight win against LSU and their national semifinal victory against Iowa,

Darrell Griffith was playing like the best player in the country, and Crum's team appeared poised to lock down some revenge on the UCLA team that had dealt them a soul-crushing overtime defeat in the Final Four five years prior.

But as the team gathered on the bus to head to Indianapolis' Market Square Arena, there arose a problem. Brown walked over to student trainer Steve Donohue and with a straight face served up a line that Donohue probably never thought he'd hear when he joined up with Louisville basketball: "Yo, man, I lost my thumb."

Brown didn't seem particularly upset by the development, but Crum was adamant that the thumb be found, especially with the program's first national title hanging in the balance. Brown had last remembered seeing his thumb on the breakfast table where he'd eaten that morning at the Hilton Hotel, so Donohue and U of L junior Randy Bufford raced back to the hotel.

The duo was immediately hit with the information they'd feared: all the tables from that morning had already been cleared, and the waste had already been tossed into the dumpster outside. After a search through the dumpster yielded no results, the group resorted to running back inside the hotel and asking anyone in the general vicinity of the dining area whether they'd recently seen a thumb. In a last-ditch effort, Bufford went back into the kitchen area to rummage through anything he could. It was there that he discovered the thumb, resting peacefully beneath a stack of pancakes, eggs, and sausage.

With his right hand as close to full strength as possible, Brown scored eight points and grabbed seven rebounds as Louisville clipped UCLA 59–54 to claim the program's first national championship.

Angel McCoughtry

When Darrell Griffith left Louisville for good after leading the Cardinals to the 1980 national championship, his school record of 2,333 points was said to be unbreakable. It took nearly three decades, but Dr. Dunkenstein finally met his match when Angel McCoughtry arrived on campus and breathed life unto the U of L women's program in the same manner that he'd jumpstarted the men's.

With McCoughtry having gone to school at St. Frances High School in Baltimore and later at Patterson Prep in Lenoir, North Carolina, her friends and family all expected her to one day wear the uniform of a perennial powerhouse like Connecticut or Tennessee. When she told these same supporters that she was instead headed to Louisville—a program, which at the time had never spent a day in the national rankings and had never made it past the opening weekend of the NCAA Tournament—she often found herself hit with blank stares or fake smiles. "I wasn't looking at the now, and everybody else was looking at the now," McCoughtry told the Associated Press in 2009. "I was looking at the whole picture. I was looking at the future and I was like, 'You know what? Maybe right now we might not be anybody. But we're going to be somebody. Just you watch.'"

Success didn't come immediately for McCoughtry, who struggled early on in her freshman season with adjusting to a life in which she wasn't the player expected to do the bulk of her team's scoring. In high school she had developed a reputation for being too outspoken and, as UConn head coach Geno Auriemma once said, "difficult to like." The rap had resulted in some power programs opting not to offer her a scholarship, and in the nascent days of her college career, it was also holding her back from enjoying instant success.

Under the direction of head coach Tom Collen, Louisville pieced together a moderately successful season that ended with the program's second consecutive trip to the NCAA Tournament. On a team loaded with veteran talent, McCoughtry had managed to see the court for only 19.9 minutes per game, but she had shown flashes of the star she would become during the season's closing weeks. She finished the year by being named to the Big East's All-Freshman team after averaging 9.4 points per game and leading the team in rebounding (9.4 rebounds per game), steals (56), and blocked shots (23).

With Louisville graduating a healthy amount of talent from its previous season, Collen opted to build his 2006–07 team around McCoughtry. She did not make him regret the move. As a sophomore, McCoughtry began demolishing everything that had been previously known about the Louisville women's basketball program. Attendance soared as she wowed the crowds inside Freedom Hall with a combination of athleticism, flair, and grace the fans had never seen before. The team climbed into the national rankings for the first time ever, as McCoughtry became just the second player in the lengthy history of the Big East to lead the league in both scoring (23.3 points per game) and rebounding (11.3 rebounds per game). She was named the conference's MVP at the end of the season and also became the first U of L women's basketball player to earn a second-team All-American nod from the Associated Press.

Although the individual accolades were terrific, McCoughtry yearned for more team success. Louisville had just put together the best season in program history thanks to its new star, winning a program-record 27 games, earning their best ever seed in the NCAA Tournament (No. 6), and securing a bid to the Big Dance for a program-record third consecutive season. But it hadn't ended

Angel McCoughtry is the most decorated Louisville women's basketball player in school history.

the way McCoughtry had wanted. After destroying BYU in the first round of the NCAA Tournament, Louisville let a 14-point lead with just 11 minutes slip away against third-seeded Arizona State. The crushing defeat had kept the Cards from crashing the Sweet 16 for the first time.

Quickly adding to the disappointment of the off-season was the news that Collen had resigned at Louisville and accepted the head coaching job at Arkansas. His replacement was someone already familiar to McCoughtry. Prior to being named the new head coach at Louisville, Jeff Walz had spent six seasons as an assistant coach at Maryland during the same time that McCoughtry had been tearing up the high school scene in Baltimore. Walz knew all about his new star player's immense talent, but he also knew about her attitude. One of the first things the new U of L coach did when he got to campus was put together a tape of McCoughtry's negative body language from the previous season. He let the All-American see for herself. "I was shocked," McCoughtry told *Sports Illustrated* in 2009. "Is this really how I look? Is this what everyone has been talking about? I had to change that and channel my energy in a more positive way."

McCoughtry fully embraced her new role as both superstar and team captain. She spent more time giving advice to the younger players and also increased her interaction with the ever-growing Angel McCoughtry fan club. She also urged U of L administrators to make her No. 35 jersey available at the school bookstore. When they obliged, it became the biggest seller on campus.

McCoughtry's evolution wasn't limited to off-the-court activities. Her scoring average rose to a career-best 23.8 points per game, and her average of 4.1 steals per game ranked second in the country. Her single season totals of 858 points and 148 steals were both school records. McCoughtry's individual success also continued to lead Louisville into uncharted territory. The Cardinals earned a No. 4 seed in the NCAA Tournament, where they knocked off Miami University and Kansas State to advance to the Sweet 16 for the first time ever. McCoughtry's 35 points and 13 rebounds nearly carried U of L to an upset of top-seeded North Carolina, but the Cards again saw their season end in heartbreak when an 18-point lead evaporated into a 78–74 defeat.

In a complete role reversal from the time she arrived, McCoughtry's senior season began with both her and the program she represented sitting squarely in the national spotlight. Both proved to be capable of handling the unexpected attention. With McCoughtry leading the way, Louisville shattered the school record for wins with 34, climbed as high as No. 5 in the national rankings, and earned a No. 3 seed in the NCAA Tournament. The real magic started in the postseason, as the Cards, who just a year prior had never been to the Sweet 16, knocked off a pair of No. 1 seeds to advance all the way to the national title game. Big East conference-mate Connecticut, which had won all 39 of its games by double-digits, proved to be too much in the championship, but McCoughtry's legacy was solidified, and U of L women's basketball was forever changed.

When the dust had fully settled, McCoughtry had finished her college career with 2,779 points, the most by any Louisville basketball player, male or female. Her first season in a Cardinals uniform had ended with a one-and-done performance in the NCAA Tournament, and her final contest had been played in that tournament's championship game. Perhaps most important, 11,000 fans had packed Freedom Hall to watch McCoughtry play on her senior night. In her first game as a Cardinal four years earlier, fewer than 1,000 had shown up.

"This is just the beginning," McCoughtry told Cardinals fans at a postseason celebration honoring the team's accomplishments. "Louisville isn't going anywhere. We got this started, but one day Louisville is going to be right there with Connecticut and Tennessee, and Coach Walz is going to be in the Hall of Fame."

McCoughtry's legacy has only grown since her days at Louisville ended. She was drafted first overall by the Atlanta Dream in the 2009 WNBA Draft and a few months later she was named the league's Rookie of the Year. From 2009 to 2016, she was named an All-Star five times, led the WNBA in scoring twice, and won two Olympic gold medals with the United States national team.

In 2010 McCoughtry became the first Louisville women's basketball player to have her jersey retired.

19 Don't Jump on the Bird

One of Louisville football's favorite modern traditions is beating down the few opponents who have dared to come into Papa John's Cardinal Stadium and stomp (or dance) on top of the midfield Cardinal bird logo before the game.

Such an occurrence has taken place five times since 2004, and it has never ended well for the visiting team.

Here's the full rundown of offending teams:

East Carolina—October 2, 2004
Final Score: Louisville 59, East Carolina 7

Cincinnati—November 27, 2004
Final Score: Louisville 70, Cincinnati 7

Rutgers—November 11, 2005
Final Score: Louisville 56, Rutgers 5

Miami—September 16, 2006
Final Score: Louisville 31, Miami 7

Kentucky—November 29, 2014
Final Score: Louisville 44, Kentucky 40

All told, the Louisville football team has beaten the five bird-stomping culprits by a combined score of 260–66.

On December 21, 2016, the Kentucky basketball team tested the crossover power of the phenomenon by jumping on top of the Cardinal bird logo that sits at midcourt inside the KFC Yum! Center. The result? Louisville native Quentin Snider scored 22 points, and the Cardinals defeated their archrivals for the first time since 2012, 73–70.

Don't jump on the bird. On second thought, keep doing it!

20 Charlie Tyra

Before Darrell Griffith or Pervis Ellison or Russ Smith, there was Charlie Tyra. After starring at Louisville's Atherton High School, Tyra arrived on U of L's campus in the fall of 1953. Three years later he would become the program's first All-American and the star of a Louisville team that would capture the National Invitational Tournament title.

Attempting to put Tyra's numbers into some sort of modern context is a futile effort. For example, in a 98–82 Louisville win at Canisius on December 10, 1955, Tyra scored 37 points, which somehow still managed to be less than his rebounding total of 38.

The closest any Cardinal has come since to matching that performance on the glass came when Ellis Myles pulled down 23 in a 2001 win over Tennessee State. Tyra's 38-rebound performance is tied for the ninth-best single game rebounding performance in the history of college basketball.

Examining Tyra's numbers are an experience, but looking at the numbers that are closest to his in the all-time Louisville record books is what really enhances it. Louisville played in just 29 games during the 1955–56 season, and yet Tyra still managed to pull down 645 rebounds, good for an average of 22.4 per game—both U of L records that will almost certainly never be approached. The second-highest single-season rebounding total in U of L basketball history belongs to Ron Thomas, who snagged 420—a mere 225 fewer than Tyra—during the 1971–72 season. Thomas also had the benefit of playing in two more games than Tyra did.

Tyra was also one of the best scorers in U of L history. Despite playing in an era in which the team never played more than 30 games, Tyra still managed to rack up 1,728 points, good for ninth on Louisville's all-time scoring list. The 95 total games Tyra played in are the fewest of any player who ranks in the top 10.

In 1955–56, the first of Tyra's two All-American seasons at Louisville, he averaged 23.8 points per game, still the highest single season average in U of L history. His 21.4 average a season later ranks fifth on that same list. Tyra also remains the school's all-time leading rebounder with 1,617 boards to his name.

From a team standpoint, Tyra will always be known for captaining Louisville's 1955–56 NIT championship squad. The title was U of L's first since making the move from the NAIB (now NAIA) to the NCAA, and at the time the NIT was viewed by many to be a more significant competition than the NCAA Tournament. Tyra scored 29 points in a semifinal victory against Saint Joseph's and then carried Louisville to a 90–83 win against No. 3 Dayton in the tournament championship game at Madison Square Garden. He was honored as the tournament's MVP following the game.

"No player in Louisville history ever worked harder than Charlie Tyra," said former *Sports Illustrated* writer and Louisville native Billy Reid. "Quiet to the point of shyness off the floor, he led by example. He never quit. He never stopped working."

The Fort Wayne Pistons selected Tyra with the second overall pick of the 1957 NBA Draft, a move which would earn him the distinction of being the highest Louisville draft pick ever. (It was an honor he would later share with Westley Unseld until Cardinals big man Pervis Ellison was selected by Sacramento with the No. 1 overall pick in 1989.) Tyra would go on to play five NBA seasons, the majority of which came with the New York Knicks, the same team he was traded to on draft night. Following his professional career, he returned home to Louisville, where he lived with his wife of 49 years and their five children until his passing in 2006. Tyra's No. 8 is one of just four numbers that Louisville basketball has retired, joining Unseld's No. 31, Ellison's No. 42, and Darrell Griffith's No. 35.

21 The First Family of Louisville Football

The rest of the country may recognize the Manning clan as the first family of football, but in Louisville it's a distinction that belongs to the Brohms.

The story begins with the family patriarch, Oscar, who was a three-sport star at now-defunct Flaget High School in Louisville from 1962 to 1965. In an era where the forward pass was as rare as the triple option is today, Brohm tossed for 1,848 yards and set a city record with 23 touchdown passes during his senior season in 1965. That record stood for nearly three decades before future U of L star Chris Redman shattered it (and just about every other city passing record) in 1993. Brohm went on to the University of Louisville, where he played quarterback from 1966 to 1969 and started a tradition that would last much longer than he could have ever imagined.

When Flaget High School closed its doors in 1974, Oscar's two oldest sons, Greg and Jeff, chose to take their teenage talents to the state's new Catholic high school power, Trinity. Greg, the oldest, became a first-team All-State receiver thanks in large part to the picture-perfect passes tossed by his younger brother by one year. Jeff was a star from day one at Trinity, becoming one of the first and still only players in the history of the state power to see varsity action as a freshman. He would eventually become one of the most highly sought-after quarterback recruits in the country after earning the state's Mr. Football honor in 1988, the same year he led Trinity to an undefeated season and a state championship.

Also a standout on the diamond, Jeff was drafted by the Montreal Expos in the seventh round of the 1989 MLB Draft but chose to temporarily put his baseball career on hold in favor of following in his father's footsteps and playing quarterback at Louisville. He would be drafted again the next year, this time in the fourth round by the Cleveland Indians, and would play two summers of minor league ball before giving up the sport for good in order to focus fully on football.

Despite having the opportunity to play for just about any school in the country, Jeff chose to stay home thanks to the fact that Howard Schnellenberger had Louisville football in as positive a place as the program had been in decades. "I was lucky enough to be recruited by a lot of big schools," Brohm said about his college decision. "The fact that coach Schnellenberger was at Louisville

Part of a great quarterback lineage, brothers Jeff (left) and Brian Brohm pose for the media in 2005.

and his experience of developing quarterbacks and winning championships at the collegiate and professional level was a big reason. The second reason was being able to play with my brother and be around family and sharing the experience with them. It's great to excel in athletics, but when you have people around you that you know and love that have been there throughout your life makes it even more fun."

After spending two seasons as the primary backup on a pair of highly successful Cardinals teams, Jeff took the starting reins in 1992 and '93. He did not disappoint. Brohm was named the team's Most Valuable Player as both a junior and a senior. In his senior season of 1993, Louisville won nine games and spent the bulk of the year in the national rankings. Brohm earned All-America accolades by tossing for 2,626 yards and 20 touchdowns, but it was his play in his final game that fans still remember most.

Playing with a steel plate and pins in the right index finger that he had broken in Louisville's regular season finale win against Tulsa, Brohm still managed to complete 19 of 29 passes and lead the Cards to a come-from-behind 18–7 win against Michigan State in below-freezing temperatures at the Liberty Bowl. He was named the game's Most Valuable Player, wrapping up a career that resulted in his jersey being one of 19 currently honored inside Papa John's Cardinal Stadium.

Though he didn't hear his name called during the 1994 NFL Draft, the same work ethic that had already made Jeff a Louisville legend led to him earning a roster spot with the San Diego Chargers, kicking off what would ultimately be a seven-year NFL career. In that first year, Brohm's Chargers advanced all the way to the Super Bowl, creating an experience that would deeply affect the entire family. Perhaps no family member was more changed by the occurrence than the youngest, eight-year-old Brian. "Jeff was the guy I always looked up, the guy I always wanted to be," Brian said. "When he went to the Super Bowl and we all went down there together to the game in Atlanta, it's really the first time that I remember falling in love with football. I watched the quarterbacks all week, the way they moved, the way they talked, everything. I decided then that this was what I wanted to be."

As had been the case with Jeff more than a decade earlier, stories of the youngest Brohm's throwing prowess began to circulate throughout Louisville well before he started making newspaper headlines. While the playbooks for most third- and fourth-grade flag football teams consisted of simple handoffs, Oscar Brohm let his youngest son air it out for the St. Bernard Wildcats.

It was at one of these youth games where the current golden boy of the city, Male High All-American Chris Redman, first encountered the young man who would one day follow in his footsteps at Louisville. Redman had been making money officiating flag football games during his senior year of high school and happened to referee one game in which the quarterback threw the ball "maybe 30 or 35 times," which was more than he'd seen the rest of the year combined. "I went home and my told my dad [legendary local high school coach, Bob Redman], 'There's this kid out there who's going to wind up being better than all of us,'" the younger Redman said. "He asked me who it was. I just told him, 'Another kid named Brohm.'"

Playing all three major sports just as his brothers and father before him had done, the youngest Brohm went on to lead Trinity High School to three straight Class 4A state championships from 2001 to 2003. He graced the cover of *Sports Illustrated* in 2002 and was named the USA Today National Offensive Player of the Year a season later. Despite being courted by every major college program in the country, Brohm ultimately chose to follow in his elders' footsteps and play his college ball at the University of Louisville.

Success continued at the next level for Brohm. He was named the Conference USA Freshman of the Year in 2004, the Big East Offensive Player of the Year the season after that, and was the MVP in Louisville's 2007 Orange Bowl victory against Wake Forest. Brohm wrapped up his Cardinals career with 10,775 yards (second all-time at U of L) and 71 touchdowns. Perhaps more impressive than the numbers was the simple fact that Brian had been able to live up to the lifelong hype created by his last name. "I'm not going to say that there wasn't pressure growing up with the last name Brohm, but it was always more good than bad," Brohm says. "My dad or one of my brothers was always one of my coaches growing up, and even when they weren't, they were always there to help. Even the pressure pushed to be better. I was very fortunate."

Brohm spent three seasons in the NFL after being selected by the Green Bay Packers as the 56th overall pick of the 2008 NFL Draft. His professional career continued in the UFL and later the CFL, where he suited up for the Hamilton Tiger Cats and Winnipeg Blue Bombers. After choosing to hang up his cleats for good in 2016, Brohm made the long-expected move to join the coaching ranks. His first gig? Coaching quarterbacks at Western Kentucky for his brother Jeff, of course.

In 2016 Jeff Brohm—with his youngest brother by his side coaching the quarterbacks and his older brother serving as his director of football operations—led the Hilltoppers to their second consecutive Conference USA championship and their third con-secutive bowl victory. When Jeff accepted the head coaching job at Purdue, an announcement soon followed that both Brian and Greg would be coming with him to West Lafayette, Indiana.

22 ACC Jubilation

There were Louisville natives and outsiders alike who, during the summer of 2014, referred to the multiple celebrations honoring U of L's official induction into the Atlantic Coast Conference as overkill.

It's true, I think, that no program or fan base has ever celebrated a move to a new conference more exhaustively than Card Nation celebrated its transition to the ACC—but there's a reason for that. Not only had Louisville fans, administrators, coaches, and athletes experienced what it feels like to be passed over, but they had all been faced with the reality of being left behind completely and been forced to stare it dead in the eyes.

By November of 2012, U of L fans had come to terms with the fact that the curious conference realignment roulette ball was never going to bounce in their favor. They hadn't been a part of the first helping of Big East-to-ACC defections that rocked the college sports landscape and then they'd lost out to West Virginia in a highly publicized battle for an invitation to the Big 12. None of this made much sense to Louisville fans, who watched their basketball, football, and baseball teams kick around the programs that were headed to greener pastures, only to spend the mornings after listening to things like television markets and airport size used as justification for another school's superiority despite their on-field inferiority.

When news broke on November 17, 2012, that Maryland and Rutgers would both soon announce moves to the Big Ten, Cardinals fans immediately expected the worst. Experience had conditioned them so well that they hardly batted an eye when every network on the planet began reporting that Connecticut was the program most likely to fill the ACC spot being left behind by the Terrapins.

Then Tom Jurich went to work. He dug up every contact he could remember, he made travel plans, and he hit the phones. Hard. "Every waking hour," Jurich said after the dust had settled. "This has been the only thing. I pulled in every marker I had in the United States. I really did. Every marker I had in 29 years as an AD I pulled in, from TV people to other league commissioners to professional sports. Anyone who could vouch for us, I asked them. You've got to sell yourself."

Six days after Maryland announced its departure plans, Louisville had become a neck-and-neck contender with UConn for that coveted ACC spot. After nine days U of L was the leader. On Day 11, the Cards were in.

The most incredible thing about the entire saga remains how, despite all the slaps in the face the program received during every awful helping of conference realignment madness, Louisville walked out of it all in the perfect situation. The ACC had always been the ideal spot for Cardinals athletics, but it felt as if it were a pipe dream—something that had never been on the table and probably would never be on the table. When it moved to the Big East in 2005, the main attraction for Louisville was that the conference was then the king of college basketball. The ACC brought that reality back—and to an even higher degree.

Duke, North Carolina, Syracuse, Pitt, N.C. State, Coach K, Roy Williams, Jim Boeheim, Tobacco Road, the Cameron Crazies. Basketball is a pretty big deal in the Derby City, so the move to a conference that is the focal point of the hoops world from November through March was always going to be more than enough to send everyone associated with Louisville athletics to cloud nine.

As far as the other major sports are concerned, there is no aspect of the football program that wasn't improved dramatically by jumping to the ACC. U of L left a conference that was relegated to being one of the have-nots for one that was always going to have a seat at the adults table. It left home games against Memphis and SMU behind for annual contests against Florida State and Miami. It no longer had to worry about competitors using conference affiliation against them on the recruiting trail and it no longer had to worry about national perception keeping it from playing for the sport's top prize.

Louisville fans should be thankful for their one season in the American Athletic Conference in 2013–14. That experience gave them firsthand experience of what could have been and what very nearly was. In that season the football team went 11–1, spent the entire season in the national rankings but was still relegated to facing an unranked opponent in the Russell Athletic Bowl. On the hardwood the Cardinals won 31 games, captured their league's regular-season and tournament titles, and were still dealt a No. 4 seed by the NCAA Tournament Selection Committee.

These are concerns that don't exist in Louisville's life in the ACC. The very next season, the Cardinals football team lost three regular-season games but still played in a high-profile bowl game against a top 15 opponent from the SEC. The basketball team lost eight regular season conference games, finished fourth in the ACC, and didn't win a game in the league tournament but still garnered enough respect to be a No. 4 seed in the Big Dance.

Listing Jurich's accomplishments since he arrived at Louisville would be enough to fill this book on its own. That said, I'm not sure the Cardinals athletic director has done any work more significant than the miracle he pulled off during those 11 days in November 2012. In moving U of L to the ACC, Jurich provided each one of his programs with the ultimate vehicle for success. The celebrations that summer were indeed justified.

23 Bobby Petrino

Not since Ross and Rachel has there been a relationship as complicated, but somehow successful, as the one between Louisville football and Bobby Petrino. The story begins in 1998. That's when Petrino, a Montana native who had spent nearly all of his playing and coaching days west of the Mississippi, came to U of L to serve as John L. Smith's first offensive coordinator. Under Petrino's tutelage junior quarterback Chris Redman made a star turn, throwing for a school-record 4,042 yards and 29 touchdowns. Petrino's offense finished the season ranked No. 1 in the country in both scoring and total offense. Largely because of the video-game-caliber numbers that the offense was able to put up, Louisville made the biggest turnaround in college football that season, going from 1–10 in 1997 to 7–5 in Smith's first season at the helm.

That one year at U of L proved to be enough for Petrino—at least for the time being. He made a jump to the NFL for the first time, coaching the quarterbacks for the Jacksonville Jaguars in 1999 and 2000 and then served as the team's offensive coordinator in 2001. After returning to the college game to serve as Auburn's offensive coordinator for the 2002 season, Petrino finally got the call he'd thought would come years earlier.

The call came from Louisville athletic director Tom Jurich, who had been sent into scramble mode thanks to an unforeseen coaching vacancy. In a breach of common protocol, Michigan State athletic director Ron Mason had contacted Smith about taking over the Spartans football program just hours before Smith was set to lead U of L onto the field in the GMAC Bowl. When news broke on ESPN during the game that Smith was headed to East

Lansing, Michigan, Jurich was forced to hold an impromptu news conference at halftime. Five days later he was introducing Petrino as his new head coach.

Under Petrino, Louisville had reached heights that had seemed like a pipe dream for the bulk of the program's existence. The 2004 Cardinals went 11–1 and knocked off unbeaten Boise State in the Liberty Bowl. With its lone defeat coming in a narrow loss on the road to powerhouse Miami, U of L finished at No. 6 in the final AP poll, the highest ranking in program history at that time. The postseason ranking was duplicated two years later when Petrino guided Louisville to a 12–1 mark, a Big East championship, and an Orange Bowl victory against Wake Forest.

Despite the success, the relationship between Petrino and his school wasn't always smooth sailing. On multiple occasions reports surfaced of Petrino either listening to pitches or actively pursuing other coaching jobs. The most infamous of those occasions was what would later became known as "JetGate," in which Auburn attempted to tab Petrino as a replacement for Tommy Tuberville. Details of the rendezvous were leaked to *The Courier-Journal*, and though Petrino initially denied that any meeting had taken place, he was forced to come clean after an admission from Auburn.

Wanting the distractions to end for good, Jurich signed Petrino to a 10-year extension in the summer of 2006. The coach said his agreement to the deal was a sign that he had finally settled and that there was nowhere else he wanted to be. "We did want to make a statement," Petrino said on the day the deal was announced. "I also wanted to make sure that everyone under-stood—and I know I've said it—that this is where my family wants to be and where I want to be. But I want everyone to really believe it when it is said."

Just six months after those words were uttered and just five days after his team's Orange Bowl win, Petrino announced that he was leaving Louisville to become the new head coach of the Atlanta Falcons.

Things didn't go swimmingly for either party in the immediate aftermath of the split. Petrino never got the chance to coach Michael Vick and left the woeful Falcons before the end of his first season on the job in a move that was widely criticized. Louisville hired Steve Kragthorpe, who failed to lead the Cardinals to a single bowl game over three woeful seasons.

In 2012 an embarrassing off-the-field incident led to Petrino's firing at Arkansas, a place where he seemed to have things rolling. Instead, the coach found himself searching for answers. He patched up his relationship with Jurich, made things right with his family, and focused on life away from football for a year. After spending one highly successful season at nearby Western Kentucky, fate intervened and gave Petrino a chance to come back to the place where he'd been the happiest.

Choosing not to heed the words of the predecessors who had advised him to hold on to his gig at Louisville for as long as he could, head coach Charlie Strong had chosen to bolt for the seemingly greener pastures of Texas in early 2013. Needing a proven winner to ensure that the program wouldn't lose any of its momentum as it transitioned into the ACC, Jurich knew the first call he had to make. "It was a tough call, but it was the right thing to do," Jurich said recently. "At first I wasn't interested in Bobby the coach, I was interested in Bobby the person, and making sure that he had made the necessary changes. Once he had proven to be that he had, I was all in. I know I'm biased, but I believe he's the best football coach in the country."

Petrino, understandably, jumped at the opportunity. He also admitted publicly for the first time that he was reckless in his first stint with the program and that he didn't fully appreciate the support and the opportunity that Jurich had given him. "When I was here before, I think I was young and inexperienced—just driven," Petrino said in a 2014 interview with CBS. "Maybe I didn't have a good idea of everything else going around. Maybe [I was] too focused and didn't enjoy it as much as I need to. I'm trying to relax a little bit more, enjoy it a littler bit more, enjoy the good times, not get so down on the bad times."

Despite the rocky patches, the highs have always outnumbered the lows when it comes to the relationship between Petrino and Louisville. Life has never been better for Cardinals football than the years under Petrino, who boasts the program's best all-time winning percentage as well as the distinction of being the only coach in school history to have multiple teams finish their seasons ranked in the top 10 of the AP poll.

The Inventors of the High Five

The 1979–80 Louisville basketball team will be forever known for the above-the-rim style of play that earned them the nickname "the Doctors of Dunk" and for bringing U of L its first national championship. But are those same Cardinals also responsible for inventing the high five? "Until someone tells me different or shows me something that proves otherwise, I'll believe we did," said Wiley Brown, a standout on 1980 championship team. "All I know is one day Derek Smith walks up to me and I was getting ready to give him a low five, and he says, 'No, up high.' We started doing it from then on. We had a lot of games on national television that year, and it kind of got out."

While both former college basketball player Lamont Sleets, current Washington Nationals manager Dusty Baker, and former Los Angeles Dodgers outfielder Glenn Burke have also made claims of either creating or playing a part in the origins of the high five, only Louisville's claim comes with video evidence.

Near the end of the Cardinals' 1980 triumph over No. 1 seed LSU in the Elite Eight, legendary announcers Al McGuire, Billy Packer, and Dick Enberg noticed the Cardinals players performing the celebratory ritual and couldn't help but comment on it. The transcript of those comments is as follows:

McGuire: "You see the handshaking above the head? You know what the guys call that? A high five."
Packer: "A high five?"
McGuire: "Yeah. A high five. They're high fiving out there right now."
Enberg: "Louisville with some high fives."

To the best of anyone's knowledge, this was the first time that the high five was ever discussed in any capacity on national television. This being the case, it's difficult to deny that at the very least, the 1979–80 Louisville basketball team took the high five mainstream.

Brown, who now serves as the head basketball coach at Indiana University Southeast, understands that there's no way to prove beyond the shadow of a doubt who deserves the credit for the invention of the cultural phenomenon. Still, that doesn't mean he's backing down from his stance that he and former teammate Smith are the rightful recipients of any origin praise. "If they want to give us the credit for it, that's fine, we'll take the publicity," Brown said. "I can't 100 percent confirm or deny anything. But I haven't seen anybody else yet prove that they [invented] it, so I'm going to stick with my story."

25 The KFC Yum! Center

When the KFC Yum! Center opened its doors on October 10, 2010, Louisville's city leaders finally got the downtown arena that they had spent years dreaming for and working toward. For the city's major university, it marked the start of a new era for both its men's and women's basketball programs, which would play all of their home games inside the state-of-the-art facility.

Built at a cost of $238 million, the 22,000-seat arena looks more like a building that should house the Los Angeles Lakers than the Louisville Cardinals. The Yum Center boasts the latest in technological advancements, including Wi-Fi within the arena bowl for patrons, as well as 72 luxury suites.

U of L's men's and women's teams have permanent locker rooms within the Yum Center, including expansive space for its coaching staffs, equipment, training room, and a lounge area for each team. There are five additional team locker rooms, two officials' locker rooms, five-star dressing rooms, a full-function media work room, and a full-sized basketball practice court on the event level. An interior truck staging area can accommodate three television production trucks and a nearby area includes four loading docks.

There are seven levels within the arena, which total a collective 721,762 square feet or roughly the area of 13 football fields. The 22,090 seats include 72 luxury suites, 70 premium boxes, more than 2,000 side-court club seats, and four party suites.

Visible from outside the arena is the Yum Center's abundant lounge, as well as a 10,000-pound section of the court from the Georgia Dome, where Louisville captured its third national championship in 2013. Four spacious donor rooms are available year-round for Cardinals fans, including three that overlook the Ohio River. The 7,000 square foot main concourse restaurant overlooks the river and a main concourse sports bar has views directly into the arena's lower bowl.

In addition to hosting Louisville games as well as NCAA Tournament games for both men's and women's basketball and volleyball, the Yum Center has established a reputation for being one of the best places in the world to see a live show. In 2016 *Pollstar* magazine reported that the Yum Center ranked seventh in the United States and 25th in the world for ticket sales by arena, selling more than 230,000 tickets in the first half of the year alone. In 2013 *Rolling Stone* named the Yum Center as the seventh-best arena or stadium in America.

Some fun facts about the KFC Yum! Center:

- The structural steel placed in the arena weighs 5,975,000 pounds—the same weight as 746 average-size Asian elephants.
- The center-hung scoreboard weighs 40,000 pounds—as much as nine Ford Explorers.
- There are 130 miles of electrical conduit and 322 miles of electrical wiring installed in the arena—enough to stretch from Louisville to Chicago.
- The overall square footage of the arena (721,762) equals approximately 13 football fields.
- 60,000 cubic yards of concrete were placed in the arena enough to fill 6,000 concrete trucks or 25 miles of concrete trucks parked bumper to bumper.
- The arena contains 58,655 square feet of exterior glass panels— the glass on the east side of the arena alone could provide for approximately 60 houses.
- The length of the arena's catwalk totals one half mile.

26 The Hiring of Rick Pitino

Tom Jurich didn't always have carte blanche at Louisville. It's true that in 1999 Jurich signed an unprecedented contract to stay the director of athletics until 2012, but that was based largely on the tremendous work he'd done on the football front. Wanting to galvanize the fan base for the program's first season at the new Papa John's Cardinal Stadium, Jurich had replaced head coach Ron Cooper with John L. Smith, who promptly produced a football team that led the nation in scoring and went to a bowl game for the first time since 1993.

To many, Louisville's other showcase sport was a different story. Jurich was still a relative newcomer in 2001, and the Cardinals basketball program was sacred ground that he needed to tread upon carefully. At least that was the way a large portion of the fan base felt. Jurich felt differently.

With the basketball team suffering through a disastrous 2000–01 season, reports began to surface in January that Jurich may have been contemplating doing the unthinkable by putting pressure on Denny Crum, the architect of Louisville basketball, to step down. The reports and the growing speculation led Crum to state publicly that he had no intention of walking away from U of L before his contract expired in 2003. Adding to the drama was the release of university memos to the *Louisville Eccentric Observer*, which fully showcased the divide between Jurich and Crum.

The published memos included a message from Jurich to Crum: "The thing that is hurting our recruiting is not Tom Jurich, but the performance of our program…To be continually attacked by you for lack of support is appalling."

And from Crum to Jurich: "Many of my colleagues have told me that they cannot believe that I have been treated like I have. If they had accomplished one-half of what I have done here, they would be heroes at their schools."

The tension led to a 90-minute meeting in Jurich's office on January 25, which seemed to resolve little. Following the meeting, each U of L powerhouse held his own press conference, and each reiterated his previous stance. Crum told the media that he had no plans to step down, and Jurich stated that he couldn't guarantee the Hall of Famer would be back. For the first time in its modern history, the Louisville basketball fan base was separated by a deep and distinct crack, and two of the most prominent men associated with the program were standing squarely opposite sides on the dividing line.

As Louisville continued its crawl toward Crum's third losing season in just 30 years, the pressure on both central figures continued to mount. For Crum, it was pressure from a segment of the fan base that was frustrated with the struggles in recruiting, the recent probation, and the fact that the Cardinals hadn't won a game in the NCAA Tournament in four years or been to a Final Four in 15. For Jurich the pressure came from both another segment of the fan base: those which believed Crum had earned the right to go out on his own terms and a group of former players who believed the same. "It's also amazing to me how things turn," said former player Junior Bridgeman. "Here's a guy who's built this program from the ground up, and the speculation just kept getting worse. I didn't like to see it." The program's most notable former player, Darrell Griffith, took it a step further. "The whole thing has been degrading and sad," he said.

In late February, when Jurich turned down a job offer to become the new athletic director at Indiana, Crum finally started to see the writing that had been on the wall for months. Jurich had the support of the U of L board of trustees and university president

John Shumaker. The next move would have to be the head coach's. After a buyout agreement was reached that would pay Crum $7 million in total and allow him to stay at U of L for 15 years in the role of "university consultant," the coach announced on March 2, 2001, that his 30th season at Louisville would be his last. It was his 64th birthday. "This is my decision. I feel really good about it," Crum said at a news conference that was also attended by Jurich and Shumaker. "I've had a lot of conversations the last few weeks with a lot of my friends. Almost to a person, they've said, 'There is a better life out there than the one you're living, and you need to come enjoy it with us.' That and the fact I'm getting married in June and I have a lot on my agenda I want to do and can do and still serve the university."

Later, when the inevitable topic of Crum's successor was able to be discussed openly for the first time, Jurich made a statement that sent a matching, if not larger, ripple through the Louisville sports world. In an era in which the established safe play in situations like this was always to defer comment to a later date, Jurich did the exact opposite. He called his shot for everyone to see. "What I've tried to focus on is who would be the best fit and who would do the best job and who I would enjoy working with," Jurich said. "I feel, at this point, Coach Pitino is really who I want to focus on."

It had been fairly well known that Rick Pitino, once Louisville's hated but highly successful archnemesis, had been on Jurich's radar for some time. Even so, to hear him speak the name…it made it real. It was also a doubling down of sorts for a still-fresh athletic director who was dealing with a fan base that was still highly uneasy about the way its most beloved figure was walking into the sunset.

To this day, Jurich maintains that there was no deal done with Pitino at the time he made that statement. In fact, the general sense at the time the press conference took place was that Pitino was likely headed to UNLV. Joanne Pitino, whose lone request during her husband's recruitment was that he not take the family anywhere too far west, put the kibosh on that.

The battle to bring Pitino back to the college game ultimately came down to Louisville and Michigan. Despite Jurich traveling to south Florida to spend some significant time selling his program to the former Cardinals rival, Pitino seemed destined to take his vaunted résumé to Ann Arbor. "The day that I committed to Louisville, I signed an agreement to be the next head coach of Michigan and I was fired up to be the coach at Michigan," Pitino said in a 2012 interview on SiriusXM's *Basketball and Beyond* radio show. "The athletic director at the time [Bill Martin], who's no longer there, was playing squash. My wife came up—she just didn't want me to go to the West Coast, UNLV, and be away from the children. She agreed, 'Okay let's go to Michigan.'"

Joanne Pitino had secretly been hoping all this time that her husband would pick Louisville, but he had expressed concern about returning to the Bluegrass State to coach his former school's archrival. She eventually convinced him to have a change of heart, expertly arguing that it was just one game out of the year. Because of Martin's squash-playing habit, Pitino would be forced to explain his decision to the Michigan athletic director via voicemail. "I tried to call the AD at Michigan between 12 and 1," he recalled. "I had a false name. I would give him a fake name, and he would call me back. I couldn't get a hold of him because he was playing squash. The secretary said he demands that he doesn't get interrupted unless it's an emergency and if you want you can leave a voicemail. I left a voicemail and went to Louisville. I'm really happy I did."

The moment Pitino signed his name on the dotted line instantly removed a year's worth of burden from Jurich's shoulders. He was once again the golden athletic director who could do not wrong, a reputation that would only grow with time. Pitino doing the unthinkable gave Jurich the cachet he needed to start making the moves that would lay the foundation for the success U of L would enjoy over the course of the next 15 years. It also began a core of trust that would evolve into one of the most important relationships in the history of Cardinals athletics.

27 Reece Gaines' Miracle Against Tennessee

When Rick Pitino was hired by Tom Jurich in 2001, Louisville was coming off a season in which it had won only 12 games. The Cardinals had not tasted victory in the NCAA Tournament since 1997. It was a steep decline for a program that *Sports Illustrated* had named its Team of the Decade for the 1980s, and the fan base was desperate for a visual piece of evidence to back up the renewed hope that Pitino's hiring had inspired.

That first bit of evidence came on December 20, 2001. Despite inheriting a team that he had described as being "the worst collection of basketball talent I had seen in all my years of coaching," Pitino had guided his first Louisville team to a 7–1 start. The Cardinals had a quality win against Ohio State, and their lone loss had come on the road against an Oregon team that went on to earn a No. 2 seed in the NCAA Tournament. Still, U of L's other six wins had come against extremely poor competition, and the loss to the Ducks was a 90–63 beatdown that was even more lopsided than the final score would indicate. The fans were looking for magic.

Magic came in the form of Tennessee owning a 70–64 lead with 31.7 seconds to play in the Cardinals' ninth game. While fans began to file out of Freedom Hall, already accepting an understandable loss to the visiting Volunteers, junior Reece Gaines banked in a shot that he had attempted from several feet behind the three-point line. Before the fans who were on the

93

way to their cars could even make a move back to their seats, Tennessee's inbounds pass was stolen by Cardinals forward Erik Brown. An instant later, walk-on guard Bryant Northern had drilled a wide-open trey to put a cap on a stunning six-second sequence that ended with the score tied at 70.

With Freedom Hall seemingly pulsating thanks to its highest decibel level in years, Tennessee calmly came up the court and handed the ball to star big man Ron Slay. Slay made an aggressive, seemingly out-of-control move to the basket, but his wraparound pass in the lane somehow wound up in the hands of fellow front-court standout Marcus Haislip, whose layup put the Volunteers back ahead by two points.

Without hesitation, Gaines rushed the ball up the court, evaded two defenders with a pair of skillful moves to his left, and let loose with a three-pointer from the left wing. When his shot ripped through the net with less than two seconds to play, it was as if the weight and frustration of the past several seasons had been lifted off the collective shoulders of the Louisville fans in attendance. "It was one of the most awesome feelings of my life," Gaines recalled in 2015. "I had a lot of great memories from my time at U of L, but that game definitely stands out."

Freedom Hall was a madhouse. Strangers hugged, the Cardinals bench burst onto the court, and only Pitino attempted to maintain order. "It's not over," Pitino furiously told his still-celebrating players. The man who was on the receiving end of Christian Laettner's famous East Regional Final shot in 1992 would certainly know.

History almost repeated itself in the cruelest of forms. Slay threw a beautiful baseball pass nearly the length of the court, which landed directly in the arms of Haislip, whose momentum was already carrying him toward the basket. An arena of 19,627 fans were momentarily sick and then instantaneously medicated by the clang of Haislip's shot off the back iron.

"I've been involved in some extraordinary games and tonight I witnessed another," Pitino said after the game. "I was privileged to coach a team [Kentucky] that came back from 30 down [against LSU] and also a huge comeback against Arkansas. I don't believe tonight. I'm so amazed and so proud of them."

Louisville basketball wasn't "back" just yet—a fact that a trip to the NIT months later would confirm—but hope certainly was. Gaines' miracle minute had left no doubt about that.

28 Visit the U of L Hall of Honor

After passing through the one-and-a-half-acre landscaped entry plaza of the KFC Yum! Center, fans can visit the 3,000-square foot U of L Hall of Honor, which is situated in the middle of the arena's lobby. The Hall of Honor features tributes to all of Louisville's former basketball greats in a number of different forms.

Designed by Workshop Design in Kansas City, the U of L Hall of Honor highlights the finest team and individual performances from the history of Louisville basketball with a number of displays and interactive features. Among the items on display are multiple trophies from the Cards' national championships, Final Fours, and conference titles.

The Hall also features a number of artifacts that basketball aficionados will appreciate regardless of their team affiliation. The artifacts range from the early 1900s to the game ball from the last game in Freedom Hall. The area also features a massive timeline that dates back 100 years studded with various pieces of Cardinals basketball history.

A multimedia 14-foot wide projection screen and six additional digital monitors within the area present visitors with a visual experience of Cardinals basketball before they get to their seats to take in the real thing. Visitors can use two touch-screen kiosks to watch highlights from some of the most memorable games in U of L's history.

Inductees to the U of L Athletics Hall of Fame are also celebrated at the Hall of Honor, and visitors can view photos and additional information on each member at a pair of interactive kiosks. A scrolling LED board continually displays all of the 1,000 point scorers in the program's history.

Perhaps the most popular attraction at the U of L Hall of Honor are the life-size images on the wall of former Cardinals greats, where fans can stop and pose to have their pictures taken next to a likeness of their favorite player from the recent or not-so-recent past.

29 Teddy Bridgewater: The Ultimate Nice Guy

Perhaps the most significant day of the Charlie Strong era at Louisville took place on December 20, 2010. The Cardinals were a day away from playing Southern Mississippi in the Beef 'O'Brady's Bowl—the program's first postseason game in four years—but what took place off the field wound up being the piece of news that would define the program's immediate future.

Teddy Bridgewater, a high school All-American at Miami Northwestern Senior High who was dubbed the second-best dual threat quarterback in the country by Rivals.com, spurned the hometown Miami Hurricanes in favor of heading north to play his college football at Louisville. What followed were three seasons of success at a level Louisville fans feared the program may never reach again after the three previous years of disaster under coach Steve Kragthorpe. Instead the Cardinals won 30 games between 2011 and 2013 and secured landmark victories against Florida in the Sugar Bowl and Miami in the Russell Athletic Bowl.

The biggest reason for all that success was Bridgewater, who left Louisville having tossed for 9,987 yards and 72 touchdowns over three seasons as the Cardinals quarterback. After earning his degree in three and-a-half years, Bridgewater opted to forego his final season of college eligibility in favor of entering the NFL draft, where he was selected by the Minnesota Vikings in the first round. Yet the numbers, the wins, and the next-level success only tell half the story when you're talking about the love affair between Louisville fans and Bridgewater.

There are few moments in life where I find myself upset that the modern sports fan ran the word "class" and all its derivatives so far into the ground that they no longer have any real meaning. Talking about Teddy Bridgewater is the most common of those rare instances. Bridgewater is why the word existed—at least the way it existed before it became a hollow battle cry for Internet sports fans looking to claim superiority over another group of people cut from an almost identical mold. Thrust into the public spotlight when he became the starting quarterback at one of the nation's most prominent high school powers as a sophomore, Bridgewater has gone from there to the NFL without a single negative off-the-field story. He's done this at a time when a high-profile athlete without at least a couple of well-known blemishes on his character is seen about as often as a phone booth.

Bridgewater wasn't the first beloved Louisville athlete, nor will he be the last. Typically though, when you meet these people or someone close to them, at least some of the shine begins to come off. There's a reason the saying "don't meet your heroes" still floats around. With Bridgewater, however, my personal experiences have only reinforced the notion that the actual man is about as close to his beloved public persona as possible.

The following are three quotes about Bridgewater given to me by a Louisville classmate, a Louisville teammate, and a Cardinals athlete from a different program. They were given in the spring of 2013, just a few months before Teddy would begin his final season at U of L:

- "I think he is legitimately the nicest human I've ever met. I can't remember him ever saying one bad thing about another person."
- "He seriously doesn't go out. All he does is practice, go to class, do schoolwork, and watch film. If it's the weekend or we don't have class, he might play video games."
- "I've never known anyone with a clearer vision of what he wants to be in life. The guy is completely, 100 percent focused on his goals and isn't going to let anything or anyone distract him. I've never seen anything like it."

If you're thinking that the behind-closed-doors Teddy Bridgewater sounds an awful lot like the public Teddy Bridgewater, well, there's a reason for that.

Louisville fans respected and cheered for Bridgewater because of what he did on the field, but they loved the quarterback for the way he carried himself off of it. His infectious smile and his incredible relationship with his mother, Rose, will always be remembered in the same light as his record-setting postseason performances.

At some point between 2011 and 2013, Bridgewater became one of Louisville's most treasured sons. And when members of the national media began tearing Teddy down in the weeks leading up to the 2014 NFL Draft, the city reacted as any suitably protective parent would.

Nice Guy Teddy: one of the best people—and players—ever to have suited up for the Cardinals.

Critics harped on the Cardinals legend's small hands and "skinny knees," questioned whether or not he had the personality to be a franchise quarterback, or if he could talk loudly enough to be a leader. They said he didn't have the oft-discussed but ever-mythical "It Factor." Louisville fans rolled their collective eyes and told them all how wrong they'd ultimately be proven.

The lesson in all of this is that, even in an era where their breed is growing increasingly rare, the nice guy can win. The nice guy can capture not only the attention but the hearts of an entire city simply by being himself.

"Never Nervous" Pervis Ellison

"The best thing about freshmen is that they become sophomores." During the 1980s, this was a saying that anyone associated with college basketball had heard at one time or another. It was also widely believed to be accurate. Newcomers weren't supposed to be impact players. They were supposed to be guys who came along slowly before eventually developing into primary contributors later on in their careers.

Long before the so-called "one-and-done rule" made freshmen dominating the college basketball landscape a relatively common-place occurrence, there was Pervis Ellison. He arrived at Louisville in the fall of 1985 as part of a recruiting class that had been ranked as the best in the country, and most had pegged it as Denny Crum's best since the arrival of Darrell Griffith nine years prior. "I never judge freshmen classes until they're juniors or seniors," Crum said on the day that U of L inked their six-player class of '85. "By then they will be known to be able to play or not to play. We're happy we got most of the players we went after, and it gives us reason for hope. As far as this being our best recruiting class since the Darrell Griffith year, we'll just have to wait and see. Signing stars doesn't always mean championships. Houston had Hakeem Olajuwon and Virginia had Ralph Sampson, and they didn't win any NCAA championships with them."

As it turned out, Ellison would prove his worth long before his junior or senior season. Crum would later admit that even before practice had started in the fall of 1985, he knew that his new freshman big man was going to be the team's starting center. At Savannah High (Georgia), Ellison had played an up-tempo, man-to-man style, developing the type of open-court skills that would allow him to flourish in Louisville's system. After the 1985–86 season, sophomore Herbert Crook was asked to pinpoint when he became aware of how good Ellison was going to be. "October 15" was the reply—the same day that the team held its first official practice of the season.

Ellison was tremendous as a freshman for the Cardinals, averaging 13.1 points and 8.2 rebounds per game for a team that was able to earn a No. 2 seed in the NCAA Tournament's West Region. It's what Ellison would do in those subsequent three weeks, however, that would make him a college hoops immortal.

By the time Louisville reached its fourth Final Four in six seasons, Ellison—who had started every game for the team—had already been labeled with the nickname of "Never Nervous Pervis." The epithet referred to both Ellison's unflappable demeanor and his propensity for making key plays during a game's most crucial moment. "Oh, I get nervous sometimes," Ellison told the Associated Press in 1986, "but you got to go off the court for me to get nervous."

Never was this more apparent than in the 1986 national championship game. With Cardinals star Milt Wagner having an uncharacteristically cold shooting night, Crum turned the focus of his offense inside, where he believed Ellison could have his way with the less-skilled Duke frontcourt. The big man responded with 25 points and 11 rebounds, as well as several key plays during the game's most crucial stretch.

With 38 seconds to play and Louisville clinging to a one-point lead, Ellison alertly caught an air ball from guard Jeff Hall and laid it in to give the Cardinals a three-point advantage. They would win the game by that margin, capturing the school's second national championship with a 72–69 triumph against the Blue Devils. After the game Ellison was named the Final Four's Most Outstanding Player, becoming just the second freshman—and the first since 1944—to earn the distinction. "I'm happy I got it," Ellison said after the game, "but what's the MVP award when you just got the national championship?"

It was that same attitude that resulted in Ellison consistently shirking the notion of making an early jump to the NBA at various points throughout his college career. Serving as Louisville's starting center for four years, he left U of L as the school's second all-time leading scorer and the only player in school history to total more than 2,000 points and 1,000 rebounds. He also became both Louisville and the Metro Conference's all-time leader in blocked shots, recording at least one block in 130 of his 136 career games. Ellison was twice named the MVP of the Metro Conference Tournament, and after a disappointing season for the Cardinals in 1987, he led them back to the Sweet 16 in 1988 and 1989.

Ellison's No. 42 was retired during a ceremony immediately following the end of his senior season. Months later, he became the first Louisville player ever to be selected with the first pick of the NBA draft. Persistent injuries kept Ellison from having the same impact at the professional level that he did in college, but he still managed to spend 11 seasons in the league and was named the NBA's Most Improved Player in 1992.

Despite everything that came afterward, "Never Nervous" will still forever be known to most hoops fans as one of the college game's first freshman heroes. Long before Kevin Durant or Anthony Davis, there was Pervis Ellison.

31 Louisville's Greatest Nicknames

Whether they were created by fans, teammates, coaches, or the players themselves, nicknames have played a huge role in Louisville athletics since the Cardinals first started competing. Here are some of the best from over the years.

AFROS (America's Finest Receivers on Saturday): Louisville wide receivers

Action: Arnold Jackson

Art-o-matic: Art Carmody

The Baby Faced Assassin: David Levitch

Big Escalade: Troy Jackson

Big Play: William Gay

Big Smooth: Barry Sumpter

Boo: James Brewer

The Bulgarian Helicopter: Simeon Naydenov

The Bullet: Elisha Justice

Chief: Felton Spencer

Cool Hand Luke: Denny Crum

Cootie: Mike Grosso

Dark Slime: Michael Baffour

The Doctors of Dunk: 1979–80 Louisville men's basketball team

Dr. Dunkenstein: Darrell Griffith

E5: Earl Clark

The Fastest Man in Football: Lenny Lyles

Flash: Lancaster Gordon

The Godfather: Rick Pitino

A great nickname for a great player, Dr. Dunkenstein is hoisted atop fans' shoulders in celebration of Louisville's 1980 national championship.

Golden Arm: Johnny Unitas
The Hammer: Robert McCune
Hard: Rodney McCray
Honey Mustard: Damian Copeland
Ice: Milt Wagner
Instant Defense: Roger Burkman
Instant Offense: Poncho Wright
Johnny U: Johnny Unitas
L.A.: LaBradford Smith
Lamarvelous: Lamar Jackson
LoZo: Lorenzo Mauldin
Mega Trez: Montrezl Harrell
Mr. Football: Johnny Unitas
The Narrow Pharaoh: Anas Mahmoud
Never Nervous: Pervis Ellison
Never Wrong: Poncho Wright
Peanut: Deantwan Whitehead
Q: Quentin Snider
Rubberband Man: Herbert Crook
Russdiculous: Russ Smith
Showtime: Shoni Schimmel
The Snowman: Marty Pulliam
Super Mario: Mario Urrutia
T-Will: Terrence Williams
Teddy Two Gloves: Teddy Bridgewater
The Vanilla Godzilla: Stephan Van Treese
Wichita: Tim Henderson
The Wizard: Jason Osborne

32 Lee Corso's Greatest Hits

Long before he was donning oversized headgear on autumn Saturday mornings for ESPN's *College GameDay*, Lee Corso was showcasing the full extent of his outrageous personality while serving as Louisville's head football coach from 1969 to 1972.

Corso led the Cardinals to an impressive 28–11–3 mark during his tenure, won at least a share of two Missouri Valley Conference championships, and took U of L to the 1970 Pasadena Bowl. Still, it's the madcap stories that are the most enduring part of Lee Corso's legacy at Louisville.

Everyone who remembers the era starts at the same place. Fan interest in Louisville football was low when Corso took over. The team hadn't won more than seven games in a season since 1957; meanwhile, the basketball program was on its way to becoming a national power. Corso was willing to try anything in order to drum up some added intrigue, so when a friend informed him that the circus was coming to town and suggested that he should ride one of the elephants that was about to arrive at the fairgrounds as a way to sell some extra season tickets, he didn't bat an eye. "I thought it was gonna be a little one," Corso recalled in a 1973 *Chicago Tribune* article. "But this elephant was so big I had to lay down so we could get under viaducts. I was supposed to wave to the crowd, but have you ever been on an elephant? They walk *blump-blump*, like a tossing ship, tilting forward. And those sharp hairs get right through your clothes. I was so scared. I've got scars on my fingers because I held onto the strap so hard. There I was, for 45 minutes, bleeding all over the elephant. Kids would come by and honk the horns on their bicycles, and I would yell at them to stop it. When we finished, I'd found I'd pulled both my groin muscles because I'd been holding on so hard with my legs. They had to help me walk to the car. I was sweaty and I stunk, and my pants were ruined—and people still think I planned it."

So was it worth it? "No," Corso answered at the annual Governor's Cup Luncheon in Louisville in 2015. "I got off the elephant, and the damn thing spit at me. Then a guy walks over to me and says, 'Congratulations, Coach, you've sold four tickets.'"

The madness didn't stop once the actual season started. The Cardinals were heavily outmanned in a November road game at rival Memphis State, a fact that mattered little to Tigers head coach Spook Murphy. Despite having the game well in hand, Murphy opted to keep his first-team offense on the field and run up the score. Corso, who had inserted his reserves when it became apparent that U of L had no shot at victory, began waving a white towel from his sideline in order to inform the opposing team that their rivals had surrendered. When Memphis State punched in a final touchdown to make the score 69–19, Corso launched the towel onto the actual playing field and shouted "SURRENDER!" at the top of his lungs. When an official informed him that the act was going to cost his team 15 yards, Corso was indignant. "Sir, the score is 69–19," he said. "How is 15 yards going to hurt us?"

A week after the beatdown in the Bluff City, Corso needed a way to revitalize his team heading into their regular season finale game against Tulsa. With the game set to be played on Thanksgiving Day, Corso opted to purchase a turkey, paint a bright red L on it, and make it the team's unofficial mascot for the week. For the next four days, he brought the turkey to practice, had it sit in on team meetings, and ostensibly become part of the team.

Corso's original idea was to call Tulsa and ask them to purchase a turkey mascot of their own so that the two birds could meet at midfield for a confrontation before the coin toss. Tulsa declined.

Undeterred, Corso chose to lie to his team. He told them that he had made a bet with the Tulsa coaches, the terms of which included the Tulsa team being able to kill the Louisville mascot turkey if the Cardinals didn't prevail.

Somehow, the players bought it. The turkey, being trotted out on a leash like a well-trained dog by the Louisville head coach himself, came off the U of L bus with the rest of the Cardinals team and accompanied them onto the field at Tulsa. The turkey also made its way to midfield with Louisville's designated team captains for the pregame coin toss. When a reminder of the new mascot's fate was brought up during a potential game-winning drive by Tulsa in the final minute, the Louisville defense found the motivation it needed to secure one final stop and come away with a 35–29 season-ending victory. Corso was carried off the field on the shoulders of the Louisville players. As was the turkey.

Louisville lost perhaps the most enigmatic figure in program history when Corso accepted the head-coaching job at Indiana in 1973. The stories stayed in the Derby City, though, and they always will.

33 Eliminate These Rivalry Words and Phrases from Your Lexicon

For all the good things about the Louisville-Kentucky rivalry, most who are directly involved with the feud in some form would likely agree that there are times when it's either exhausting or just downright annoying. The social media era has exacerbated this, of course, as the fringe fans now have more ability than ever to let their thoughts be heard...and heard...and heard...and heard.

Rivalry dos and don'ts are always difficult to lay out due to the inherently subjective nature of fandom. Even so, here's a handy guide to several words or phrases that all Cardinals and Wildcats fans should avoid at all costs.

"I couldn't care less about Louisville/Kentucky."

This might be the aspect of the modern rivalry that is the most grating. There are fans on Twitter who have more tweets about how little they care about Kentucky or Louisville than they do supporting the team they root for. Website proprietors on both sides have all likely seen at least one instance of a fan taking the time to read the site, sign up for am account, and then start writing comments detailing just how little they care about their rival.

This is a rivalry. Obviously it's okay for both sets of fans to admit that they don't like the other side, that they pay attention to them, and that they'd prefer—so long as it doesn't have a negative impact on their own team—that they lose.

Louisville fans shouldn't have a problem with Kentucky fans who watch Cardinals games hoping that the team in red is going to lose and vice versa. They should have a big problem with the fans who do it and feel the need to lie about it.

"Irrelevant"

Yes, Kentucky basketball has more wins and more national championships than Louisville, but U of L is still widely regarded as the sixth or seventh best program in the history of the sport. If Louisville isn't relevant in college basketball, then it's a game with five teams that are worth paying attention to and 346 that don't matter at all. Both programs are relevant enough that this putdown should be deemed irrelevant forever.

"Loserville"

At this point, what's the goal when you serve up this gem? When you type it or say it out loud, are you thinking, *Someone's about to read or hear this insanely brilliant modification, and I am going to blow their freaking mind?* Or do you think that Louisville fans are going to be so insulted and floored by the gravitas of such an overwhelmingly brilliant insult that they're going to finally see the light, burn their Cardinals garb, and don a UK starter jacket? The only thing "Loserville" does effectively is let people know that they're free to stop reading or stop listening.

"Kensucky" (or any variation)

Ditto.

"Little Brother"

Here's how one of these conversations typically goes after a Louisville win.

"You're still little brother."

"Well, we won."

"Doesn't matter, you're still little brother."

"Well, we've [insert statistic detailing superiority]."

"Doesn't matter, you're always going to be little brother."

It's tired, it doesn't have any impact anymore, and it doesn't really make any sense.

"Tards"

The fact that is still utilized and accepted by any portion of Kentucky's fan base is ridiculous.

"Class"

There was probably a time when "class," "classy," and all the other derivatives had legitimate meaning, but it's a time I'm not familiar with. The only use of "class" most of us know anymore is a hollow battle cry for Internet sports fans looking to claim superiority over another group of people cut from an almost identical mold.

"Thugs"

Like the "class" spiel, this goes for all sports fans. Everyone knows what you're actually saying. Stop.

"Troll/Trolling" (when used incorrectly)

If you're using it right, that's totally fine, but I'm not sure that anyone really understands the proper usage anymore. A Kentucky fan throwing a beer bottle at a Cardinals fan (or vice versa) isn't "trolling" Louisville. It's just being an awful person who probably shouldn't attend sporting events. At some point in the Internet era, all annoying fan behavior became qualified as "trolling," and it has gotten very old, very quickly.

There is nothing wrong with disliking the other side in this rivalry and doing some smack talking in the days leading up to the game (or for no reason in the middle of summer). Just make it clever and fun, not tired and offensive.

34 The Doctors of Dunk vs. Phi Slama Jama

When it happened, Louisville's 1983 "Dream Game" win over Kentucky seemed destined to be remembered just as much for being a precursor to the Cardinals' second national title as it was for its role in the evolution of college basketball's most heated rivalry. Then one thing kept that from happening: Texas' tallest fraternity.

Phi Slama Jama, the nickname given to the Houston Cougars basketball team from 1982 to 1984, was the only collection of basketball talent in the country that seemed to spend as much time above the rim as Louisville's Doctors of Dunk. With Cinderella teams North Carolina State and Georgia squaring off in the other national semifinal, the Final Four game between Louisville and Houston was viewed not only a spectacle of next-level athletes, but also as a de facto national championship game.

The story line leading up to the game was whether or not the 4,958-foot altitude at Albuquerque's The Pit arena would affect the air show that fans were hoping to take in. Of particular note was how the lack of oxygen would affect a Louisville team that only liked to go six men deep on most nights.

The answer to the first question was served up early, as both teams got up and down the court without any issue in the game's opening minutes. To the surprise of many, Houston opted not to employ its trademark pressure man-to-man defense and instead sat back in a zone, forcing Louisville to try and score from the outside. Cardinals guards Milt Wagner and Lancaster Gordon were up to the challenge, connecting on shot after shot and combining for 20 first half points.

With a little more than six minutes left in the first half, Houston finally began to feel the effects of Louisville's full-court pressure. Cougars point guard Alvin Franklin threw a pass right to U of L's Jeff Hall, who went the other way for a dunk that gave the Cardinals a lead they would hold onto for more than 15 minutes. Moments after Hall's dunk, Wagner hit Scooter McCray for another slam that sent the Louisville fans in New Mexico into a frenzy. McCray then recorded a steal near midcourt and took off again toward the Cardinals basket, which is when one of the game's most significant, and unquestionably its most bizarre, moments occurred.

Perhaps feeling the pressure after his team's disappointing Final Four loss to North Carolina the year before, Houston coach Guy V. Lewis snapped and threw his towel at McCray during his drive to the basket. The game was brought to a halt as fans, players, and coaches alike attempted to make sense of what they'd just witnessed. "What do you say in a situation like that?" Lewis asked rhetorically during an ESPN interview. "It didn't hurt too much because they missed their technicals. It was stupid, but I was frustrated."

In reality, Gordon connected on one of the two technical free-throws, giving Louisville a 41–36 advantage that it would take into halftime. The Cardinals, despite being the smaller team and having the thinner bench, were surprisingly outrebounding Houston, 24–14.

The trend continued early on in the second half, as a Rodney McCray dunk and a Wagner jumper extended U of L's lead to 57–49. The Cardinals had also managed to foul out 6'9" Larry Micheaux, one of Houston's best frontcourt players. It was at this moment that Lewis called on the player who would eventually blossom into one of the NBA's most dominant centers to step his game up. "That's when I told Hakeem [Olajuwon] that he had to get every defensive rebound from then on," Lewis said after the game. "I told him he was the guy who had to do it for us. And he did it."

Olajuwon's second half wound up being the finest 20 minutes of his basketball career up to that point. Though he finished the evening with 22 rebounds and 21 points, 15 and 13 of those, respectively, came in the second half. Olajuwon also recorded four of his game-high eight blocked shots after halftime. His post presence completely changed the game and also allowed Houston to get out on the break again after Louisville's missed shots.

Whether it was the elevation or the pace of the game, near the midway point of the second half, Louisville clearly appeared to hit a wall. "You hear the stories about the elevation, how it's all mental," Rodney McCray said. "But I got so winded I just couldn't get where I wanted to go. My mind was saying 'get back on D,' but my legs were like I was running on the beach."

Houston had dunked just four times in the game's first 27 minutes, but with their opponents now appearing noticeably gassed, the Cougars went into attack mode. UH got out onto the break and dunked on three consecutive possessions, the last of which was a vicious one-handed slam from the Cougars' Benny Anders on top of Louisville big man Charles Jones.

Anders' slam brought Houston within two, but the highlight reel dunks at Jones' expense weren't over yet. Moments later, Anders came up with a steal and found teammate Clyde Drexler streaking down the wing. "The Glide" then proceeded to bring the house down with a play that would show up in March Madness highlight reels for decades to come. He leapt toward the basket, appearing poised to try and dunk with just his right hand, and then clutched the ball with both hands before bringing the world down on Jones yet again. "I wanted to make him think first that I was going to dunk it," Drexler said after the game. "Then, if he thought that, I would bring it down and pass it. Then I went on and dunked it. Then we were both confused."

Louisville, which to that point had answered every highlight reel play from Houston with one of their own, appeared to have used up all of its appropriate responses. When the dust settled, the Cougars had gone on a 21–1 run that turned an eight-point deficit into a 70–58 advantage. The Cardinals did manage to make one final run but lost all their momentum when freshman Billy Thompson lost control of the ball on a fast-break dunk with nobody else around him.

In the end, Houston dunked 13 times and pulled off a 94–81 victory that many believe ushered in a new style of basketball to the college game and also laid the foundation for the sport's television success over the next few decades. Somewhat ironically, the most anticipated game of the tournament at the time has had a shadow cast upon it because of what happened to Louisville in the round before and what would happen to Houston two days later.

For Louisville fans, the legacy of the game for those who weren't alive when it took place or were too young to remember will always be the message that has been passed down (and passed down and passed down) by their elders: if Houston had played anyone other than U of L in the Final Four, they wouldn't have been stunned by Jim Valvano's N.C. State team in the national championship. "I do think that had to have played a part in it," Denny Crum said about Houston's apparent fatigue in the championship game. "How could you not be tired after a game like that? Of course, I also think that if the [semifinal] game had been played at sea level, then we would have won."

35 The Greatest Upset

Without too much difficulty, you can make the case that March 31, 2013, is the most eventful day in the history of Louisville basketball. On the men's side, Kevin Ware suffered a gruesome leg injury that a national television audience watched live, but the Cardinals overcame that pull off an Elite Eight win against Duke to set up their third national championship. And just about an hour after that game wrapped up, the U of L women's team pulled off perhaps the greatest upset in the history of their sport.

Led by one of the most dominant players in the history of men's or women's college basketball, Baylor had superstar center Brittney Griner and was expected by most to roll to a second straight national championship in 2013. The Bears had returned every starter from a team that went undefeated in 2011–12 and were the 32–1 overall No. 1 seed entering the big dance a year later. Through two rounds of play, Griner and company certainly looked the part of a dynasty team that would have little issue winning six consecutive single elimination games for a second straight year. Baylor destroyed Prairie View A&M 82–40 in round one and then hammered eighth-seeded Florida State 85–47 two days later. Those wins set up a Sweet 16 date with Louisville, a No. 5 seed whose road to the tournament's second weekend had been greatly aided by being able to play its two opening weekend games on its home court. The common thought was that the plucky Cardinals, who had lost three starters to injury throughout the course of the season, would have no more of an answer for Griner than any of the other teams that had stood in her way for the past two years.

With the odds stacked remarkably high against his team, Louisville head coach Jeff Walz devised a high risk, high reward strategy that he believed gave his team its only opportunity to win. Instead of playing the Bears straight up, the Cardinals would launch three-pointers at a much higher rate than usual on the offensive end and put two defenders on Griner at all times on the defensive end. "We do some crazy things here," Walz said. "We're not your conventional team, and I don't try to be a conventional coach. We simply chose not to guard a few of their players. I rolled the dice and said, 'I know what Brittney Griner can do, and if these other players can beat us without her, then they beat us.'"

The strategy made Walz look like a genius right from the opening tip. The Cardinals connected on 15 of their first 20 three-pointers and held Griner, the only player in NCAA basketball history to score more than 2,000 points and block more than 500 shots, without a basket in the first half.

With nine minutes to go in the game, Walz's plan had resulted in a 68–50 lead that had the nation's attention. "I saw the lead keep growing to 16 points, to 18 points," Walz recalled. "I just kept looking at my staff going, 'It's not enough.'"

Walz's premonition proved to be accurate. Baylor staged a furious rally that turned a 68–50 deficit with under nine minutes to play into an 81–80 lead with just 9.1 seconds left. With his team's season on the line, the head coach turned to his most experienced guard. Monique Reid, a Louisville product out of Fern Creek High School who had battled injuries through the bulk of her career, made a brilliant drive to the basket, drew a foul from Griner, and calmly sank two free throws to push the advantage back in the Cardinals' favor. A last second prayer from Baylor went unanswered, and the celebration was on. Louisville, which had been a 24-point underdog heading into the game, had done the unthinkable.

Griner, who had averaged 33 points in Baylor's first two tournament games, finished with just 14 on 4 of 10 shooting. U of L finished the game a scorching 16 of 25 from behind the three-point line and shot 48.2 percent from the field overall. "Every three that they hit when we would cut the lead made it that much tougher," Baylor coach Kim Mulkey said in her postgame press conference. "You keep thinking through the course of the game that they're going to start missing some. But they never did."

The upset of the year wound up resulting in Louisville marching all the way to its second national championship game appearance, where the Cardinals saw their dream die at the hands of Geno Auriemma and Connecticut.

36 Peck Hickman

Before Rick Pitino cemented his Hall of Fame legacy or Denny Crum turned Louisville basketball into a bona fide national powerhouse, there was Bernard "Peck" Hickman. The native of Central City, Kentucky, played three years as a guard for Western Kentucky University and was hired by U of L in 1944 to take over a program that had gone just 21–67 over its previous five seasons. The Cardinals were also dealing with the limitations of playing inside Belknap Gymnasium, which had bleacher seating on only one side of the floor and could only seat at most 600 spectators.

When Hickman accepted the head coaching job at Louisville in 1944, he did so despite the fact that it would pay him $600 less than his previous gig at Valley High School and despite the fact that he was told he would have to line the gym floor and wash the team's towels. Hickman was just 33 years old and had never coached a college game.

Regardless of the fact that Louisville had produced winning seasons only 11 times in 33 years, Hickman found success with the Cardinals right out of the gate. His first U of L team went 16–4, kicking off an era when all 23 of Hickman's Cardinals squads would win more than half their games. In his very first game as Louisville's head coach, the Cardinals destroyed Georgetown College 99–27, producing a margin of victory that still exists as the largest in the history of the program.

In 1948, while Louisville was playing in the National Association of Intercollegiate Basketball—the forerunner of the NAIA—Hickman led the Cardinals to the NAIB title with an 82–70 win against Indiana State. The victory represented U of L's first basketball national title of any sort and sparked the program's move to the Ohio Valley Conference and the NCAA the next season.

Playing in an era where the National Invitational Tournament was viewed as just as big, if not bigger, than the NCAA Tournament, Hickman led the Cards to five consecutive NIT appearances between 1952 and 1956. In the last of those appearances, All-American Charlie Tyra carried Louisville to three double-digit victories, including a 93–80 triumph against Dayton inside Madison Square Garden to give U of L its first NIT title.

With two different championships already notched, Hickman turned his full focus on capturing the third. "My goals were very simple," Hickman would later say about his time at Louisville. "I wanted to win what I called the triple crown: the NAIB, the NIT, and the NCAA. I'd be the only coach to win all three."

He very nearly pulled off the feat in 1959 when his 19-win Cardinals team advanced to the program's first Final Four. Louisville sent shock waves across the commonwealth by defeating Kentucky 76–61 in the Mideast Regional Semifinals and then knocked off another national power, Michigan State, to win the regional. The Cardinals had the added benefit of playing the 1959 Final Four inside their own Freedom Hall, but that still wasn't enough to knock off Jerry West and West Virginia, who ended Louisville's national championship dreams with a 94–79 defeat.

From 1954 to 1967, Hickman pulled double duty as Louisville's basketball coach and athletic director, a position he would hold on to until his retirement in 1973. His notable accomplishments as AD included bringing in Lee Corso to revive the football program, transitioning the basketball program from that 600-seat Belknap Gymnasium to 16,000-seat Freedom Hall, and hiring Denny Crum, the man who would go on to guide Cardinal basketball to six Final Fours and its first two national championships.

Hickman would take Louisville to the NCAA Tournament three more times, but the Cardinals would never again advance past the Sweet 16 under his watch, which ended after a 23–5 season in 1966–67. Hickman won 70.8 percent of his games (443–183) over 24 years. He also graduated 82 percent of his players and was the first college coach in the state of Kentucky to break the color barrier when he recruited and signed Eddie Whitehead and Wade Houston in 1962.

In addition to being a member of the athletic Halls of Fame of both the University of Louisville and Western Kentucky University, Hickman was inducted into the Helms Athletic Foundation Hall of Fame in 1967 and to the National Association of Collegiate Directors of Athletics Hall in 1981.

37 The Dunk Heard 'Round the Derby City

One of Louisville's most storied sports traditions, the "Dirt Bowl" originally began as the brain child of two college kids who were bored while back home for summer break. In 1969, Ben Watkins—a former standout basketball player at Louisville's Central High—and Janis Carter—a former cheerleader at Shawnee High—were looking for ways to spice up their summer internship with Louisville Parks and Recreation. That curiosity led to the Dirt Bowl, a double elimination basketball tournament held at Algonquin Park, where the courts were typically populated with the state's best ballers. The Dirt Bowl eventually moved to Shawnee Park, but the spirit of the event has remained the same for nearly five decades. Each summer Louisvillians get together to celebrate some of their favorite pastimes: warm weather, their community, and basketball.

That's the Dirt Bowl's legitimate origin story. To most hoopheads around the city, however, the event was actually born in 1972. That's the summer when a teenage kid named Darrell Griffith made his first audible statement to everyone in Louisville that he was going to be something special. "We played on a team called Chocolate City," Griffith said. "We didn't have any pros on our team and so we always finished as the runners-up in the pro division of the Dirt Bowl. This is when pros and NCAA guys could play, so we had people from the [ABA's Kentucky] Colonels who were there, guys from the [Indiana] Pacers would come down, and all the top notch college players played. The Dirt Bowl at that time rivaled the Rucker Park league."

One of the pros participating in the event that particular year was Artis Gilmore, the 7'2" Kentucky Colonels center who was in the second year of what would wind up being a Hall of Fame career. With Gilmore's and Griffith's teams locked in a tough battle, the man who had just been named the ABA's Rookie of the Year saw his outlet pass intercepted by a kid who was set to start his freshman year at Male High School in just a few months. "Gilmore was underneath the basket," Griffith recounts. "He's looking at me like I'm just this little eighth grade guy, and so I'm going to pull up on him. But he didn't realize that I didn't have no conscience. I went straight at the rim and dunked the ball because that's the way I grew up playing the game. The park went crazy. That was a very memorable moment for me as a kid."

It was a memorable moment for everyone who witnessed it (the number of whom seems to grow with the legend as time passes). It was also the moment that Griffith went from a kid who the local basketball community had heard whispers about to the one who had just written the first chapter of the Dr. Dunkenstein legend.

38 Howard Schnellenberger

When Louisville hired Howard Schnellenberger on December 2, 1984, to be its new head football coach, most felt the struggling program was in need of a miracle. Luckily, Schnellenberger was the man who had already made such a thing happen.

In 1979 Schnellenberger had taken over a Miami program that seemed to be on its last legs. He then pulled off what was deemed "the Miracle at Miami" by recruiting the city harder than any of his predecessors had done and installing a boot camp methodology and a pro-style offense. Soon, the Hurricanes were experiencing the best days of their program's history, and it was capped off by a national championship in 1983.

Following that season Schnellenberger tearfully announced that he was departing for the newly formed United States Football League. There, he was set to become part-owner, general manager, and head coach of the Spirit of Miami. Then one of the deal's primary supporters backed out of the deal at the last minute, the franchise was moved to Orlando, and Schnellenberger was not retained.

After spending a year away from coaching, Schnellenberger was given an opportunity by a program in Louisville that, like Miami before it, had recently considered dropping football entirely. "Very few coaches in their lifetime have an opportunity to take Cinderella to the ball twice," Schnellenberger said during his introductory press conference. "I've been there once and I think I have the opportunity to do it here again."

He then took things a step further and uttered what would become one of the most memorable quotes in U of L sports history. "The University of Louisville is on a collision course with the national championship. The only variable is time."

The statement didn't seem any less ridiculous after Schnellenberger's first few seasons on the job than it had at that press conference. The Cardinals struggled to a 2–9 record in Schnellenberger's debut season and then won just one more game in each of his next two. Despite an 8–24–1 overall record through three seasons, the Cardinals head coach remained steadfast in his belief that great days were coming. "You have to understand that what we're doing here is the biggest thing that's ever been done in college football," Schnellenberger told the Associated Press after his team's 3–7–1 season in 1987. "And when we make it happen, Paul Bryant going to Texas A&M and Alabama and winning national championships won't be this big. Knute Rockne taking that little

Catholic school on the plain in South Bend and making a nationally prominent program won't be as big as this."

That confidence began to carry over onto the field. Louisville went 8–3 in 1988 and then fielded another winning team in 1989, when the Cardinals went 6–5. Then in 1990 Schnellenberger's prophecy finally felt more like a potential reality than a hollow rallying cry. Led by the play of star quarterback Browning Nagle, the 1990 Louisville team rolled to its best season in school history, a 10–1–1 campaign that was capped off by a 34–7 demolition of mighty Alabama in the Fiesta Bowl. The victory marked the program's first-ever win in a New Year's Day bowl and resulted in its first-ever appearance in a final Associated Press Top 25 poll (14th).

After a pair of down seasons in 1991 and 1992, the good times returned to the gridiron in 1993. Nagle's heir apparent, local product Jeff Brohm, quarterbacked the Cardinals back into the national rankings after a 5–0 start that was highlighted by a 41–10 stomping of Texas and a 35–17 upset of No. 23 Arizona State. Louisville finished the season with a 9–3 record and ranked No. 25 after defeating Michigan State in the Liberty Bowl.

The Liberty Bowl win would prove to be the final high note for the Howard Schnellenberger era at Louisville. In 1994 U of L had made known its plans to join the newly formed Conference USA in all sports. This included football, a sport in which the Cardinals had competed as an independent for the duration of Schnellenberger's tenure. Schnellenberger, who had been open and outspoken about his desire to not join Conference USA, accepted the head coaching job at Oklahoma on December 16, 1994. "I didn't leave because of money," Schnellenberger recalled. "I left because of that conference. I didn't want to coach in a conference where I felt like we couldn't compete for a national championship. That was always the goal."

At Oklahoma, Schnellenberger drew the ire of his players right away with public criticisms of their lack of conditioning. He then drew the ire of his fan base after a lackluster performance in conference play that included embarrassing losses to both Kansas and Kansas State. After posting a 5–5–1 record, Schnellenberger resigned after just one season with the Sooners.

Howard Schnellenberger, who won 54 football games at Louisville, enjoys the 2005 Kentucky Derby.

Despite his departure from the program (and the fact that he later went to the University of Kentucky), Schnellenberger has remained consistently beloved in Louisville. It's a fact that both surprised and warmed the heart of the head coach in his later years. "I divorced them when I took that job at Oklahoma, and it was the biggest mistake of my life," Schnellenberger said. "But when I came back to my hometown as a lost son, they turned me into a prodigal son. From the bottom of my heart, I thank Louisville fans for that. They never turned their backs on me, even though it may have seemed like I turned my back on them. They always loved me, and I'll always love them."

39 Howard Schnellenberger Meets Mick Jagger

Howard Schnellenberger was known for a number of things during his time at Louisville, but perhaps three things above all others: He won football games, he ran an extremely tight ship, and he cursed like a sailor after one or eight too many drinks. The last two of those qualities would come together on one glorious autumn day that Mick Jagger would never forget.

Louisville's 1989 season had gotten off to a solid start. The team had gone on the road for each of its first two games and had managed to secure close victories against both Kansas and Wyoming. After a week off, the Cards were finally going to play a home game at Cardinal Stadium, and the opponent was a West Virginia team that was unbeaten and ranked ninth in the country. To no one's surprise, Schnellenberger was on edge.

Adding to the excitement in the city of Louisville that week was the fact that the Rolling Stones were coming to town for the ninth stop on their Steel Wheels Tour. The legendary band would play at Cardinal Stadium four days before U of L would. With a complex set needing to be built in preparation for the show, the Stones' roadies took over the visitor's locker room inside the stadium. With that move came a pinball machine, a Ping-Pong table, and a number of similar items that began to distract U of L players attempting to work out in the adjoining weight room. Schnellenberger was furious but willing to contain his anger to those within earshot.

A boiling point arrived on the day before the show, when Schnellenberger noticed an unfamiliar face strolling around his facility unsupervised. To everyone else in the building, the man was Mick Jagger, one of the biggest music stars in the world. To Schnellenberger, a man never shy about admitting that he had little interest in music or any other type of popular culture, he was just a stranger walking somewhere he wasn't supposed to be.

A member of Louisville's staff at the time, who still wishes to remain anonymous, recalled what transpired next: "Howard had been fed up all week, and this was just the last straw. So he screams at the top of his lungs, 'Hey, boy! Get the fuck out of my weight room!' Without any hesitation, Mick Jagger goes scurrying off. And he looked terrified."

When members of the staff informed Schnellenberger of the name of the man he had just run off, the head coach remained unimpressed. "He pointed right at us and said, 'I don't give a fuck if he's Mickey Mouse, get him out of my goddamn weight room.'"

The staff members broke it down even further. They explained to Schnellenberger that Mick Jagger was the front man of one of the most popular musical acts in the world, one that had made millions and millions of dollars. The last fact seemed to impress the head coach, who walked away without saying anything more.

Scene two came about 30 minutes later. "About a half hour later, we see Schnellenberger walking with his arm around Mick

Jagger saying, 'Let me show you our Hall of Fame, Mickey.' He was giving him the same tour that he gave to all our potential donors at the time, I guess because he thought he might be able to get some money out of him."

Of course, the softer side of Schnelly could only accomplish so much. "Mick Jagger still looked scared shitless. He definitely didn't give us any money."

40 Louisville's Fiesta Bowl Thrashing of Alabama

Out of all the matchups, a New Year's Day bowl game would have seemed like one of the least likely ways for Louisville and Alabama to square off against one another in an athletic contest. Yet thanks to the presence of a coach with a knack for jumpstarting programs and a few odd, extenuating circumstances, that's exactly what took place at the 1991 Fiesta Bowl.

Playing as a college football independent, Louisville had reeled off perhaps the best season in program history. The Cardinals had gone 9–1–1, a mark that included road wins against West Virginia, Pittsburgh, and Cincinnati. Alabama, meanwhile, had limped out to an 0–3 start before winning seven of their final eight regular-season games. The Crimson Tide were nationally ranked at No. 25 but had only landed in the Fiesta Bowl after multiple other programs had rejected a bid because of Arizona's rejection of a state holiday in honor of Dr. Martin Luther King Jr.

Despite its overwhelming success that season, and its loftier national ranking, Louisville was still viewed as an underdog heading into the game. It was understandable given the hot streak that Alabama was riding, and the fact that the Cardinals hadn't won a bowl game since 1958—or even played in one since 1977.

U of L coach Howard Schnellenberger, who years earlier had vowed to somehow turn the Cardinals into a national powerhouse, played up the narrative during his pregame speech. He told his team that they were "givers," a group of players who programs like Alabama had passed over during recruiting and who were looked down upon by the sport's national powers. The Crimson Tide, on the other hand, were "takers." Whether it was scheduling, recruiting, or national perception, Alabama could take whatever they wanted without reprimand.

Whether it was Schnellenberger's fiery speech or the mere fact that Louisville was simply a much better team than its SEC foe is up for debate. What isn't up for debate is that the Cardinals absolutely dominated the Crimson Tide for four quarters. U of L senior quarterback Browning Nagle ended his college career in style, tossing a Fiesta Bowl record 451 yards. By comparison, Alabama could only manage 189 yards in total offense as a team, and just 95 yards of that came through the air.

When the final whistle blew, Louisville had scored a dominating 34–7 victory in front of 69,098 fans at Sun Devil Stadium. At the time, the loss was Alabama's second-most-lopsided defeat ever in a bowl game.

For Schnellenberger, the victory wasn't quite the realization of the national championship dream that he had preached about during his introductory press conference in 1994. It was, however, a reinforcement of the notion that such an achievement was possible for a program like Louisville. "We had to come so far, and it took so long and it was so hard," Schnellenberger said during his postgame press conference. "It was super. I'm so proud of them."

41 Louisville's All-Americans

Though Louisville has yet to produce a national champion in a team sport other than men's basketball, the program has produced a healthy number of individuals across a number of sports who have been recognized as first-team All-Americans.

Baseball

2016—Zack Burdi (National Collegiate Baseball Writers Association First Team)

2016—Drew Harrington (Louisville Slugger First Team, NCBWA First Team)

2016—Kade McClure (NCBWA First Team)

2016—Brendan McKay (American Baseball Coaches Association First Team, Baseball America First Team, D-I Baseball First Team, NCBWA First Team)

2016—Corey Ray (ABCA First Team, D-I Baseball First Team, NCBWA First Team, Perfect Game First Team, Baseball)

2016—Nick Solak (D-I Baseball Second Team, NCBWA Second Team, Perfect Game Second Team, Baseball America

2015—Brendan McKay (Baseball America First Team, D-I Baseball First Team, NCBWA First Team, Perfect Game First Team)

2014—Nick Burdi (Louisville Slugger First Team, NCBWA First Team, Perfect Game First Team, ABCA First Team)

2013—Nick Burdi (Perfect Game First Team, NCBWA First Team)

2010—Neil Holland (NCBWA First Team)

2009—Chris Dominguez (Baseball America First Team, Louisville Slugger First Team)

2017—Brendan McKay (Consensus First Team/Consensus National Player of the Year)

Men's Basketball

2013–14—Russ Smith (Consensus First Team)

1993–94—Clifford Rozier (Consensus First Team)

1988–89—Pervis Ellison (Consensus First Team)

1979–80—Darrell Griffith (Consensus First Team, John Wooden Award winner)

1978–79—Darrell Griffith (Sporting News, Citizens Athletic Foundation, Converse)

1966–67—Wes Unseld (Associated Press, United Press International, National Association of Basketball Coaches, Helms, United States Basketball Writers Association, Converse)

1967–68—Wes Unseld (Associated Press, United Press International, National Association of Basketball Coaches, Helms, United States Basketball Writers Association, Converse)

Women's Basketball

2008–09—Angel McCoughtry (Consensus First Team)

Men's Cross Country

2015—Ernest Kibet

2014—Edwin Kibichiy

2014—Ernest Kibet

2013—Tyler Byrne

2009—Cory Thorne

2007—Wesley Korir

2007—Cory Thorne

Field Hockey

2014—Alyssa Voelmle (Longstreth/National Field Hockey Coaches First Team)

2005—Jessica Javelet (National Field Hockey Coaches First Team)

Football

2016—Lamar Jackson (Consensus First Team, Heisman Trophy winner)

2014—Gerod Holliman (Consensus First Team)

2005—Elvis Dumervil (Consensus First Team)

1979—Otis Wilson (Sporting News First Team)

1972—Tom Jackson (Walter Camp First Team)

1957—Lenny Lyles (AP First Team)

1949—Tom Lucia (AP First Team)

As undeniably dapper as he is talented, All-American Lamar Jackson accepts the Heisman Trophy in 2016.

Women's Lacrosse

2016—Kaylin Morissette (Intercollegiate Women's Lacrosse Coaches Association First Team, Lacrosse Magazine First Team)

2015—Kaylin Morissette (IWLCA First Team, Lacrosse Magazine First Team)

2014—Nikki Boltja (IWLCA First Team)

Men's Soccer

2012—Andrew Farrell (National Soccer Coaches Association of America First Team, College Soccer News First Team)

2010—Colin Rolfe (Consensus First Team)

2009—Colin Rolfe (NSCAA First Team)

Women's Swimming & Diving

2016—Kelsi Worrell (200 fly, 100 fly, 50 free, 400 medley relay, 200 medley relay, 400 free relay)

2016—Andrea Cottrell (400 medley relay, 100 breast, 200 medley relay)

2016—Mallory Comerford (800 free relay, 500 free, 400 medley relay, 200 free, 200 medley relay, 400 free relay)

2016—Andrea Kneppers (800 free relay, 400 medley relay, 200 medley relay, 400 free relay)

2016—Abigail Houck (800 free relay)

2016—Alex Sellers (400 free relay)

2016—Marah Pugh (800 free relay)

2015—Maggie Patterson (200 free relay)

2015—Rachel Grooms (200 free relay)

2015—Andrea Kneppers (200 free relay, 400 medley relay, 200 medley)

2015—Andrea Cottrell (400 medley relay, 200 medley)

2015—Tanja Kylliainen (200 free relay, 200 individual medley, 400 medley relay, 200 medley relay, 200 fly, 400 IM)

2015—Kelsi Worrell (200 free relay, 50 free, 400 medley relay, 200 medley relay, 100 fly, 200 fly, 400 free relay)

2014—Kelsi Worrell (200 fly, 100 fly)

2013—Kelsi Worrell (100 fly)

2013—Tanja Kylliainen (200 fly)

2012—Gisselle Kohoyda (200 breast)

2009—Whitney Campbell (200 free relay)

2009—Nicole Landisch (200 free relay)

2009—Anna Dishuck (200 free relay)

2009—Liz Halet (200 free relay)

Men's Swimming & Diving

2016—Trevor Carroll (800 free relay, 400 medley relay, 200 medley relay)

2016—Grigory Tarasevich (100 back, 200 medley relay, 400 medley relay, 800 free relay, 200 medley relay)

2016—Nolan Tesone (400 individual medley)

2016—Carlos Claverie (100 breast, 200 breast, 400 medley relay, 200 medley relay)

2016—Zach Harting (800 free relay)

2016—Matthias Lindenbauer (800 free relay)

2016—Josh Quallen (200 medley relay)

2016—Pedro Coutinho (400 medley relay)

2015—Josh Quallen (200 medley relay)

2015—Grigory Tarasevich (200 medley relay)

2015—Rudy Edelen (400 free relay)

2015—Matthias Lindenbauer (400 free relay)

2015—Trevor Carroll (200 medley relay, 400 free relay)

2015—Thomas Dahlia (200 medley relay, 400 free relay, 100 breast)

2014—Joao De Lucca (100 freestyle, 200 freestyle)

2013—Joao De Lucca (200 freestyle, 400 free relay, 100 freestyle)

2013—Caryle Blondell (400 free relay)

2013—Alex Burtch (400 free relay)

2013—Sam Hoekstra (400 free relay)

2012—Carlos Almeida (100 breast, 200 breast, 200 medley relay, 400 medley relay)

2012—Brendon Andrews (200 free relay, 200 medley relay, 400 medley relay)

2012—Tim Collins (200 medley relay, 400 medley relay)

2012—Joao De Lucca (100 free, 200 free, 200 free relay, 200 medley relay, 400 medley relay)

2012—Samuel Hoekstra (200 free relay)

2012—Matt Schlytter (200 free relay)

2011—Carlos Almeida (100 breast, 200 breast)

2010—Carlos Almeida (200 breast)

Men's Tennis

2015—Sebastian Stiefelmeyer (NCAA Singles)

2011—Austen Childs (NCAA Singles, Doubles)

2011—Viktor Maksimcuk (NCAA Doubles)

2010—Austen Childs (NCAA Singles)

1998—Michael Mather (NCAA Singles)

Men's Indoor Track & Field

2016—Ben Williams (triple jump)

2016—Damar Robinson (high jump)

2015—Ben Williams (triple jump)

2014—Ben Williams (triple jump)

2010—Tone Belt (high jump)

2010—Tone Belt (long jump)

2010—Andre Black (triple jump)

2007—Tone Belt (long jump)

2007—Andre Black (triple jump)

2007—Arthur Turland (weight throw)

Men's Outdoor Track & Field

2016—Edwin Kibichiy (3,000m steeplechase)

2015—Ben Williams (triple jump)

2013—Mattias Wolter (3,000m SC)

2011—Matt Hughes (3,000m SC)

2010—Matt Hughes (3,000m SC)

2010—Andre Black (triple jump)

2009—Tone Belt (high jump)

2009—Andrew Hackney (discus)

2009—Cory Thorne (3,000m SC)

2008—Andre Black (triple jump)

2008—Michael Eaton (10,000m)

2007—Wesley Korir (5,000m)

2007—Andre Black (triple jump)

2007—Tone Belt (long jump)

2006—Tone Belt (high jump, long jump)

1999—James Dennis (discus)

1997—James Dennis (discus)

Women's Indoor Track & Field

2016—Dolly Nyemah (weight throw, first team)

2011—D'Ana McCarty (weight throw, first team)

Women's Outdoor Track & Field

2015—Emmonnie Henderson (discus, first team)

2012—Chinwe Okoro (shot put, first team)

2012—Michelle Kinsella (high jump, first team)

2011—Rachel Gehret (high jump, first team)

2011—D'Ana McCarty (hammer throw, first team)

2006—Kelley Bowman (high jump, first team)

1995—Michelle Borgert (10,000m, first team)

42 Go! Cards! Beat! Purdue?

During the 1980s, a recurring event during Louisville basketball games at Freedom Hall was the Cardinals cheerleaders leading the fans in a cheer that included both U of L and the team on the opposite bench. The cheerleaders would show a card with one word to one of the four sections of the crowd, and that section would shout the word on the card in unison. Three of the cards were always the same. The first one said Go, the second CARDS, and the third BEAT. The fourth card, as you may have already deduced, always had the name of Louisville's opponent. Not the most groundbreaking of cheers, sure, but the people enjoyed it.

On December 7, 1985, Louisville played its first home game of the season and claimed a 77–58 win against Purdue that seemed relatively forgettable at the time. What transpired afterward, however, would etch the game in Cardinals lore forever.

U of L was back inside Freedom Hall three days later for another early-season matchup, and much to the delight of the home crowd, the Cardinals were having their way with visiting Iona. With Louisville comfortably ahead and a timeout on the floor, it was time for the cheerleaders to lead the spectators in the familiar cheer. The first three parts of the performance went off without a hitch, but when it came time for the grand finale, there was a problem. The opponent card had not been switched out from the previous game. The result was that 19,000 highly amused fans inside Freedom Hall screamed *Go! Cards! Beat! PURDUE!* before anyone on the court could figure out what was going on and make the proper adjustment.

There was no similar faux pas the next time the Cardinals played inside Freedom Hall. The fourth card very clearly read

WESTERN KENTUCKY. And yet, the cheer remained the same: *Go! Cards! Beat! PURDUE!*

It was apparent then that this was going to be an issue.

For the rest of the season—which would end with Louisville winning its second national championship—Cardinals fans would ignore the name of the opponent that was actually in their building and cheer for the home team to defeat Purdue. The cheer never ceased to elicit looks of bewilderment from the visiting players, coaches, and fans and continued to do so until the U of L spirit groups finally gave it up for good.

Gone, but never forgotten, the chant made a triumphant return on March 6, 2010, when Louisville played its final game at Freedom Hall before moving into the new KFC Yum! Center. The opponent was No. 1 Syracuse, and the game was one the up-and-down Cardinals desperately needed to win, but with 7:23 remaining in the first half, the cheer was the same. *Go! Cards! Beat! PURDUE!*

43 The Dream Game That Almost Was

The mere thought of Louisville and Kentucky meeting in the championship game of the NCAA Tournament is enough to set the entire state afire. The reality is that the rivalry game to end all rivalry games very nearly came to pass in 1975.

With Kentucky having already defeated Syracuse by 16 in the first national semifinal on March 29 in San Diego, the burden of completing the setup for the all–Bluegrass State title game fell on the Cardinals. The obstacle in the way was UCLA, owners of a 26–3 record and champions of 10 of the last 12 NCAA

Tournaments. Legendary head coach John Wooden, who also just so happened to be the former boss and mentor of Louisville head coach Denny Crum, was also coaching in his last season (a fact that was unbeknownst to everyone at the time).

Crum, who had also played at UCLA, had brought all of Coach Wooden's systems and teaching philosophies with him to Louisville, which made the Cardinals a pretty easy team to scout for the Bruins. But knowing what U of L was going to do and knowing how to stop them proved to be two very different challenges for Wooden's team. Louisville knocked down eight of its first 10 shots to race out to a 23–13 lead. UCLA responded with a run of its own, but the Cardinals were still able to carry a 37–33 advantage into the locker room at halftime. The situation represented uncharted territory for UCLA, which had not trailed at halftime of a single NCAA Tournament game between 1963 and 1974.

The Cardinals remained in front for nearly the entire second half and, despite letting a 65–61 lead slip away in the final minute of regulation, there was reason for Louisville to feel optimistic heading into the overtime period. Two of UCLA's primary front-court players, Ralph Drollinger and Pete Trgovich, had both fouled out near the end of regulation. This would force Wooden to do something he hated to do, especially in March: rely heavily on the poise of a pair of freshmen, Wilbert Olinde and Jim Spillane.

In the extra period, Louisville again took control early and was able to maintain its advantage. The Cardinals were ahead 74–71 before a pair of free throws from UCLA's Dave Meyers cut the lead to one with just 57 seconds to play. With no shot clock at the time, Crum directed his team to get the ball to free throw specialist Terry Howard, who had connected on all 28 of his attempts from the charity stripe that season.

Howard dribbled expertly around the UCLA defenders as Wooden shouted from the bench for his players to try and steal the ball or force him to pass it to a teammate. Finally, with 20 seconds remaining on the game clock, the Bruins relented and sent Howard to the free-throw line for a 1-and-1.

To this day, Howard seems perplexed that his first attempt didn't earn him the bonus. "It hit the right side of the rim, then the left side of the rim," Howard said in *The Rivalry: Red v. Blue*. "It went in…and then it bounced out. It still comes up in my life every single day."

UCLA's plan following the miss was to get the ball in the hands of Richard Washington, who had connected in his last six straight field goal attempts in the game. Despite Louisville's best attempt to deny Washington the ball, Marques Johnson fed the junior forward a beautiful pass just outside the key. Washington took one dribble and buried a 10-foot jumper with just two seconds to go.

After Allen Murphy's prayer went unanswered, the mostly UCLA blue crowd, which had been stunned the year before when the Bruins were defeated in the national semifinals, stormed the San Diego Sports Arena court. Little did they know that it was in those celebratory moments that Wooden made the decision that his next game coaching would be his last.

In the book *The Ultimate Book of March Madness: The Players, Games, and Cinderellas That Captivated a Nation*, Drollinger recounted how Wooden broke the news to them in the locker room. "He said, 'You know, alumni just told me, 'Thanks, Coach, you owed us that one from last year.' And he just had a guarded disgust in his voice that was somewhat the precursor of the motive for saying I'm bowing out. In other words, if that's what my spoiled alumni think, I don't need any more of this. And that was the somewhat underlying tenor of the retirement announcement, which turned out to be very motivational."

Wooden announced his decision minutes later during his post-game press conference, and the media uncharacteristically gave him a standing ovation. Two days later, UCLA sent Wooden out on top with a 92–85 win against Kentucky.

Louisville defeated Syracuse 96–88 in the third-place game, and Howard finished the season as the nation's leader in free throw percentage at 96.5 percent. U of L would earn its revenge five years later, when Crum and the Cardinals defeated UCLA 59–54 in the 1980 national championship game.

44 Papa John's Cardinal Stadium

Cardinal Stadium—now commonly referred to as "Old Cardinal Stadium"—holds a special place in the heart of every U of L fan of a certain age. At the same time, it also serves as a "look at how far we've come" reminder. The same fan who expresses reverence for the old stadium is just as likely to echo some form of "I was going to games when we were playing in a decrepit old minor league baseball stadium" later on in the same conversation.

Louisville football finally made the move out of the old minor league baseball stadium—complete with its AstroTurf and blue, green, yellow, and red seating—in 1998. That's the year that Papa John's Cardinal Stadium opened, a move that perhaps uncoincidentally happened to coincide with the start of an era of unprecedented success for the Cardinals football program.

Although U of L was able to keep the "Cardinal Stadium" portion of its old moniker, they offered up the other portion of its stadium's new name to interested corporations. Papa John's founder John Schnatter, who grew up in nearby Jeffersonville, Indiana, and whose business is headquartered just outside Louisville, jumped at the opportunity. He donated $5 million initially and then tossed in another $10 million for the stadium's expansion, a move that also extended the naming rights through the year 2040.

Although some both in and outside the city have scoffed at the corporate name, Louisville athletic director Tom Jurich has embraced it since the beginning. "I've always liked it," Jurich said in response to a question about a move to make the name of the stadium more visible from the air. "How many college football stadium names can the average person name? Probably not all that many, but I bet ours is one of them. I think that's a good thing."

The move had an immediate impact. In 1997, when the new stadium opened, Louisville was coming off of a dismal 1–10 season. A year later, the Cardinals lost just one home game and began a streak of consecutive bowl game appearances that would last until 2007.

Since its opening the stadium has undergone two major expansions. In 2010 U of L completed an expansion project that increased capacity inside the stadium from 42,000 to 55,000 by adding "the UPS Flight Deck" as well as 33 new luxury suites. Another fan-friendly aspect of the expansion was the construction of the Norton Terrace. The Terrace connects the east and west sides of the stadium seating bowls via a 60-foot-wide concourse veranda overlooking the playing field.

The second major addition to Papa John's Cardinal Stadium was put into motion in 2016. The $63 million project will enclose the stadium, add field level suites, and increase the total capacity to 65,000. "Anyone can add bleachers," Jurich said just before the official expansion announcement. "We don't do that here. This is going to have all the bells and whistles. We don't do anything if we can't do it first class. That's been our stance since we first started building things here."

45 Kevin Ware's Injury

Heading into the 2013 Midwest Regional final between top-seeded Louisville and No. 2 seed Duke, there was a sense that viewers might be in for an afternoon they would never forget. These were the top two teams remaining in the NCAA Tournament, and the victor was all but guaranteed to be the favorite at the following weekend's Final Four. On top of all that, the Cardinals and Blue Devils had played a terrific game—won by Duke—in the championship of the Battle 4 Atlantis Tournament three months prior. The game did indeed turn out to be one that no one watching will ever forget. Just not for any of the reasons people anticipated.

With 6:33 remaining in the first half, U of L sophomore guard Kevin Ware attempted to block a three-point shot by Duke's Tyler Thornton. The shot went in, and the Blue Devils cut their deficit to 21–20. Ware landed awkwardly, fell to the court, and stayed there. Moments later, his teammates joined him on the ground. Their hands were over their faces as they refused to believe what they had just seen.

Ware had just suffered one of the most gruesome injuries ever seen during a live sporting event. His right leg had snapped, and nearly six inches of bone were visible for all the world to see. At least for an instant. Ware had to look at it for much longer. "It was one of those things where I couldn't believe it," Ware told ABC News four days later. "I honestly didn't feel the pain. It was more a shock."

The inability of head coach Rick Pitino to play it cool when he saw Ware's leg for the first time didn't help matters. "He went to help me up, he glanced at my leg, and his eyes got huge," Ware said. "I looked down at my leg, and it was just automatic shock."

Teammate Luke Hancock was the first player off the Louisville bench to comfort Ware. Members of the U of L medical staff were close behind. The commotion gave Ware an opportunity to compose his thoughts. There was only one thing going through his mind: just win the game. "The bone's six inches out of his leg, and all he's yelling is, 'Win the game, win the game,'" Pitino told ESPN. "I've not seen that in my life. Pretty special young man."

Ware remembered things the same way. "I said it probably 15 times, 'Coach, I'm going to be good. You just got to win this game.'"

The inspiration of Ware's words proved to be enough to over-whelm the shock of his injury. The Cardinals overwhelmed Duke in the second half, outscoring them by 19 points and punching their ticket to the Final Four with a convincing 85–63 win. In the postgame celebration, teammates held up Ware's No. 5 jersey as the crowd chanted the name "Kevin" repeatedly.

After the team's postgame commitments were finished, Pitino left Lucas Oil Stadium and went straight to the Indianapolis hospital where Ware had already undergone surgery to repair the gruesome fracture. Pitino brought the Midwest Regional champi-onship trophy with him, but he didn't leave with it. "He was real excited about the trophy," Pitino said. "I said to him, 'You want me to bring it back or stay with you?' He said, 'It's staying with me.' I said, 'All right, just make sure you don't lose it.'"

Ware's injury and the grace with which he handled his new-found fame became the premier storyline of the next week. But as Louisville prepared to head to Atlanta to try and win its third national title, the injury was affecting them in a much simpler and straightforward way. Ware hadn't made much of an impact as a freshman, and his sophomore season had been something of a roller coaster up until late February. But he had been playing the best basketball of his life at the time of his injury, emerging as the first guard off the Louisville bench during the team's run to the Big East tournament title and posting a season-high 11 points in the team's Sweet 16 win against Oregon.

The injury to Ware was an emotional blow to the entire Louisville team, but it also left Pitino without his top backcourt reserve heading into the biggest weekend of the season. That became an increasingly bitter pill to swallow as he saw his team trailing by 12 points to Wichita State and his struggling star shooting guard Russ Smith saddled with three fouls.

With Ware unavailable, Pitino was forced to turn to Tim Henderson, a seldom-used walk-on who had scored just 16 points all season. Without hesitation, Henderson buried back-to-back three-pointers that cut Wichita State's lead in half and sparked a furious second-half rally that carried Louisville on to the national championship game. "It meant everything," Ware said after the game of Henderson's heroics in his place. "Tim's been working hard all year. He gets chewed out because he's guarding Peyton and Russ all practice. But when he gets his moment, he always does his thing. That was clutch."

Louisville would go on to top Michigan in the title game two nights later, and Ware would get one final moment in the national spotlight. All cameras were on him as the goal was lowered, and he was handed the scissors to make the final snip on the Georgia Dome net. He wore the net around his neck and smiled brightly as the most emotional eight days of his life came to a close.

46 Attend the Louisville Football Card March

Two hours and 15 minutes prior to the announced kickoff time of any Louisville football home game, thousands of fans form a line, and the U of L marching band plays as the Cardinals players and coaches make the approximately 10-minute walk from the team buses to the inside of Papa John's Cardinal Stadium.

The tradition was born in 2003 when first-year head coach Bobby Petrino wanted to create a way for the fans and players to share in the excitement of the pregame atmosphere. U of L left the naming the rights up to the fan base, which chose "Card March" from a lengthy list of possible titles. Though Petrino left in 2007, both Steve Kragthorpe and Charlie Strong chose to keep the tradition alive as part of their routine before home games (though it must be noted that Strong's propensity for canceling the parade when inclement weather hit drew the ire of many fans).

The route has changed a bit over the years. The team is no longer dropped off at the Denny Crum overpass; instead the buses now let the players and coaches off at Floyd Street at the south end of the stadium, where they proceed through the crush of fans before entering the stadium through Gate 4.

Though the route may have changed, the pageantry remains the same. The band plays, the cheerleaders cheer, the Ladybirds dance, and the fans shake hands with the players and wish them good luck. It's an event that adds to the game-day experience of any Cardinals tailgater.

47 The Keg of Nails

Perhaps the most overtly masculine of all college football rivalry trophies, the Keg of Nails has been awarded to the winner of the rivalry game between Louisville and Cincinnati since 1929.

According to both schools, the trophy is a replica of the type of keg that is used to ship nails. The exchange of the odd trophy between the two programs is believed to have been initiated by fraternity chapters on the UC and U of L campuses, signifying that the winning players in the game were "tough as nails."

The present keg is actually a replacement for the original award, which was misplaced by Louisville—ironically lost during the construction of office facilities. The keg is adorned with the logos of both schools and the scores of the series games. According to multiple players who inspected the keg, there are no actual nails inside.

For 40 years from 1929 to 1969, the keg remained in Cincinnati as the Bearcats claimed each of their first 12 meetings with Louisville. The rivalry evened out over time, and the Cardinals prevailed in 22 of the next 41 games.

Playing for the final time before Louisville left Cincinnati behind to join the Atlantic Coast Conference, the Cardinals pulled out one of the most dramatic wins in series history with a 31–24 overtime triumph at Nippert Stadium in 2013. Teddy Bridgewater made several improbable plays down the stretch, including a blind heave to wide receiver Damian Copeland for a late touchdown that sent the game into overtime. The victory allowed the Cards to clinch the American Athletic Conference championship in their only season in the league and also marked the second straight year that they had defeated their rivals in overtime.

48 Muhammad Ali and U of L

Though he never suited up for the Cardinals, Muhammad Ali, Louisville's favorite son, was a lifelong fan of U of L athletics.

The Greatest of All Time was a fixture at major Cardinals sporting events, following the football team to Miami for the Orange Bowl in 2007 and to New Orleans for the Sugar Bowl in 2013. He was also a routine visitor to Jim Patterson Stadium, when his son, Asaad, played for the Louisville baseball team from 2009 to 2012. "I always knew he was from Louisville, but I didn't realize how connected he was to the university until I got here," Cardinals baseball coach Dan McDonnell said. "He loved baseball and he loved supporting this program."

In 2016 the Ali family introduced the Muhammad Ali Leadership Scholarship, an honor given annually to a player on the baseball team who best exhibits the same leadership qualities for which Ali was famous. The inaugural recipient, first baseman Danny Rosenbaum, hit two home runs in an NCAA Tournament win against Ohio State the day after Ali's passing and wound up earning a spot on the All-Regional Team.

Ali was never one to hide his love for his hometown, and his feelings about the Louisville Cardinals were equally transparent. "He never turned down a request to attend a game," longtime friend and Louisville radio show host John Ramsey said. "He loved the energy of the fans and he loved the spirit of Cardinal athletics. If you asked him to show up at a game, he was going to show up at the game."

One such occasion came in 1991, when Louisville was hosting No. 11 Tennessee in a football game at Cardinal Stadium. Sensing that the crowd wasn't as revved up as they ought to be for a game of that magnitude, Ali made his way out to midfield and engaged in an impromptu sparring match with the Cardinal bird mascot. The act sent the fans into a frenzy.

After his death in 2016, Louisville's athletic teams honored him with Ali patches on their uniforms as well as a number of different warm-up shirts bearing his most famous phrases. An intro video showcasing some of Ali's greatest sayings and clips from his greatest fights was shown before every home Cardinals football and basketball game. "I always said he was the best example of the human spirit that I'd ever seen," Ramsey said. "But he was also the best example of the Louisville spirit that I ever saw."

The Greatest and U of L will forever be linked.

49 Louisville Honors Ali, Destroys Florida State

Just a little more than three months after Muhammad Ali's death, Lonnie Ali walked into Papa John's Cardinal Stadium for the first time as a widow. There were reminders of her husband everywhere.

On the field there was a 30-foot graphic of a butterfly with the word ALI painted behind one of the end zones. The same graphic would appear on the back of every Louisville player's red helmet that day. The Cardinals student section was loaded with fans decked out in commemorative Ali T-shirts, and the team's pregame hype video on the big screen featured numerous quotes and highlights from the career of Louisville's favorite son.

As Lonnie Ali walked onto the field to be introduced to the crowd, she looked at the visitor's sideline. It was loaded with massive human beings decked out in gold and garnet. They carried themselves with all the confidence of a champion heavyweight cocksure about retaining his crown. "These guys are supposed to be pretty good, right?" Ali asked local radio show host and longtime family friend John Ramsey.

They were. The Seminoles were the No. 2 team in the country. They had won a national title three years earlier and had participated in the first College Football Playoff the season after that. What's more, Florida State had dominated its series with Louisville, winning 14 of its 16 all-time meetings.

As Lonnie Ali looked around the stadium and heard the cheer as they introduced her to the home crowd, she was overwhelmed by the same feeling that had overwhelmed her ever since she first met Muhammad Ali in 1963 as a young girl in Louisville.

"Not today," she said to Ramsey. "Not today." Ali may have known what was about to happen next, but that made her the only one. With ESPN's *College GameDay* program in town for the first time, 10th-ranked Louisville could do no wrong for four quarters. The Cardinals didn't just deal Florida State its first loss of the season, they dismantled the Seminoles in historic fashion.

In a performance that would prove to be the turning point of his Heisman Trophy campaign, Lamar Jackson shined more brightly than any other Cardinals star on the field. He threw for 216 yards and a touchdown, rushed for 146 yards and four more, and then watched nearly the entire final quarter from the sideline as his team put the finishing touches on a 63–20 win that stunned the college football world.

50 The Power of the InfraReds

With all due respect to Louisville's Final Four run in 2005 and its journey to the national championship in 2013, it's not difficult to make the case that the most significant month in the Rick Pitino era at U of L was March 2012.

At the time, Pitino was far from the most popular man in Louisville. His top-seeded 2008–09 team had been upset in the Elite Eight by Michigan State, and the months that followed had brought with them the embarrassing details that led to the extortion trial and conviction of Karen Sypher. After back-to-back one-and-done performances in the 2010 and 2011 NCAA Tournaments, Cardinals fans felt like they needed to see major results from a 2011–12 squad that had begun the season ranked in the top 10 of both major polls. Yet as the regular season began to draw to a close, the results weren't matching up with expectations.

After winning 20 of its first 25 games, Louisville entered the postseason having dropped four of its last six. The two most recent were the most troubling because they seemed to offer little hope of any sort of turnaround. The Cardinals were held to 51 points in an embarrassing seven-point Senior Night loss to South Florida, the first Senior Night defeat in Pitino's tenure at U of L. The head coach was so mad that he didn't let his team go through the postgame traditions that typically go with the event, including the departing players' final addresses to the home crowd. Nothing happened to calm his nerves three days later, when Louisville went on the road and managed just 49 points in an embarrassingly ugly 58–49 loss to Syracuse in the regular-season finale.

If any sort of postseason run was going to take place, Louisville needed either divine intervention or a new player capable of putting the ball in the basket with some degree of regularity. What they got instead were new uniforms from Adidas.

The uniforms could best be described as having a blinding orange-pink hue, a look that seemed better suited for Syracuse or Tennessee. Adidas dubbed them "infraRed," and had created an entire line of similarly bright postseason creations for its other schools. Traditional powers Kansas and Indiana had said thanks but no thanks to the looks, and Pitino had wanted to follow suit. His players convinced him otherwise. "I thought they were just about the ugliest things that I had ever seen in my life," Pitino recalled.

"A lot of people don't like them because they say we look like highlighters," Louisville point guard Peyton Siva said in March 2012. "Coach P doesn't like change. He likes constants in whatever he does. The players liked it, we talked Coach P into wearing them and we won the first game, so we had to wear them the second game."

That first game had been an ugly, grind-it-out Big East Tournament victory for the seventh-seeded Cardinals, who dispatched of Seton Hall 61–55. On night two, Louisville miraculously found its offensive footing and pulled off a stunning 84–71 upset of ninth-ranked and second-seeded Marquette. A U of L team that hadn't scored more than 61 points in six of its most recent seven games hung 50 points on the Golden Eagles... in the first half. It was a performance that sent the Cards into the semifinals, but perhaps even more important, it restored a belief that an even bigger run was at least possible. "We didn't want to go back to Louisville and have it where if the fans looked at us, we had to look down," said sophomore center Gorgui Dieng after the Marquette win. "We want to give it all we have. There's just one option: win it."

Since the Cardinals were the higher-seeded team against Marquette, the game had also marked the first time Louisville had been forced to wear the infraRed visiting uniforms. "I told my teammates before the game, 'You need to tell me what color this is so I know what to tell people after the game,'" Dieng said.

The infraReds were back a night later for the semifinal game, which saw Louisville pull off another major upset—a 64–50 takedown of third-seeded Notre Dame. The uniforms also made an appearance in the championship game, which pitted U of L against longtime rival Cincinnati. Though both teams were relative newcomers to the Big East, they played the 2012 title game in the aggressive fighting style for which the conference was so well known. When the Madison Square Garden glass had finally been chipped for the last time, U of L had emerged with a 50–44 victory and its 17th—and perhaps most unlikely—all-time conference tournament championship.

Whatever Adidas had put into those strange uniforms wasn't working just for Louisville. Baylor had ridden its neon green look all the way to a Big 12 Tournament title. The only other team that had received (and accepted) the specialty uniforms was the Cincinnati team the Cardinals had knocked off for the Big East title.

Given the turnaround, abandoning the uniforms would have been borderline sacrilegious, and so the infraReds were approved by Pitino to come along for the NCAA Tournament ride as well. That tournament ride would prove to be just as entertaining as the one in New York had been. After pulling off narrow victories against Davidson and New Mexico to make its first Sweet 16 appearance since 2009, Louisville was poised to pull off its biggest shocker. Sporting the same unusual look that had by that point become well known nationwide, the infra-Cardinals made the Michigan State Spartans the first No. 1 seed in the tournament to fall, winning with a lockdown 57–44 effort. The 44 points scored by Tom Izzo's team were the fewest ever by a No. 1 seed in the shot clock era.

The infraReds would have to be shelved for the West Regional Final in favor of the home whites. The Cardinals were suddenly in the unusual role as favorites, going up against the seventh-seeded Florida Gators coached by former Pitino player and assistant Billy Donovan. The dream appeared to fleeting with Louisville trailing by 11 and just over eight minutes to play. Sparked by the sophomore duo of Russ Smith and Chane Behanan, however, U of L scored 18 of the game's final 21 points and punched its ticket to the most unlikely Final Four appearance in program history with a 72–68 win. "We're in the Final Four with the infraRed jerseys," Siva said in the aftermath of the win over Florida. "So if anybody has any problems, I think they need to chop that up. It might be Louisville's new colors. If we win the whole thing, it might be the uniforms next year."

That vision never became a reality, as the glowing Cardinals gave Kentucky the toughest test of its national title run but ultimately saw its miracle March end with a 69–61 defeat in New

Orleans. Despite the season coming to an end at the hands of a bitter rival, Louisville and its much-maligned uniforms gave the U of L fan base one of the most enjoyable four-week runs in the program's history. They had also laid the foundation for a national championship that would come 12 months later.

51 Louisville's Greatest Football Wins over Kentucky

While Louisville-Kentucky will likely forever be known first as a basketball rivalry, the two programs have also had some classic matchups on the gridiron since their annual series was resumed in 1994. Here are U of L's three most memorable football victories over their archrivals.

September 2, 2000: Louisville 40, Kentucky 34 (OT)

The contest is still and will likely forever be known as simply "the Lightning Game." Kentucky led 19–14 midway through the quarter before a nasty lightning storm forced the game to be delayed for over an hour. When play resumed the teams exchanged leads until things became knotted up at 34. The Wildcats appeared to have victory in hand, but a chip-shot field goal was blocked by Louisville's Curry Burns as the regulation clock expired. After Anthony Floyd intercepted a Jared Lorenzen pass on the first series of overtime, Tony Stallings took the ball 25 yards to the house on U of L's first play to secure the dramatic win.

November 29, 2014—Louisville 44, Kentucky 40

One of the most bizarre and exciting games in series history featured a pair of pregame scuffles, five personal foul penalties, and a third-string quarterback from Lexington leading Louisville to a miraculous victory in an unexpected shootout. With the Cardinals trailing 13–0 in the second quarter, starting quarterback Reggie Bonnafon left the game with an injured knee. With Will Gardner already done for the season, that left only redshirt freshman Kyle Bolin (a Lexington Catholic product) to command the U of L offense. Bolin responded by tossing 381 yards and three touchdowns, all of which were hauled in by DeVante Parker. The game was sealed by Gerod Holliman's 14th interception of the season, which tied a longstanding NCAA record.

September 17, 2011: Louisville 24, Kentucky 17
In what turned out to be the beginning of the Teddy Bridgewater era at Louisville, the true freshman came off the bench to replace an injured Will Stein and led the Cardinals to their first win against Kentucky since 2006. Charlie Strong famously told his team after the game that they would never lose to UK again, a proclamation he made good on before bolting for Texas after the 2013 season.

52 Battle for the Governor's Cup Traditions

After meeting six times between 1912 and 1924, Louisville and Kentucky went 70 years before playing one another again on the gridiron. After much poking and prodding resulted in the series being renewed, the Governor's Cup, a trophy which would be given to the winner of the annual rivalry game, was created.

Donated by the Kroger Company at a cost of $23,000, the Governor's Cup stands 33 inches tall and weighs 110 pounds. The trophy's base and upright columns are hand-milled black marble.

The glass components are optic-grade crystal. All metal parts are 23-karat-gold-plated brass. The cup itself is made of pewter and has a 23-karat gold-plated finish.

In addition to the traveling trophy, the series also has its own Most Valuable Player of the Year Award. Beginning in 2010 the series began handing out the Howard Schnellenberger Award, which would be given to the best player on the field for that year's game. Cardinals quarterback Teddy Bridgewater is the only player to take home the honor in back-to-back seasons, earning the hardware in 2012 and 2013.

Schnellenberger was honored due to his ties to both schools. In addition to serving as Louisville's head coach from 1985–1994, Schnellenberger graduated from Kentucky in 1956 after playing for the Wildcats under coach Bear Bryant. After his playing days had ended, Schnellenberger got his start in coaching at UK, where he was in charge of the wide receivers and tight ends for the 1959 and 1960 seasons.

53 Louisville's 2005 Final Four Run

Selection Sunday came with a mighty surprise for Louisville in 2005. The Cardinals had just won the Conference USA Tournament title over Memphis in dramatic fashion, they owned a sparkling 29–4 overall record, and had been ranked No. 6 in the AP poll that was released before the start of league tournament play. The general sense was that while U of L probably deserved a No. 1 seed in the NCAA Tournament their lack of conference strength would relegate the Cardinals to the second line. The cruelest scenario of all had seemed to be a slip all the way down to a No. 3

seed, a status unfitting of a team most believed was one of the three or four best in the country.

When Louisville popped up as the No. 4 seed in the Albuquerque Regional, the shock was not contained to the Derby City. Particularly upsetting for the participants involved was that the draw had set up a second-round showdown between the Cardinals and fifth-seeded Georgia Tech. The Yellow Jackets were coming off a national title game appearance in 2004, and after narrowly losing to Duke in the ACC title game, many believed Paul Hewitt's team was fully capable of advancing to the season's final weekend again.

While Rick Pitino chose to deflect comments about the job the selection committee had done, Hewitt was far more upfront about his lack of appreciation for the bracket that had been made. "Peter Zaharis does our scouting report," Hewitt told the media the day before his team faced Louisville. "When he got on the bus last night, he said that this is more a Sweet 16 or Final Four kind of game. We're seeded where we should have been, but Louisville probably should have been a two or a three seed at worst. They could have made a case for getting a top seed."

Hewitt's worst fears were realized the next day, when Louisville put on a shooting clinic in front of a mostly red-clad crowd inside the Gaylord Entertainment Center in Nashville. The Cardinals connected on their first five field goal attempts, four of which were heavily contested three-pointers, and built a 23–8 lead that would never be overcome. All-American Francisco Garcia dropped 18 points in the opening half before finishing with a game-high 21, as U of L advanced to its first Sweet 16 in eight years with a 76–54 drubbing of the reigning national runners-up.

After the game Pitino was finally ready to address the perceived snub that the rest of the country had spent the past week talking about. "We never harped on seeding," the Louisville coach said. "We know we should have been a two seed. We know. They made a mistake. It was like *Runaway Jury*…and they made a mistake. Now you look at all the twos and threes getting knocked off. What does it matter?"

Hewitt was less willing to simply brush aside the bad hand he felt his team had been dealt. "I don't want to tick anybody off, but somebody told me this is a four seed. You're nuts. You're absolutely nuts," Hewitt said. "They're as good as anybody we've played this year. Washington got a bum steer getting two No. 1 in their bracket because these guys are a No. 1. We weren't good enough to beat them. That's why they're going to move on. That's going to be a good game next week."

Billed as the most anticipated of the eight regional semifinal games, fourth-seeded Louisville and top-seeded Washington brought two of college basketball's most potent offenses with them to Albuquerque. The matchup was also enticing because the Huskies had been easily the most criticized of the four No. 1 seeds, making U of L—which had not lost since January 8—an underdog by the numbers but a favorite in the eyes of the public.

The public's hunch proved to be correct, as Louisville treated Washington no differently than it had treated Georgia Tech the weekend before. U of L's dynamic duo of Garcia and point guard Taquan Dean splashed five three-pointers apiece as the Cardinals rolled to a 93–79 win that ended the Huskies' dream season. As a team Louisville connected on 11 shots from beyond the arc, tying a school record for made three-pointers in an NCAA Tournament game. "You wonder what it would've been like if they hadn't been making all the threes," Washington coach Lorenzo Romar said. "But they've won 31 other times this year. I'm sure there are 31 other teams who have said that."

If Louisville fans are being honest, most can admit today that the Washington victory was treated as though the Cardinals had just punched the program's first Final Four ticket in 19 years. Outside of the Huskies, the biggest threat to Louisville's chances of being the last team standing in Albuquerque had seemed to be Chris Paul and second-seeded Wake Forest. And that fear had disintegrated on opening weekend, when the Demon Deacons were stunned by No. 7 seed West Virginia in a 111–105 double-overtime thriller.

With all due respect to West Virginia, no rational U of L fan would have placed the Mountaineers in their top five if they had been ranking tournament teams most likely to eliminate the Cardinals. So when Louisville's lone roadblock on the ride to St. Louis and the Final Four was John Beilein's team, it felt to many as if the job had already been done.

West Virginia erased that notion right out of the gate on Elite Eight Sunday. The Mountaineers hit an absurd 10 three-pointers in the first half on their way to building a seemingly insurmountable 38–18 lead. Doing the lion's share of the damage was 6'11" forward Kevin Pittsnogle, who drilled six treys and finished with a game-high 25 points.

A Mountaineers fan sitting close to the court and holding up a sign that read YOU JUST GOT PITTSNOGLED was featured prominently during the CBS broadcast of the game. That was as good a term as any to describe what had happened to a Louisville team that had not been forced to weather an offensive flurry that extreme all season.

West Virginia missed just seven shots in the first half, carrying a 13-point advantage into the locker room. Knowing that he needed to deliver a cinema quality halftime speech in order for his team to have any shot at pulling off a miracle comeback, Pitino channeled his inner Al Pacino and delivered. He told his players that to be down just 13 after a performance like that from their opponent was "the best thing I've ever seen as a coach." He said that the deficit was nothing and told stories from his coaching career of teams overcoming seemingly much more insurmountable odds. "By the time we left that locker room, we believed we were coming back, no problem," Garcia said after the game.

But did Pitino actually believe the message he was delivering? Not entirely. "You're not always believing what you're saying, but you're citing the truth," the coach said. "I told them I had seen this. I had been here before. I had seen so many comebacks. I told them I had no doubt that we were going to win the game. That was the only mistruth."

Either way, the spreading of mistruth worked—but not because West Virginia cooled off. Despite U of L's best attempts to take away the Mountaineers' outside barrage, Pittsnogle and company continued to light it up, missing just eight shots in the second half and finishing an incredible 18 of 24 from behind the three-point line. Louisville's only shot was to be even better on offense.

Dean made three triples during a 24–14 stretch to open the second half and help pull Louisville to within three at 54–51. But West Virginia, who would finish with the second-most made three-pointers ever in a tournament game, always seemed to have the answer. It wasn't until a Larry O'Bannon layup with 38 seconds left that the Cardinals finally pulled even at 77 all. After Louisville guard Brandon Jenkins blocked a potential go-ahead shot by West Virginia's J.D. Collins, Dean had an opportunity to send the Cards to St. Louis himself. His fall-away buzzer-beater from the left corner came up short, and U of L fans would be forced to sweat out another five minutes.

Despite the missed shot at the buzzer and the fact that Garcia had fouled out of the game, Pitino surged onto the court pumping his fists as the team prepared to huddle. "We felt at that point there was no way we were losing," Dean said.

Dean fought through cramps in the extra period and buried a crucial three-pointer that gave Louisville a 82–78 advantage. For the first time all day, West Virginia's shots started to come up short. Big men Ellis Myles and Juan Palacios made sure there were no second chances and converted at the free-throw line on the other end to seal the deal. When the final horn sounded,

Louisville had pulled off an almost impossible-to-explain victory that had punched the program's first Final Four ticket in nearly two decades.

When the Cardinals players returned to their locker room, Pitino had written a clear message on the team's white board: GREATEST COMEBACK EVER. YOU ARE NOW PART OF LEGEND.

"I've been a part of some great comebacks," the coach told the press after the game. "But none has ever been so big or satisfying as this one."

54 Louisville's First Bowl Win

Being a program that existed in relative obscurity for most of the 20th century and more than once toyed with the idea of dropping the program entirely, it's fitting that Louisville's first bowl game appearance and victory came over an opponent which no longer plays the game at the FBS level.

On January 1, 1958, Cardinals football made its postseason debut in the 23rd edition of the Sun Bowl from El Paso, Texas. The game featured Frank Camp's 8–1 Louisville squad taking on the 7–1 Drake Bulldogs. Despite the similar records, Drake entered the game with national rankings in both the AP (13) and coaches' (17) polls, while U of L was unranked. The Cardinals did, however, lay claim to the nation's leading rusher in Lenny Lyles.

The Cardinals were expected to ride Lyles for four quarters, but that plan was thwarted when the All-American suffered a leg injury on a kick return near the beginning of the game. With Lyles out, U of L turned to fullback Ken Porco, who wound up being named the C.M. Hendricks Most Valuable Player after carrying the ball 20 times for 119 yards and one touchdown.

Drake came to Tempe with one of the nation's most feared aerial attacks, but the Cardinals defense forced Bulldogs quarterback Roger La Brasca to connect on just 10 of 33 passes for a meager 140 yards.

With the game tied at 14 in the second half, Cardinals wide receiver Ed Young caught the first of two touchdown passes to break the tie and start a string of 21 unanswered Louisville points that would put the game away. U of L's quarterback tandem of Dale Orem and true freshman Pete Bryant combined to complete 6 of 10 passes for 148 yards and a pair of scores.

Though Lyles would go on to be the only player on the roster drafted, Louisville's 1957 squad still has a legitimate claim as one of the best in program history. The Cardinals finished 9–1—with their lone defeat coming in a 13–7 tussle with Kent State—and outscored their 10 opponents by a combined total of 350–106.

The Sun Bowl victory would have to tide Cardinals fans over for a long time, as Louisville would not make another bowl appearance until 1970 and wouldn't win another postseason game until their 1991 Fiesta Bowl triumph against Alabama.

55 Kelsi Worrell Wins Gold

It may not have gone down exactly how she imagined it when she left for Rio, but in the end Kelsi Worrell returned to Louisville in the summer of 2016 with the title she had always dreamed of attaining: Olympic gold medalist.

Worrell, who had already established herself as the most deco-rated individual athlete in the history of U of L athletics before she embarked on her Olympic adventure, carved her place in Olympic history by being a part of the United States women's 4 x 100 medley relay team. She swam the 100 butterfly in the preliminary race with a time of 56.47 seconds to help the U.S. win the semi-final heat and then watched as Lilly Ling, Kathleen Baker, Dana Vollmer, and Simone Manuel topped the rest of the world in the finals.

"I responded to all my texts, I had probably 200 people reach out to me, but I haven't gotten through the Facebook messages. I'm not sure I ever could," Worrell told the Associated Press. "It's been incredible. For example, my neighbor when I was two months old wants to be my friend. My life is a lot different right now."

A four-time NCAA champion, Worrell was the first Louisville Cardinals swimmer ever to win an Olympic medal. Still, her time in Rio didn't come without some misfortune. Earlier that summer, in front of a national television audience on NBC, Worrell became the first American swimmer ever from Louisville to qualify for the Olympics when she swam the second-fastest 100 fly in the world that year. In the finals of the event, Worrell bested Dana Vollmer, the 2012 gold medalist in the event. The upset instantly made Worrell one of the faces of USA swimming's youth movement and one of the favorites to medal in the 100 fly in Rio.

After winning her first-round heat with a time of 56.97 seconds, Worrell swam a 57.54 in the event semifinals. That time left her a heartbreaking 0.03 seconds short of qualifying for the last spot in the final. Sweden's Sarah Sjostrom went on to win the gold medal in the event, and Vollmer claimed the bronze. "It obvi-ously wasn't what we planned for," Louisville swim and dive coach Arthur Albiero said. "That's just athletics. I couldn't be prouder of her for getting to this point. She's the ultimate team player, and

Kelsi Worrell suits up for the Cards in the 2016 NCAA Women's Swimming and Diving Championship.

her first concern afterward was Team USA and feeling like she let those people down. Obviously, this was a bitter pill for her to swallow, but this is just the beginning of Kelsi's journey, and she knows that."

Despite the disappointment, Worrell wasn't about to let failing to medal in the 100 fly ruin her Olympic experience. Her presence cheering on her U.S. teammates in the pool was a common sight throughout NBC's coverage of the swimming events. She even made it back into the national news thanks to some crowd photos with NBA superstars/fellow USA swim fanatics including Kevin Durant, DeAndre Jordan, and Draymond Green.

When Worrell got the call to get back in the pool during week two of the games, she was ready. Her gold medal days later was the icing on top of what had been without question the most successful swimming year to date.

Worrell's monster 2015–16 season began when she won three medals, including a gold in the 100 fly, at the 2015 Pan American Games. She then became a world record holder in the 400 meter short course medley relay thanks to her team's performance at the 2015 Duel in the Pool in Indianapolis. For good measure she tossed in a pair of NCAA championships, another year of All-America honors, the first woman in history to swim the 100-yard butterfly in under 50 seconds (an American record), and finally, a gold medal.

Worrell's resilience and grace on the grandest of all stages served as an enjoyable finish to a 2015–16 Louisville athletics season that had given Cardinals fans more downs than ups.

56 Tom Jurich and Bobby Petrino's Secret Meeting

Following a very public scandal that cost him his job at Arkansas and which he feared may cost him his family, Bobby Petrino needed someone to talk to. The only person he could think of was the man who had been the most loyal to him in his professional career, even when Petrino hadn't returned the favor.

When Louisville athletic director Tom Jurich picked up the phone, he wasn't sure what to expect. Jurich and Petrino had not communicated for years after the football coach had bolted from U of L under circumstances that left his former boss less than thrilled. It hadn't been until relatively recently that the two had been in any sort of contact, and even then, they were far from being on close terms.

Petrino informed Jurich that he wanted to talk to him. He needed to talk him. And it had to be face-to-face. "I told him that I was willing to do it, but I let him know that I wasn't going to hold back," Jurich recalled. "I let him know that he probably wasn't going to like what he heard. He said he still wanted to come meet me."

"Come meet me" didn't mean sometime in the future; it meant as soon as possible. It meant right now. Right after he hung up the phone, Petrino hopped in his car and began the 625 mile trek from Fayetteville, Arkansas, to Louisville. He drove through the night before arriving at the place where he had been given his first head coaching gig nearly a decade earlier. Jurich was waiting for him in his box at Papa John's Cardinal Stadium, and the two began a candid discussion that lasted three hours.

They didn't talk at all about football. Instead, Petrino talked about his current situation. He apologized for the past, he wept.

Jurich admitted how angry and disappointed the coach's departure had left him, but he also listened and offered counsel to a man in desperate need of some. When he walked out of Jurich's suite after those three hours, Petrino still had no idea what the future held for him, but he knew that he'd gone a long way toward mending a relationship that was very important to him. For the time being, that was enough.

Jurich and Petrino stayed in touch after the meeting. When the head coaching job opened up at Western Kentucky a year later, Jurich put in a good word for Petrino to WKU athletic director Todd Stewart. Fate then intervened one year later, when Charlie Strong abruptly left Louisville to accept the head coaching job at Texas. Jurich wasn't immediately sold on the idea of bringing back the man who had taken the Cardinals to unprecedented heights only to leave them out in the cold. Could he really have changed that much? "It's well documented what type of person he was back then," Jurich told ESPN in 2014. "He was focused on one thing and one thing only. That's why I'm so impressed with him now— the person he has become through all of this."

After meeting with Petrino and those closest to him, Jurich determined that the person Petrino had become through all of this was "Bobby 2.0." He still possessed all the fire and coaching acumen that had made him so successful during his first go-round at Louisville but had shed the distractions that led to his first term being cut off so abruptly.

The announcement was made on January 9, 2014, that Petrino would be returning to U of L for a second stint as football coach. It may have never happened if Tom Jurich hadn't answered one phone call two years earlier.

57 Youth, David Letterman, and the Louisville-Cincinnati Basketball Rivalry

In my surely flawed mind, 90 percent of the games Louisville played against Cincinnati in the 1990s took place on Thursday nights at 9:00 PM on ESPN. Both teams always had legitimate national title aspirations, and every game between the pair rivaled Game 5 of the 1976 NBA Finals.

Most people experience several drastic life changes in their twenties, thirties, and forties, but there's a sense of familiarity inherent in established adulthood that makes all the changes feel as if they belong to the same "era," for lack of a better term. The same can't be said for youth, where the span from ages 6 to 13 essentially encompasses three or four different lives. It's likely this phenomenon that has made late Thursday night games against Cincinnati feel to me like more of a staple of Cardinals basketball in the '90s than they do to other generations.

Still, the memories feel fresh to me. This was a period when Cincinnati was consistently one of the best team in college basketball and almost always the baddest. The rivalry between the Cardinals and Bearcats defined Conference USA basketball, and it always demanded a national audience. In the days leading up to a game against UC, my friends and I would update each other on the status of our persuasive attempts to earn permission to attend the game or at least stay up to watch it. Some would celebrate an unparalleled triumph of youth, while others would shed tears and be relegated to an early morning update from their father or *The Courier-Journal*.

The one memory I have that stands out above all others from this period was basking in the glow of the 1996 victory in the old living room at my parents' house and realizing that *The Late Show with David Letterman* was on. Letterman viewings at this point in my life were typically reserved for the summertime, when my brother, Oliver, more than 10 years my senior, was home from college. Oliver was cool, Dave was cool, and staying up with him until midnight as an 11-year-old was definitely cool.

Watching Letterman give fake orders while going through drive-through lines was a privilege reserved for July, when life's only responsibility was, at its most demanding, a Little League game the next evening. A Thursday night in the dead of winter? That was special. *The Cards just beat Cincinnati, Letterman's on, I've got school tomorrow, and holy mother of God I'm still awake.* It may have been the most celestial moment of my childhood.

The rivalry with Cincinnati was never on par with Kentucky (nothing is), but it certainly had its own place. While disdain for the wild brand of cats is an almost inherent aspect of being a Louisville fan, the Bearcats earned it. The players were dirty and didn't care. Kenyon Martin is still the most intimidating human being I've ever been in the presence of. Bob Huggins' antics made him perhaps the ultimate U of L villain of the '90s. And more times than not they got the better of our beloved Cardinals. All of these factors made the twice-annual games the biggest events Louisville winters, and made the victories incredibly special.

Ultimately, because of conference shakeups having more to do with football than basketball, the rivalry followed the same pitiless path that youth itself always takes: it changed dramatically overnight and then it disappeared forever. Just a couple of years after that, Letterman's status as a late-night television staple did the same.

The rivalry series and the show are both gone, but thoughts of Danny Fortson, Freedom Hall, Denny Crum, Bob Huggins, childhood in Louisville, endless summer nights, and one magical Thursday night will allow them to exist in a different form for me for a while longer.

58 Lenny Lyles

While what Johnny Unitas would go on to do in the NFL would later make him a household name, there was no bigger football star at Louisville in the 1950s than running back Lenny Lyles.

A product of Louisville Central High School, Lyles became the first African American to play football for the Cardinals when he suited up in 1954. By the start of his senior year, Lyles had earned the reputation and the nickname of the "Fastest Man in Football." That year Lyles led U of L to its first bowl game appearance and became the first Louisville football player to rush for more than 1,000 yards in a single season. His 1,207 yards not only earned him Little All-America acclaim, but also led all of college football in 1957.

Lyles left Louisville as the school's all-time leading rusher and currently stands No. 3 behind Walter Peacock and Nathan Poole. His career marks of 42 touchdowns and 7.0 yards per carry are still both still U of L records. In Lyles' four seasons, Louisville produced an overall record of 25–12, marking an unprecedented era of success for the program at the time.

Following graduation, Lyles was selected in the first round of the 1958 NFL Draft by the Baltimore Colts, for which he planned on sharing a backfield with Unitas. Instead, Lyles was moved to cornerback, and in his rookie season he played in the famous 1958 NFL Championship Game—what some call "the greatest game ever played"—in which the Colts defeated the New York Giants 23–17 in sudden death overtime.

After a successful 12-year stint in the NFL, in which he racked up 2,161 return yards and averaged 26.7 yards per return, Lyles went on to an equally successful career in business. He spent 27 years as an executive with Brown & Williamson in Louisville and was a hero to many in the city for being one of the first Louisvillians to invest a substantial portion of his business earnings into the city's West End.

Like Unitas, Lyles' legacy is honored at U of L with a statue bearing his likeness. The Lenny Lyles statue at Louisville's Cardinal Park was dedicated on October 12, 2000, and still stands there today.

59 Russ Smith, Louisville's Most Unlikely All-American

Being wrong isn't nearly as bad as its rap. This is something that happens to anyone with a properly functioning brain at least 100 times a day. Allow me to say this: I have never been as wrong about anything as I was about Russ Smith. The best evidence of this extreme fallacy that I can think of is a late-2010 phone call with a friend, who shall remain nameless. I will attempt to recreate the conversation as best I can remember:

> **Equally wrong friend:** So, does Russ leave at the end of the semester or at the end of the season?
>
> **Me:** I think he'll make it through the year, but yeah…
>
> **EWF:** I'm not sure we've ever had a less-Louisville player.
>
> **M:** Yeah, he might be the most predictable transfer we've ever had.
>
> **EWF:** Don't get me wrong, I think he could be an average player in the MAAC or a bottom-tier A-10 school, but he'll never see the court here. He has to know this.

M: Couldn't agree more. Two years from now, Russ Smith will be an up-and-down player at Duquesne.

Russ Smith did not transfer to an MAAC program and he did not become an up-and-down player at Duquesne. Instead, Russ Smith became the breakout star of a Cardinals squad that went to the Final Four, the leading scorer on U of L's first national championship team in 27 years, a player who cracked the top five on Louisville's all-time scoring list, and the program's first consensus first team All-American in more two decades.

So I was wrong.

The worst thing about this particular wrong is how much Louisville fans would have been deprived had I been right. And I don't even have to say that I'm not just talking about on-the-court stuff because invariably any conversation about Russ Smith winds up being just as much about his personality as anything else.

For the duration of his first season as a Louisville Cardinal, fans knew little about Smith. They knew he took bad shots, knew he turned the ball over, knew he tweeted a lot, and knew that he was the most likely transfer candidate on the U of L roster. That was Russ Smith encapsulated from the summer of 2010 to the end of the season in 2011.

Things changed, and I'm still not entirely sure how, but I know it happened quickly. Long before the 2011–12 season began, Rick Pitino had already told Smith's father that they were going to give this one more year, and that if it didn't work out, he'd help the younger Russ pick out a new school. All arrows pointed toward the latter scenario playing out. Then Louisville got stabbed ("bitten" is far too friendly) by the injury bug. This meant Russ would see extended court time during the team's summer trip to the Bahamas, where he would be tried out as a two guard for the first time. He scored an unbelievable amount of points, and everyone, his head coach included, thought it was hilarious.

Getting buckets against the hotel bellhop (a true story, not a joke) isn't exactly the same as beating a Big East guard off the bounce or finishing around the rim against Connecticut's front line. Russ hadn't really proven anything, but he'd done enough to at least warrant a shot in a game that mattered. Maybe if everyone had been healthy, the story doesn't even get that far, and all the skeptics, myself included, chalk up their prognostication as an easy win. There are more comforting things to think about.

It's difficult to get my mind back to a place where I can remember just how unfathomable the first few weeks of "RussellMania" were. It was this odd, but great mixture of joy and humor, and Cardinals fans couldn't figure out whether it was the product of an unbelievable run that was destined to end soon or the ever-increasing likelihood that we were all completely wrong about this kid.

Russ Smith became the single biggest reason why, from 2011 to 2014, Louisville basketball became more fun to follow than ever before—at least during my stint on this planet. That's a pretty significant thing.

An effectively reckless mind-set on the court coupled with an equally captivating and equally unfiltered persona off it has helped him gain the adoration of Louisville and college basketball fans alike. But it's also masked the most overlooked (or dismissed) aspect of Russ: he is one of the more intelligent people to ever put on a Cardinals uniform. Maturity can be just as evident in a player starting to let people see a previously hidden side of himself as it can in a dramatically improved assist-to-turnover ratio. Both of those things happened with him during his senior season, and that only added to the fun.

The two-star recruit who became a first team All-American. The kid a basketball-obsessed fan base knew nothing about for a year who became the biggest and perhaps most-talked about personality in the city. The freshman who couldn't make a shot or keep from turning the ball over in a gym by himself who became one of the best pure scorers and arguably the most unstoppable penetrator in the history of U of L basketball. The Dr. Frankenstein of Rick Pitino's softer "Louisville First" persona. The non-native Louisvillian who never needs to be called by more than one name in the city. The national champion. The most unlikely Cardinals All-American. I still don't know how any of that happened. All I know is that I did not predict it.

60 Russ Smith's Best Quotes

In addition to being the leading scorer on Louisville's 2012–13 national championship team and the Cardinals' first consensus first-team All-American in two decades, Russ Smith will also forever be known as one of the best quotes in the history of U of L basketball.

Here are the 10 best from his four years as a Cardinals player:

10. His pregame breakdown of Louisville's 2013 Sweet 16 game against Oregon:
"Pretty much whoever gets more confused is going to lose the game."

9. After Louisville's second-round win against Seton Hall in the 2012 Big East Tournament:
Peyton Siva: "Me and Russ have a little steal battle going on. I had six tonight, I don't know how many he had."
Russ: "I didn't have none."

8. **On waiting to see who Louisville was going to play in the 2012 Final Four and which of the two teams he'd prefer:**

"I want UK because of the in-state rivalry, but I want Baylor because they got the infra-green uniforms."

7. **On talking to the ref after not getting what looked like an obvious foul call in the 2012 Sweet 16 game against Michigan State:**

"I went to the basket, and Adreian Payne just shoved me. Like, that was ridiculous. I was like, 'Dag' and then I told him that was probably the makeup no-call for all the times that I done flopped so that was a great call."

6. **On how he was the reason for Rick Pitino's longstanding ban on Twitter for everyone associated with Louisville basketball:**

"When I was on Twitter as a freshman, I was ridiculous. I was using profanity, just being all-out reckless. I would tweet at such a high rate, and so recklessly, that it was just like, 'Russ has to stop.' I got in trouble from Coach P. so many times…I was injured, not playing, so it didn't even feel like I was part of the team yet—I didn't think it would matter what I said. But the [coaches] printed out all my tweets and showed me how bad they were, and after that it was no Twitter allowed."

5. **On whether there was a specific tweet of his that led to the ban:**

"No, not a specific one, it was just more the volume of them. But I guess I did once tweet something like, 'All right, I'm about to take a shit.' That was probably the one."

4. On some of the criticisms from NBA scouts:

"I was critiqued unfairly. If you talk about me as a point guard, obviously other guards had a better ratio, but I wasn't playing that position. That wasn't my job. My job was to win games, and that means putting the ball into the basket. A better assist-to-turnover ratio would've helped me, but I don't play for me, I play for the team. And if I have to take some ill-advised shots to kickstart the team, well, I'm not about to leave these guys stranded because I'm only focused on improving my draft stock."

3. On the criticism from some that he was an inefficient player:

"People say I'm not efficient, and I won the [Ken Pomeroy] efficiency award last year. I just play basketball and I make people's lists sometimes. I am efficient. I can't become efficient in their opinion because they probably never played basketball before. If you win the Efficiency of the Year award, then you're efficient. I mean, two plus two is four."

2. On being in Rick Pitino's doghouse early in his college career:

"He was just very unhappy. It got to the point where he was in my face yelling, and I was like, 'All right, coach, all right coach. What I could really use now is a hug.'"

1. On his own assist during an intrasquad scrimmage:

"Nice pass, Russ."

61 Louisville Blacks Out West Virginia

The most apparent incident of Cardinals fans moving their hearts from midcourt to the 50-yard line came during the week of November 2, 2006. Led by the stellar play of junior quarterback Brian Brohm, Louisville had raced out to a 7–0 start that had landed the Cards in the top five of the AP poll for the first time in program history. Despite losing Brohm's fellow homegrown star and Heisman Trophy candidate senior running back Michael Bush for the year to a broken leg during the team's season-opening win over Kentucky, U of L had won all but one of its games by 15 points or more. Included in that total was a 31–7 thrashing of No. 15 Miami, in which Bobby Petrino's team had announced to the rest of the country its status as a legitimate national title contender.

The next audible statement was made on the first Thursday of November, when new conference rival and third-ranked West Virginia came to Papa John's Cardinal Stadium. The Mountaineers had upset Louisville in a triple overtime thriller the season before, setting the stage for a magical 11–1 season that ended with a Sugar Bowl victory against Georgia. The bulk of the playmakers from that team had returned to Morgantown, and the bar was set even higher for 2006.

Even so, heading into November it appeared as though that bar may have been set laughably low for the Mountaineers. No team on WVU's schedule to that point had shown any ability to slow down the two-headed ground attack of quarterback Pat White and running back Steve Slaton, who had led the team to a 7–0 start in which every win had come by at least 17 points and all but one had come by more than three touchdowns.

Something had to give on the night of November 2, and a record crowd dressed in all black at Papa John's Cardinal Stadium hoped that it would be the visitors' national title chances. All week long in the city, things had felt different than they ever had before. There was a noticeable buzz, something most Cardinals fans assumed was a constant in places such as Columbus or Tuscaloosa. For Louisville, however, it wasn't ordinary to see one out of three kids on the playground sporting a Cardinals football jersey or to hear talk about that week's game on the local top 40 radio station. But there they were. It felt as though the program was building up to a game that would change everything forever.

Whether or not that's what wound up taking place is up for debate. What isn't is that the Cardinals secured what was at the time the most significant regular-season win in program history. The Louisville offense seemed capable of doing whatever it wanted from the opening kickoff. Brohm threw for 354 yards, and the Cardinals defense took advantage of a generous Mountaineers rushing attack that lost fumbles on three separate occasions. In the end, the fans stormed the field after a monumental 44–34 U of L victory that appeared to pave a clear path toward the program's first national championship game appearance. "It's been a dream since I was a kid for Louisville to be on a stage like this," Brohm said after the game. "These people have been waiting for a team to be on the national stage so they could come and cheer them on."

Sadly, Louisville's dream of a national championship died a week later with a last-second Thursday night road loss to Rutgers. The dream season, however, continued, and the Cardinals made their first BCS game appearance, knocking off Wake Forest 24–13 in the Orange Bowl.

Perhaps more important than any of the wins or champion-ships was the fact that the 2006 Cardinals made an entire chunk of the program's fan base fall head over heels in love with football for the first time. It was a beautiful four-month run that laid the foundation for its future success.

62 Crawford Gymnasium

When it was originally erected in 1964, Matthew H. Crawford Gymnasium was notable only for the way it looked. "The unusual roof will be the first elliptical paraboloid in this part of the United States," an October 20, 1963, article in *The Courier-Journal* heralded. "The form of the U of L gym is not just an experiment in shaping geometric designs in concrete, the shape has real practical advantages."

The intent of the revolutionary design was to create the largest possible amount of usable space for the least amount of money (the structure wound up costing $1.1 million). The result was a rare design that wound up commonly referred to as a "saucer." It also ended up being home to some of the most competitive basketball the city of Louisville has ever seen.

Though it lacked any of the bells and whistles commonly associated with major college athletic facilities, Crawford Gym served as the practice home of U of L basketball. Because of its open door policy when the Cardinals weren't practicing, it was also home to pickup games that were more intense and better attended than anyone would believe today. "We would be there playing, and there would be 600 people there watching us play a pickup game," Darrell Griffith said. "You had to get you a good team when you got there because if you didn't you weren't going to stay on the court. There might have been four or five teams waiting to play, so if you lost once, that was it. That's how much talent was coming to Crawford back then."

Spanning all ages, the best players in the area would always find their way over to Crawford in order to participate in the city's most competitive unofficial games. Players for all the area colleges, including Louisville and Kentucky, were frequent visitors, as were the best high school players in the area. With the Kentucky Colonels occupying the city as well, it also wasn't unusual to see some of the ABA's biggest stars drop by. "Those days were special because it was always open, and there would usually end up being standing room-only there inside Crawford Gym," former Louisville player Wiley Brown said. "You had to bring your competitive nature into every battle there at Crawford Gym or else you were going to get embarrassed in front of a crowd. There [were] some battles in there. Guys would get dunked on, people would talk trash—people would always talk trash. It was never anything personal. There were just a lot of All-Americans in there, and everybody wanted to prove they were the best."

Crawford Gym opened with two basketball courts but neither air conditioning nor industrial fans. The fact that the state's largest indoor swimming pool (at the time) also existed in the building did nothing to help quell the heat. "It was the hottest place I've ever been inside in my entire life," said former Cardinals player Robbie Valentine, a member of the 1986 championship team. "An absolute sweat box. All it took was one trip up and down the court for you to be drenched in sweat from head to toe. We tried not to start games until 9:00 PM so it would be a little bit cooler."

One face you wouldn't typically see inside Crawford Gym was Denny Crum's. NCAA rules at the time prohibited Crum from being in the building at the same time that his players were taking part in pickup games. So he would have to come up with excuses to walk by the gym and take quick glances through the open doors.

For everyone else associated with Louisville basketball, Crawford was a hoops sanctuary. "When I came here for the first time, I saw Crawford Gym before I ever saw the campus," Brown said. "At the time, our facilities weren't the best, but it was all about the people and their competitive nature. I walked in that first day with Derek Smith, and we were ready to battle because we came here from Georgia without any publicity since that was a football state. The first person I saw was Darrell Griffith. The reason I'd come to Louisville was because of Darrell Griffith. I hadn't met him yet, but I'd seen him on TV dunk over a big, seven-foot Russian guy. I watched him, and he just played above the rim on every single play. He was Michael Jordan before Michael Jordan. That was my first experience in Crawford Gym, but there were so many more."

On September 8, 2016, Crawford Gymnasium was demolished in order to make room for a new academic building on campus. A month earlier, a large gathering of former players, coaches, and fans had showed up at the gym to say good-bye. They took pictures, told stories, and even cut down one of the old nets.

As he looked over a group of players who had help him win two national championships and get inducted into the Hall of Fame, Crum served up the definitive quote on the building that had helped make it all happen: "We made a home here."

63 Samaki Walker's Triple-Double

Nine games into his Louisville career, things had not gone according to plan for Samaki Walker. Walker was supposed to be the heir apparent to Cliff Rozier. He was supposed to be the man who made losing a first-team consensus All-American center and the 16th overall pick in the 1994 NBA Draft no big deal. Instead, both Walker and his new team had been a disappointment in the season's opening five weeks.

After losing the bulk of their star power from the previous season's Sweet 16 team, Louisville started its 1994–95 campaign with a disappointing 1–2 showing at the Great Alaska Shootout in Anchorage. They then returned home and were promptly dealt an 85–71 loss by Michigan State that dropped the Cardinals to 1–3. The Louisville guards and forwards had trusted Rozier in a way that they didn't yet appear to trust Walker. The result was a number of stagnant offensive possessions that ended in contested jump shots from the outside.

Louisville had righted the ship and won five straight games against relatively lackluster competition by the time No. 5 Kentucky came to Freedom Hall on New Year's Day. At 6–1 the fifth-ranked Wildcats would be the ultimate barometer for just how much the Cardinals had improved since the start of the season. Also on the line was the avoidance of a dubious distinction for head coach Denny Crum. The recent Naismith Hall of Fame inductee had lost the Battle of the Bluegrass four straight times to Kentucky. In his long and distinguished coaching career, Crum had never lost to the same opponent five consecutive times.

From the opening tip, Walker appeared possessed with the desire to make sure that streak wasn't broken. He dominated the paint, scoring with ease and protecting the rim against a Kentucky team that refused to stop driving to the basket. "That game is the only one from those years that sticks out in my memory," Rick Pitino said about his memories of the rivalry during his time at Kentucky. "I kept calling timeouts just to yell at my guys and tell them 'stop driving at that guy, stop driving at that guy!' Clearly, the message never got through."

At least one of Pitino's players agreed with his coach's sentiment. "I think he blocked my shot about 100 times," Kentucky's Jeff Sheppard said about Walker.

In reality, Walker's block total was a mere 11. When you tossed that in with his 14 points and his 10 rebounds, you had the first triple-double in the 83-year history of Louisville basketball. Perhaps more important, you also had an 88–86 upset of Kentucky. He may have been making Cardinals history on the court, but because of the high drama in playing the game, he wasn't aware. "I had no idea I had that many blocks," he said. "I was shocked when they told me that after the game. And then they told me that I had Louisville's first triple-double, and it really started to hit me that I had done something special."

"I had a lot of great memories from my time at Louisville, but that game and the triple-double was definitely the highlight," Walker said. "Everybody at that time just wanted to be Cliff Rozier, and that was the first time where I really felt like everybody started to believe that I could do it."

Walker's performance against Kentucky stood alone as the only triple-double in Louisville basketball history until 2005, when Ellis Myles scored 10 points, grabbed 10 rebounds, and handed out 10 assists in an 85–61 Cardinals victory against TCU in the Conference USA Tournament quarterfinals. Terrence Williams joined the club in 2007–08, when he posted triple-doubles against both Hartford and Seton Hall.

64 Eric Wood's Favorite Stories

Though he would go on to start 49 consecutive games at Louisville, hear his name called in the first round of the 2009 NFL Draft, and develop into a Pro Bowl center for the Buffalo Bills, there was a time when Eric Wood couldn't get major college football programs to pay any attention to him.

Appropriately enough for a college hoops freak who would eventually attend Louisville, it was basketball that was to blame for Wood's relatively anonymous reputation coming out of high school. "I believe if I had 'played the game' as far as recruiting goes, I probably would have picked up a few more scholarship offers," Wood says. "I didn't do any of the summer camps or any of the high school combines, mostly because I was constantly playing basketball in the summer. It sounds sort of stupid now, especially with how year-round every major sport is, but playing basketball was what I loved to do. I was actually offered by Louisville after a few of the coaches came to watch me play in one of my basketball games. I never sent out a highlight film for football, so I guess that the best way for them to see my athleticism and potential was on the basketball court. I will always remember joking with my buddies after committing to Louisville how I could hopefully make the Cincinnati Bengals practice squad one day and earn $80,000 a year. Things worked out a lot better than I could have imagined."

At Louisville, Wood would wind up becoming a first-team Freshman All-American, a three-time All-Big East performer, and the rock of a Louisville offense that would put up astronomical numbers and win the Orange Bowl to cap off the 2006 season.

Always calm and eloquent off the field, Wood quickly earned a reputation at U of L for being fiery and nasty on it. That same intensity led to him becoming one of Louisville fans' favorite all-time personalities. It also led to Wood having a treasure trove of stories from his college days.

Here are a few of Wood's favorites.

On almost attacking the wrong teammate in the middle of a rivalry game

"We were playing a close game against Kentucky in 2007, and we had just converted on a really important quarterback sneak that had been waved off because of a penalty. I thought Pat Carter had lined up off the ball, and it literally took the other four offensive linemen to keep me from killing him on the sideline. I finally sat down and caught my breath, and then realized that it was Harry Douglas who had gotten the penalty."

On the unfortunate placement of Brent Myers

"I gave up a quarterback hit during a game my junior year. I can't even remember who it was against, but I'll always remember what happened on the sideline. I slammed this Gatorade bottle down right in front of me, completely unaware that our offensive line coach, Brent Myers, was standing right there. He was drenched from head to toe, but I was still too pissed to laugh or apologize.

"My senior year, Hunter Cantwell had thrown an interception, and I was chasing the defensive player out of bounds on our sidelines. I'm not the most graceful of dudes so my momentum carried me right into my boy Coach Myers, who ended up getting a concussion."

On taking the sidelines seriously

"We were losing at home my senior year, and I noticed this woman who I had never seen before laughing and joking. I was a senior captain and I had a little bit of pull at that time, so I went off and had her removed from the sideline. I never saw her again or I would have apologized. She shouldn't have been laughing though."

On becoming a water boy

"We were getting destroyed down in Tampa the second-to-last game of my junior season. I think the score was 55–17, and the trainers decided to start packing things up early. This annoyed me to no end, so I started serving water to the other offensive players myself, and then I threw the entire water tray when I was done. Some of the South Florida fans started heckling me, and so I did the only thing my immature mind could think to do and I called one of the guy's wives ugly. I regret it."

On being especially attached to his helmet

"This guy for Pitt would not stop ripping my helmet off, so I did what I used to do in those situations and just blatantly choked him. We ended up getting a 15-yard penalty that ruined the two-minute drill that we'd been in the middle of. I thought I was going to get chewed out by the coaches when I got over to the sideline, but they had my back. Looking back, that was nice of them."

On his affinity for practice fights

"I'm pretty sure I set the Louisville record for most fights during practice in a career. I'm almost positive. I had to have. I texted a bunch of my college friends and teammates from Louisville when I got into my first fight in the NFL, and they all responded by saying they'd seen the video already on the NFL Network. The lesson I learned was to not fight people on the days when the NFL Network is filming at practice. It's a valuable one. Better to learn it young."

65 DeJuan Wheat

Louisville fans, who were either not alive or too young to experience the magic of Cardinals basketball in the 1980s, never had the experiences that made their fathers light up of watching Darrell Griffith play firsthand.

What they did have was DeJuan Wheat. A local product with an outside shooting form so sweet that it begged to be mimicked by '90s kids across the Derby City, Wheat remains the brightest spot from the second half of the Denny Crum era at Louisville. Of course that's only a portion of his legacy.

Despite being a two-time All-State Tournament team pick who averaged 22.8 points per game as a senior at Louisville power Ballard High School, Wheat was something of an afterthought when he arrived on U of L's campus as a freshman in the fall of 1993. That's because it was another Louisville freshman and native, Jason Osborne, who was receiving too much attention to share. Osborne had attended Male High School, the same school as Cardinals legend Darrell Griffith, and had been the first Male player in a decade to be named a McDonald's All-American. Osborne also had been named Kentucky's Mr. Basketball in 1993, and the hype surrounding his arrival at Louisville seemed to be justified. "I guarantee this one will be as strong a representative as any we've had at Male," Male coach Maurice Payne told *The Courier-Journal* after Osborne was named Mr. Basketball. "I don't think there's ever been a more complete player. At 6'8" he can rebound, pass, and shoot. He is proficient at all the skills you're looking for."

The reviews for Wheat, who stood just 6'0", 160 pounds, were less flattering and far less frequent. Cardinals fans had been excited about Wheat's arrival the year before, but the diminutive point guard had failed to qualify academically. As a result, he spent the year taking classes at U of L in order to avoid losing a year of eligibility and in the process he slipped out of the minds of most of those who followed Cardinals basketball.

When he became just the fifth true freshman starter of the Crum era, Wheat wasn't just back in the minds of Cardinals fans, he was at the forefront. On a team loaded with veteran talent at nearly every position, Wheat still managed to stand out. He emerged as the team's most consistent three-point threat, was the team's fourth-leading scorer at 12.6 points per game, and was the captain of an offense that helped earn U of L a No. 3 seed in the NCAA Tournament and a trip to the Sweet 16.

With the veterans moving on to the NBA and Osborne appearing increasingly unable to evolve into the player the whole city had thought he would be, Wheat found himself having to shoulder more and more of the offensive workload. As a sophomore Wheat shot a sparkling 43.1 percent from beyond the arc and led Louisville in scoring at 16.5 points per game. A year later, with Osborne now gone from the program, Wheat cemented his status as one of the country's elite point guards by averaging career bests in points (17.7 per game) and assists (3.9 per game).

Wheat's final chapter at Louisville would prove to be his most memorable. Serving as Louisville's leading scorer and assist man for a third straight season, Wheat almost singlehandedly carried the Cardinals into the Sweet 16 of the NCAA Tournament for a second straight season. He outdueled the vaunted UMass backcourt of Carmelo Travieso and Edgar Padilla in round one, scoring a game-high 16 points in a 65–57 win. Two days later he was the only U of L player to score in double figures, dropping 22 points in a 64–63 upset of third-seeded New Mexico.

Louisville's magic continued into the tournament's second weekend with a 78–63 win against Texas, sending the Cards to their first regional final since 1986. The news wasn't all positive, however, as Wheat had suffered a severely sprained ankle that had forced him to miss most of the second half and appeared certain to keep him sidelined for the team's Elite Eight game against North Carolina. For Wheat, a player who had not just seen the court but had started in all 135 of Louisville's games in the past four seasons, sitting out No. 136 simply was not an option. "He came over to me after we were almost done warming up," Crum said after the game. "I told him it was up to him, that I had no way to determine his ability to play. He said he wanted to play. He'd started every game in his career."

U of L's star played valiantly on one good ankle, and when it was obvious that his shot wasn't falling the way it typically did when he was able to get his full lift on it, Wheat changed up his game. He assisted on a game-high eight Louisville baskets, leading a furious second-half rally where the Cardinals cut a 21-point half-time deficit to just three with 8:19 to play. Ultimately, Wheat's inability to get any offense going for himself left Louisville short of being able to make the shots necessary to crash their first Final Four in over a decade.

Despite the disappointing final game, the legacy of Louisville's No. 32 had already been etched in stone. Wheat left college basketball as the only player in NCAA history to amass career totals of 2,000 points, 450 assists, 300 three-pointers, and 200 steals. He ranked as the school's second all-time leading scorer (trailing only Griffith) with 2,183 points and was the first player in U of L history to lead the team in both scoring and assists in three different seasons. Wheat was inducted into the University of Louisville Athletics Hall of Fame in 2014.

66 The Miracle of Dan McDonnell

Near the beginning of his brilliant documentary *Baseball*, Ken Burns speaks about the mythical contradictions present in the sport of his focus. Perhaps it is these same inherent ironies that have always made me feel like baseball and the city of Louisville are so compatible. A city with both Southern and Northern roots that is technically considered Midwestern and a highly engaging democratic sport that tolerates cheating. A blue city in an overwhelmingly red state and a profoundly conservative game that has often proved to be years ahead of its time. Though today synonymous with basketball and horse racing, there was a time—from which we aren't so far removed—when America's pastime was king in these parts.

One of the first Major League Baseball cities in America, Louisville's Colonels played in the American Association from 1882 to 1891. The club won the pennant in 1890 and went on to play in an early version of the World Series, in which they tied the Brooklyn Bridegrooms at three games apiece. Though irrelevant in the broad scheme of things—and absurd because it ended in a tie—the series is historically important because legend has it that during one of these games Colonels star Pete Browning used a bat made by young Bud Hillerich at his father's woodworking shop. This first bat would eventually evolve into the Louisville Slugger brand that now dominates the game at every level.

The greatest Louisvillian of all, Muhammad Ali, exuded courage throughout his career, but one of the most noble acts in the history of sport occurred in the summer of 1947 when universally respected Dodgers captain—and Louisville native—Pee Wee Reese walked outside of his dugout and draped his arm around a rookie named Jackie Robinson, who was being given a particularly hard time by the home crowd in Cincinnati. Though he would be inducted into the Hall of Fame in 1984 for his stellar playing career, it was this act—as well as his refusal to sign a petition started by Dodgers players during spring training in 1947 that said they would boycott the season if Robinson was brought up—more than anything he did on the field that made him one of the most revered men in the history of baseball.

Of course times of changed and modern Louisville has become less receptive to the sport than it once was. Being a baseball fan requires commitment, and watching a game on television demands constant attention and involvement—things the average working American is often unwilling to give. In an age where one-liners are far preferred to lengthy statements that actually address concrete issues, it's no wonder that high-action, low-involvement sports such as football and basketball are thriving, and baseball worshipers continue to convert or denounce the religion entirely.

Still, there's something special about baseball in Louisville, something that anyone who has dedicated a solid chunk of his life to the sport could tell you. From Reese to sold-out minor league games at Louisville Slugger Field to Valley Sports Little League winning a world championship to the always hyper-competitive sixth and seventh regions at the high school level, an enthusiasm and a prowess for baseball has long been one of the Derby City's best-kept secrets.

It's not much of a secret anymore, and that's mostly thanks to the rapid rise to prominence of Dan McDonnell's U of L baseball program. For all intents and purposes, the McDonnell era at Louisville represents the entirety of the program's history. Before McDonnell arrived the Cardinals had been to exactly one NCAA Tournament (2002) and won exactly zero games in the Big Dance. Since McDonnell's arrival U of L has missed the tournament just once, crashed the College World Series four times, captured seven regional titles, and earned one of the eight national seeds for the NCAA Tournament four times.

The Cardinals hosting Regionals and Super Regionals at Jim Patterson Stadium has become such a norm that athletic director Tom Jurich now refers to the opening two rounds of the NCAA

The architect of Louisville baseball's success, Dan McDonnell has every reason to smile.

Tournament as "the annual two-week celebration in the city of Louisville." It's a festival that few would have predicted a decade ago.

Playing in a city that's known for college basketball and the Kentucky Derby as much as anything else, Louisville baseball has always been inherently tasked with a seemingly impossible assignment: capture the hearts and minds of the local fans while competing during the spring months. With all due respect to free admission and dollar beers, winning big at the highest level was the only way to make that happen, and that had never come close to happening. And yet the program currently exists as one of the country's elite.

Somehow Louisville fans have reached the point where they expect "the Cardinal Nine" to be the biggest story in the area come late May and early June, when overflow crowds at Jim Patterson Stadium have become a tradition every bit as celebrated as Memorial Day cookouts and Waterfront Wednesdays on the Big Four Lawn. For all the incredible success with which the Jurich era has blessed U of L fans, perhaps none compares to the miracle on the diamond.

67 U.S. Reed's Half-Court Shot

It seems improbable, if not downright wrong, that a basketball program's most gut-wrenching defeat (or at least one of them) could come in the season immediately following its first national championship. Such is the case with the end of the season for the 1980–81 Louisville Cardinals.

Louisville had started off the season struggling mightily to adjust to life without Darrell Griffith. The Cardinals played a brutal nonconference slate to begin their campaign, and the return of Derek Smith, Jerry Eaves, and Rodney McCray, three key contributors from the national championship team, were far from enough to avoid a disastrous start. U of L lost its first three games and then following an upset of fourth-ranked Maryland dropped three more in a row after that.

By January 5 the Cardinals were 2–7 and seemed like a long shot to even make the NCAA Tournament. Miraculously, everything changed for U of L once it began Metro Conference play. The veterans returned to form, and increased contributions from sophomore Scooter McCray and freshman Lancaster Gordon made a world of difference.

After an overtime loss at Memphis State on January 22, the Cards earned a program-record 14 consecutive victories. The streak propelled U of L to its second straight Metro Conference regular-season and tournament championship. It also resulted in the Cardinals earning a No. 4 seed on Selection Sunday and capable of becoming college basketball's first repeat national champion since UCLA's streak of seven consecutive titles had been snapped in 1974.

U of L's first opponent on its quest to maintain its status as college basketball's king would be Arkansas. Eddie Sutton's team had earned a No. 5 seed after going 23–7 in the regular season and had fended off a pesky Mercer team by six in round one to advance to play Louisville in the second round. (Top four seeds earned a first-round bye, thanks to the tournament's then–48-team format.)

In the first half of the game against the Razorbacks, Louisville was uncharacteristically sloppy, turning over the ball a whopping 14 times. The result of that was that, despite shooting a sizzling 66.7 percent from the field, the Cardinals went into the half trailing 37–33 because they'd only managed to attempt 18 shots.

Louisville took better care of the ball in the second half, but still found itself playing catch-up thanks to an Arkansas zone that was forcing the Cardinals to take outside shots and allowing the

Razorbacks to control the rebounding battle. Thanks to a furious final-minute rally, U of L was able to grab a 73–72 lead on Smith's acrobatic 10-foot jumper with only five seconds to play.

That proved to be too much time. Sutton's plan was simple: get the ball to Ulysses "U.S." Reed. The junior guard had shown a knack for late-game heroics throughout his career and had beaten Texas in a similar situation the year before. Reed's original plan was to advance the ball as close as he could to the basket with a pass to future NBA big man Scott Hastings. When it was clear that Hastings wasn't open and Reed had already used up way too much of the five seconds to look for another option, he had no choice but to hoist up a 49-foot prayer. "It looked like it was going to at least hit iron," Sutton told ESPN in 2009. "And then when it went in, I thought the Louisville coaches were going to have a heart attack." Reed's miracle shot proved to be the first of three NCAA Tournament buzzer-beaters on a day that most credit with ushering in the "March Madness" brand that would begin to be used by CBS a year later.

For Louisville, the loss was not just the end of the team's dream to repeat as national champion but a cruel reversal of fate from the year before. (The Cardinals had also started slow in the 1980 NCAA Tournament, winning their first two games in overtime before hitting their stride and winning the national title.)

"We were tentative," Smith said after the game. "I don't feel we'd have played this badly if we'd gotten past this game. We were just so unlucky. I guess that's a turnaround from last year. But I think this team was probably better than last year's."

After the game Sutton predicted that Reed would become a lifelong Arkansas legend, claiming he was "more popular than our two senators or our governor." The prognosis proved to be accurate, as Reed's name and video of his shot are resurrected every March, a trend that is likely to continue so long as the NCAA Tournament remains an American staple.

68 Railroad Roots

Due to the fact that the Kentucky General Assembly was unable to provide any public funding, the construction of Papa John's Cardinal Stadium began with private funds. This included the reclamation of land that had previously served as a rail yard and switching station for Louisville & Nashville Railroad.

When the stadium construction on that land neared its conclusion, the overseers of the project wanted to find a way to pay tribute to the site's origin. They saved the rail yard's shift horn and later installed it at the stadium's north end zone scoreboard. Now, whenever the Louisville football team scores a point inside Papa John's Cardinal Stadium, the horn blares to the stadium crowd and beyond. "I hate that horn," South Florida tight end Cedric Hill told *The Tampa Tribune* in 2008. "We want to silence that horn."

The location's roots of the area are also honored when it comes to Cardinals tailgating. Next to the stadium's Green Lot are several nonfunctioning train cars that have been remade into luxury tailgating suites. The cars are known as the Cardinal Express, and they sit together on a railroad track behind the stadium. In the spring, fans have also been known to sit atop the cars to watch baseball games from behind the right field wall of Jim Patterson Stadium.

Whether he knew it or not, then–Louisville defensive coordinator Vance Bedford played right along with an established U of L theme when he game a passionate speech during the program's 2011 Media Day. "We've got it rolling," Bedford said. "Get on the train right now because Coach [Charlie] Strong's got it rolling. It's not safe. All you people on the side, it's not safe. I can't tell you what's going to happen this season. All I can tell you is that it's coming in the future. It's coming. The train is coming. Get on board or get out the way."

All that was missing was the shift horn sounding off.

69 The Curse of the Black Uniforms

The University of Louisville's official school colors are listed as red, black, yellow, and gray, with red and black serving as the primary hues for the school's athletic teams. If you followed Cardinals basketball for the bulk of its existence, however, you would have understandably thought otherwise.

It wasn't a mistake. There was just supernatural stuff going on—or at least that was the perception. "When I got to Louisville I was all excited to wear these black uniforms that they kept making them for us," said Marques Maybin, a star Louisville basketball player from 1997 to 2001. "But at that time they kept telling us that we couldn't because of 'the curse.' I wasn't a part of any curse, I hadn't lost any games in those jerseys, so I was mad about it. I wanted to wear the black uniforms."

The ongoing relationship between sports and superstition has been well documented over the years. Assuming that most participants involved are rational enough to understand that there are no actual supernatural forces at play, the explanation of phenomenon takes on an identity that is equal parts "this is why sports are fun" and "I know this isn't real, but just to be safe…"

When it comes to Louisville basketball's early history with black uniforms, it's easy to see why rationality was eventually put aside for good. Despite fielding its first team in 1911–12, Louisville basketball never sported black as the primary color on one of its uniforms until December 19, 1992, for the Kuppenheimer Classic doubleheader in Atlanta. What happened that evening gave Denny Crum justifiable cause to put the uniforms away for another 80 years.

The Cardinals had trailed No. 16 Georgia Tech by as many as 10 points in the second half, but a late rally and a pair of free throws by guard Greg Minor gave U of L an 85–84 advantage with only 2.7 seconds to play. It took only those 2.7 seconds to birth Louisville basketball's most famous curse, when Bryan Hill threw an inbounds pass to James Forrest, who buried a deep three-pointer just before the buzzer sounded to deal the Cardinals a crushing 87–85 defeat. The three-pointer was just the second of Forrest's career, and he would make only one more over the course of his final 74 collegiate games.

As it was, the black uniforms were put away for more than a year until Crum agreed to break them out again for Louisville's Sweet 16 game against Arizona in 1994 NCAA Tournament. The thought was that the uniforms might serve as an emotional boost for a highly talented Cardinals squad that had too often seemed as if it was content to coast on its natural ability alone. Of particular note was the fact that the uniforms featured the players' last names on the back, a move that Crum—who consistently preached that the only name that mattered was the one on the front of the uniform—had been vehemently opposed to his entire coaching career.

If the move had an effect, it was negligible. Third-seeded U of L was pasted by the Wildcats 82–70, and after the game, Crum swore that one of his teams would never be seen wearing black uniforms again. He proved to be a man of his word. "We had always heard rumors about there being black uniforms that were made for us that Coach Crum wouldn't let us wear," Maybin said. "My sophomore year, we actually saw them. It was like seeing a unicorn. Of course, we never got to wear them."

Crum's successor, Rick Pitino, proved to be more willing to try the black uniforms. During his first year and a half on the job, Pitino sent his team out in black uniforms on four occasions, and all four times Louisville was handed defeat. Included among that group was the 2001 rivalry game against Kentucky in which Pitino returned to Rupp Arena for the first time as the coach of the enemy. The Cardinals were defeated handily 82–62.

In true mythical fashion, it took an extraordinarily positive finish to break a curse that was born from an extraordinarily heartbreaking finish. Second-ranked Louisville had just seen its program-record 18-game winning streak snapped by Saint Louis earlier in the week. When the Cardinals showed up to the Bradley Center wearing all black before their showdown with a Marquette team that was ranked No. 11 and had won 28 straight games at home, some U of L fans were ready to an accept a winless week. It didn't play out that way, as Reece Gaines' incredible 25-footer with just a second left proved to be the difference in a 73–70 Louisville victory.

Even though U of L lost the next three times it sported its black uniforms, the curse had been broken that day in Milwaukee. Louisville donned the look for most of its run to the 2005 Final Four, and it has been a staple of the team's road attire ever since. And as far as a success rate, in the 14 seasons after Gaines' heroics against Marquette, Louisville won a whopping 52 games when sporting all black.

70 The Billy Minardi Classic

The notion that everything changed on September 11, 2001, has become something of a cliché in the years that have passed since the terrorist attacks of that day. For Rick Pitino, the change was deeply personal. Pitino's best friend and brother-in-law, Billy Minardi, was killed while working in the North Tower of the World Trade Center that day. The event nearly delayed what was supposed to be Pitino's triumphant return to college basketball.

He briefly considered taking the season—set to be his first at Louisville—off to get him emotions together, but quickly realized that wasn't a realistic course of action. "The only solace I get is when I'm on the court four hours a day for individual instruction," Pitino said in his first public statement after 9/11. "That's my only escape. I wish my wife had that escape."

Later tributes would come, but the first thing Pitino did to honor his fallen friend and family member was create an annual basketball event that would honor Minardi's legacy. Each season since 2001–02, Louisville has hosted the Billy Minardi Classic. The event has existed in both tournament and single-game forms, but the constants have always been that a champion is crowned, a Most Valuable Player is named, and members of the Minardi and Pitino families are there to take part in the festivities.

Pitino handpicks the opponents each year for the Billy Minardi Classic. The teams involved always include people who either knew Minardi personally or who have heard countless stories about him through Pitino. "We've tried to do it over the years with guys who knew Billy really well," Pitino said. "Guys like Billy Donovan or Mark Pope, who coaches Utah Valley and was part of the '96 championship team and knew Billy really well. Or like Kevin

Keatts and Kareem Richardson, who know of him. We try to get people who know about the legacy. It's a very special tournament."

In the first 15 years of the event, Louisville was defeated just once—by a 72–68 defeat at the hands of Massachusetts in 2006. Other memorable moments in the event's history came in 2003, when Louisville took down No. 1 Florida and in 2012 when Pitino coached against son Richard, then the coach of Florida International, for the first time.

Later, a new dormitory on the University of Louisville campus was named after Minardi, as well as the creation of a statue of Minardi on his favorite golf course. "We have a beautiful statue of Billy with one of his best friends, Timmy Coughlin, at the highest point at Hulman Memorial Country Club in Tampa, Florida, where Billy loved to play," Pitino said. "It's at the highest ground and it's an interesting statue. He's got his arms raised and he's with Timmy, who also died in 9/11. When people come off the 10th green there, everybody from the caddies, guests—and 98 percent of the people don't know who they are—but it's a custom for everybody to slap Timmy on the chest and high-five Billy. And then if you get a birdie, you leave the ball there at the bottom of the statue. It's really a cool thing."

Like so many others, Pitino and his family can't get back what they lost on September 11. But the tributes and the time together as a family help fill the void as much as possible. "We knew after that day that life was never going to be the same for any of us," Pitino said. "And it's not. Life will never be as good as it was when Billy was alive. But the best way for us to deal with this is to honor him and to enjoy life the way that he enjoyed life, and that's what we're trying to do."

71 Doug Buffone

Doug Buffone will likely be best-known to most for spending 14 seasons as a linebacker with the Chicago Bears. He was a defensive captain for the team in eight of those seasons and retired in 1980 with more than 1,200 career tackles and as the all-time leader in games played for the Bears. His retirement signified the end of a major era in Chicago, as Buffone was the last active Bear who had played for the legendary George Halas.

Before all of that, Buffone had been a standout at Louisville from 1962 to 1965. He is one of only four players to lead U of L in tackles in three consecutive seasons and he still ranks third on the school's all-time tackles list. Although his defensive prowess has been well documented, he also played on the other side of the ball during his time at Louisville, starting for the Cardinals at center.

Louisville was far from a national power at that point in time, so despite Buffone's tremendous college career he was still relegated to the fourth round of the 1966 NFL Draft and the eighth round of the American Football League Draft. He settled on signing with the NFL team, the Bears, and packed up for Chicago. From there, he never left.

Buffone thrived in Chicago following his retirement. He became one of the founders of the Arena Football League and worked in radio and television right up until his death in 2015. When that happened, the tributes to Buffone's legacy, both on and off the field, poured in. "Not only a great football player, a great person on the radio but more than anything, just a great individual," said Mitch Rosen, the operations director at the Chicago radio station where Buffone spent his late years as a host.

"Somebody that everybody loved. When you met Doug Buffone you fell in love with him, and that's how we feel."

Former teammates echoed the same sentiment. "Everybody knew who Walter [Payton)] was, but I was fascinated with this dude," former Bears defensive lineman Dan Hampton told the *Chicago Tribune*. "He was like the Dos Equis guy [the Most Interesting Man in the World]. He was cool. He was the big man on Rush Street and he was larger than life. It didn't take you long, going through two-a-days, and you knew he was the old, broken-down horse. But he was a wonderfully valuable member of the team in his 14th year and he was so selfless and had such a great sense of humor."

Steven Schweickert, one of the proprietors of the Bears blog Windy City Gridiron, went so far as to say that Buffone was the only Chicago athlete he'd never heard anything bad about.

Even for Louisville fans of a different generation who never saw him play with their own eyes, Buffone's legacy is a source of pride. He did the types of things that all fans hope to see from representatives of their team: he played hard on the field, he cared for others off it, and he always made sure he was living life to the fullest.

72 The Legend of Juan Palacios' Goggles

A starter on Louisville's 2004–05 Final Four team who Rick Pitino once compared to Jamal Mashburn, Juan Diego Palacios never had a chance to reach his full potential at U of L (or beyond) because of a string of unfortunate injuries. There was a lingering foot injury that derailed his sophomore season, a back injury that did the same to his senior campaign, and a pair of knee injuries that also forced him to miss extended time.

Then again, there were also two injuries that greatly *benefitted* Palacios. Or, if nothing else, benefitted his place in Cardinal lore. During Louisville's December 18, 2004, game against archrival Kentucky, Palacios was scratched in the eye by Louisville native and future NBA All-Star Rajon Rondo. The result was a contusion and corneal scratch to Palacios' eye, a pair of injuries that would force the former five-star recruit to wear protective eyewear, or goggles, for the rest of the season.

The goofy looking eyewear became a nightly fixture, as Palacios and Louisville took flight. The freshman solidified his starting spot on a team loaded with veterans and boasted solid averages of 9.7 points and 6.5 rebounds per game. Those averages helped U of L churn out a 33–5 record, a Conference USA Tournament and regular-season championship, and the program's first trip to the Final Four since 1986.

Louisville began the 2005–06 season, its first in the Big East, with a top five preseason national ranking and expectations to compete for another trip to the Final Four. Palacios, his eye now fully healed, took to the court without his now-trademark eyewear. The results were disastrous. The Cardinals went just 6–10 in their first season in the Big East, struggling just to make the conference tournament. They lost in the first round to Pittsburgh, and the result was a trip to the NIT. It was a disappointing end to a season that had kicked off with so much excitement. Palacios, who had suffered an injury to his right foot while playing in a pickup game the summer before, never regained the fine form he'd enjoyed as a freshman.

At first the notion that Palacios' sophomore struggles had a direct correlation to his lack of eyewear was tossed around as a joke. But the more Louisville lost and the more Palacios struggled, the more he heard about the need to bring back the goggles. He wasn't amused. "All the fans think that if I wear the goggles we go to the

Final Four," Palacios said in response to a lighthearted question in 2008. "It's not like that."

After another goggle-less season in 2006–07 resulted in an up-and-down season in which the Cardinals were bounced out of the NCAA Tournament in the second round by Texas A&M, fate may have intervened. While playing in a pick-up game during the summer of 2007, Palacios once again found himself on the receiving end of an inadvertent eye scratch. A trip to the optometrist hours later confirmed Palacios' worst fear: his least favorite joke wasn't dead after all. The goggles were coming back. "I can't afford to miss a game if I get poked in the eye, so I'm wearing them," a defeated Palacios explained in the preseason.

If Palacios didn't want the fans to make his goggles "a thing," he certainly didn't do himself any favors. In his first game sporting the look in over two years, Palacios lit up IUPUI with 25 points and 10 rebounds, playing one of the best games of his Cardinals career. He added to the legend weeks later when he scored 17 points and grabbed six rebounds in a win against Kentucky, Louisville's first in Palacios' four years as a Cardinals player.

The prophecy of the goggles leading Louisville back to the Final Four was cut heartbreakingly short when the Cardinals were defeated by North Carolina in the 2008 East Regional Final. Still, the legend still exists in the form of the lopsided record over Palacios' four-year career at Louisville:

Louisville's Record with Juan Palacios Wearing His Goggles: 48–8

Louisville's Record without Juan Palacios Wearing His Goggles: 46–24

The Exodus of Wade and Allan Houston

It's always an impossible, and typically foolish, task to point to one particular occurrence or event as the catalyst for the complete downfall of something great that had taken years and years to construct. But ask Louisville basketball fans about the reason the Cardinals weren't soaring as high in the second half of Denny Crum's tenure as they were in the first, and plenty will give an answer in just two names: Wade and Allan Houston.

In 1962 Wade Houston became one of the first three African American basketball players to be recruited by Louisville head coach Peck Hickman. Houston, Sam Smith, and Eddie Whitehead would go on to become the first African Americans to suit up for a basketball team of a predominantly white college in the state of Kentucky. And Houston would be the first to earn a scholarship at U of L, where he lettered from 1963 to 1966.

After coaching Louisville's Male High School to a Kentucky state championship in 1975, Houston was added to Denny Crum's coaching staff at U of L as a full-time assistant. He coached the Cardinals for 14 of the most successful seasons in program history, eventually working his way up to become Crum's top assistant.

During those years Wade's son, Allan, became Louisville's unofficial mascot. Players such as Darrell Griffith and Derek Smith loved playing with the youngster after practice and even gave him a nickname just like they had for each of their teammates. For Allan it was "Big Al's Used Cars," a wordy name he wasn't especially fond of. When the Cardinals captured their first national title in 1980, Big Al's Used Cars rode the bus back from Indianapolis to Louisville just like Dr. Dunkenstein did.

By age 13, it was becoming apparent that the younger Houston was going to be a player. When the team found itself in need of bodies during the season, Crum would enlist the help of his assistant's skinny son. Houston had earned the right to see the court in Crum's eyes because he had swept the floors and done all the other tasks that the head coach asked his actual players to perform.

When it was time for Allan to start his basketball career at Louisville's Ballard High School, the word was already out that the city's next Darrell Griffith was about to take the state by storm. Houston wound up being even better than advertised. He led the Bruins to a state runner-up finish as a sophomore, went one step further and captured the state crown as a junior, earned Kentucky's Mr. Basketball honors as a senior, and left Ballard as the school's all-time leading scorer after netting 2,276 points over his four years.

The next stop for Allan? Louisville, of course. U of L already had Houston's signed letter of intent in hand when an issue they never saw coming arose. In 1989 Wade Houston was offered the head coaching job at the University of Tennessee. It was a job that not only gave Houston the opportunity to return to his home state, but also the chance to become the first African American basketball coach in the history of the SEC. He jumped at the opportunity. The issue was that Allan, who now claimed that his desire to play for his father had always been greater than his desire to play for Louisville, wanted to jump too.

After a brief period of pushback, U of L allowed its star recruit to back out of his signed letter of intent and go play for his father at Tennessee. Allan Houston would go on to become a two-time All-American, the Volunteers' all-time leading scorer with 2,801 points, and the second-leading all-time scorer in the history of the SEC.

Unfortunately for Wade Houston, his son's individual success didn't do much to help a team that didn't have much else going on for it. Tennessee never made the NCAA Tournament under

Houston's direction and twice it tied the school record for most losses in a season with 22. After amassing a 65–90 record over five seasons, Houston was fired by Tennessee in 1994. He would never be a head basketball coach again, instead choosing to return to Louisville and try his hand at business.

The move made by Tennessee to fire his father is still one that doesn't sit well with Allan Houston. "I appreciate being able to get a college degree and I have a lot of great college memories," Houston told the *New York Daily News* in 1998. "But if it wasn't for my father, I would have played at Louisville. He deserved better."

Allan would go on to enjoy a 12-year NBA career, spent mostly with the New York Knicks. He was named an NBA All-Star twice, earned a gold medal while playing for Team USA at the 2000 Olympics, and left the NBA in 2005 after scoring 14,551 career points.

Without Houston, Louisville would fail to make it out of the first round of the NCAA Tournament in 1990 and post the first losing season of Crum's career a year later. Though the Cardinals would be far from dismal for the next 10 years, they would never regain the magic or the success that they had known throughout the 1980s. Perhaps Wade and Allan Houston could have changed that.

74 The Original White Suit Game

In addition to his gaudy win totals and numerous championships, Rick Pitino also spent decades earning a reputation for as one of the best-dressed coaches in all of basketball. Perhaps Pitino's best-known piece of sideline sartorial splendor is an all-white suit, which he has made a habit of busting out for Louisville's annual "White Out" game.

Once a year, Louisville fans are asked to wear all white to a home game, typically a weekend contest against a marquee opponent. The team also sports all-white uniforms to coordinate with the environment.

What became commonplace during the second half of Pitino's Cardinals tenure was initially a shock to the home crowd when it debuted on February 9, 2008. It was a shock that produced a jolt the fan base desperately needed. Louisville's 2005 trip to the Final Four was supposed to be a glimpse into the better days for the Cardinals basketball program that lay ahead. Instead, U of L had turned a preseason top five ranking into a trip to the NIT in 2005–06 and had been bounced in the second round of the NCAA Tournament a season later. These performances had been excused by Cardinals fans mostly because the stage had appeared to be set for a monster 2007–08. For the first three months of the season, however, Louisville had not looked anything like a national title contender, and the natives in the Derby City were growing restless.

Louisville had started to snap out of their season-long funk a little bit by the time a Saturday night showdown with Big East–leading Georgetown rolled around on February 9. Still, the Cardinals were unranked and in desperate need of a signature win. The Hoyas, meanwhile, were 19–2 and ranked No. 6 in the country. ESPN's *College GameDay* had set up shop inside Freedom Hall, and the city had been buzzing all week long with anticipation.

The atmosphere inside Freedom Hall had been electric since the moment fans had started filing in, but when Pitino strolled out of the locker room just before the pregame introductions looking like Tom Wolfe, the place nearly shook to the ground. "I haven't worn a white linen suit since my communion," Pitino said after the game. "Nobody told me that you can't wear a white suit with

Rick Pitino's all-white ensemble inspired Louisville's White Out games.

blue [underwear]. When I got out there, I started sweating, the blue started to bleed through, and that's not a good look."

It was supposedly for that reason—and not the fact that Louisville trailed 31–23 at halftime—that Pitino came out of the locker room sporting a more traditional look for the game's final 20 minutes. Regardless, the Cardinals looked like a different team in the second half, dominating the glass and forcing the bigger Georgetown team to settle for outside jump shots. Senior center David Padgett got the better of NBA-bound big man Roy Hibbert, scoring a game-high 18 points to go along with four assists. "It was a different game the second half," said Georgetown coach John Thompson III. "I don't want to negate anything they did. They were extremely attentive and they turned up the heat a little bit, but I think it was lapses on our part. We never really got started; too many times we were just playing catch out there instead of getting into situations where we knew what we were doing."

When the final horn sounded, Louisville had pulled off a much-needed 59–51 victory. Pitino lied to ESPN reporter Erin Andrews after the game about the wardrobe change, claiming it was the product of a spilled drink. He then came clean with the media during his postgame press conference.

Either way, the big night proved to be a spark that ignited a nine-game winning streak for the Cardinals, one which, ironically, ended with a regular season finale loss at Georgetown. The run proved to be a catalyst for Louisville earning a No. 3 seed in the NCAA Tournament and, ultimately, a trip to the Elite Eight.

The event also signaled the beginning of an annual tradition. Though Louisville's first "White Out" game actually took place in 2007, most Cardinals fans remember the "Pitino Suit Game" as the event's genesis. Through 2017 U of L produced eight victories in 12 "White Out" games, the majority of which came against nationally ranked conference foes at critical junctures in the season.

75 The Top 10 T-Willisims

Perhaps the best athlete of the Rick Pitino era also happened to be most apt when it came to holding court with the media. Never shy around the camera or short on words, Terrence "T-Will" Williams wowed the home crowd for four years with his tremendous passing and remarkable dunks. He became the driving force on a 2008–09 team that won both the Big East's regular-season and tournament titles and earned the No. 1 overall seed for the NCAA Tournament. He also cemented his status as one of the most humorous players ever to don the red and black.

Here are the 10 most amusing things that came out of T-Will's mouth between 2005 and his graduation in 2009.

10. On Louisville's midseason winning streak in 2008–09

"I've realized that if we just keep winning games, eventually we'll win the national championship"

9. Explaining how he followed an 0-for-4 first half with an 8-for-16 second half against Massachusetts as a freshman

"Before, I was thinking about the scouting report and how they are a great shot-blocking team, and I was just trying to get the ball up there. But then I was like, 'Terrence,'—I call myself Terrence; I don't call myself T-Will—I was like, 'Terrence, you jump too high to be nervous about somebody else.'"

8. **On the importance of senior captain David Padgett in 2007–08**

"David Padgett is the T-shirt of this team. You wouldn't go outside without your T-shirt on, and we don't go out on the court without David Padgett."

7. **Celebrating the return of seniors Juan Palacios and David Padgett from injuries in 2007–08**

"You go out into a game in which you know you've got [Palacios] and David playing, your swagger's a lot different. You walk different, you talk different, you talk to a girl different...You know they're going to back you up. They're going to say, 'Yeah, he's a great guy.'"

6. **Explaining why he didn't declare for the NBA draft after his junior season**

"There are too many sharks in the water in this year's draft. Next year there's a lot of fish and seaweed. Hopefully, I can be one of those sharks next year."

5. **Finding the silver lining in a groin strain his senior season**

"It's a good thing because I really like massages and now I'm getting massages all the time."

4. **On trying to lead newcomers as a senior captain**

"Talking to these freshman is like talking to a pond: just because the water moves doesn't mean it's listening."

3. **On breaking out of a shooting slump with a big game from beyond the arc**

"No, I'm not surprised at how I shot today. If it's two in the afternoon and it's dark outside, then I'd be surprised."

Terrence Williams, who scored 1,565 points during his Louisville career, dribbles up the court during his freshman season.

2. **On how much the team fed off of David Padgett in 2007–08**
"How much do people eat off plates? We feed off him a lot because he's our point center, our point forward, our point shooting guard. He's everything because he rebounds the ball, he passes the ball, he leads us. He could lead us out of the closet, lead us to the ocean. He's just our everything."

1. **On coach Rick Pitino's powers of persuasion**
"He's the type of man where, if a dog couldn't talk—which a dog can't talk—he would make a dog think it can talk. That dog would keep barking for a long time thinking it was talking."

76 Kenny Klein

Every time Rick Pitino tries to explain why it is that he loves the University of Louisville so much, he can't help but bring up the name of Kenny Klein. "All you have to do, if you want to know about how special this place is, is to look at Kenny Klein. Kenny is the very best at what he does and he could have taken any number of jobs over the years, probably could have wound up being an athletic director somewhere. Instead he chose to stay here because he sees, just like I do, how special a place this is to work. And I'm glad he did because he's one of my best friends."

Klein's career at U of L predates just about everyone else who occupies an office on Floyd Street. He graduated from Murray State in 1981 with a degree in journalism and then just two years later accepted the sports information director position at Louisville. Just 23 years old, Klein was the youngest SID at an NCAA

Division I football institution. "I felt incredibly prepared," Klein told *The Courier-Journal* in 2014. "The man I'd worked under at Austin Peay and Murray State, Doug Vance, is now the executive director for the College Sports Information Directors of America. I learned under a great person. But it was a bit overwhelming because really it was [me], one student assistant, and Kathy Tronzo, who's my assistant to this day. My first year at Louisville I was so excited because *Street & Smith*'s college yearbook sent out a letter asking for material and I sent them some pictures of Milt Wagner and said, 'Hey, you might consider these for your cover.' And it was the cover. I was so thrilled. Man, I was so pumped to see that."

Since that year, Klein has been a fixture at the center of U of L athletics. In addition to serving as Louisville's SID, Klein now holds the title of senior associate athletic director for media relations. His sterling reputation has also rewarded him with the opportunity to coordinate the computerized statistics operations at every NCAA Final Four since 1987.

Klein is more than willing to reciprocate the affection thrown in his direction by Pitino. "We really kind of hit it off from the start," Klein said. "When [athletic director Tom Jurich] was basically recruiting him, Tom kind of shoved me into the process, so from the start we spent a lot of time together just to be sure we were doing things the way he wanted. I just had a great relationship with him. I've had other people reach out and say 'Goodness, I've never seen two guys like this.' We're good friends and we work together, and I know I can call him about anything, and he can call me about anything."

Like Pitino, Klein is also a Hall of Famer. He was inducted into the College Sports Information Directors of America Hall of Fame in 2015 and into the Kentucky Athletic Hall of Fame in 2017.

77 Louisville and Marquette's Fantastic Games

In an age where rivalry became synonymous with in-state bragging rights, rich multisport history, or just pure, unadulterated hate, Louisville/Marquette never seemed to make much sense.

The universities—one a Jesuit school in the Midwest and the other a Southern state school—are separated by 400 miles. They began playing each other in 1951, but both have multiple series with other programs that date back even further. Each program already had an established in-state rival (Kentucky and Wisconsin, respectively) and a secondary conference rival (Cincinnati and Notre Dame, respectively). Louisville/Marquette was never a rivalry built out of necessity; it was simply unavoidable. When two high-profile programs from the same conference play memorable game after memorable game for a prolonged period of time, it automatically becomes something much more than it was before, whether the parties involved like it or not.

Louisville and Marquette are two of just 37 programs to taste the sweet joy of a Division I college basketball national championship. Al McGuire took MU to the Promised Land in 1977, while Denny Crum made U of L the Team of the '80s and captured national titles in both 1980 and 1986. The two have maintained their relevance since then by advancing to a Final Four in the past decade, making the move together to perhaps the most prominent college basketball conference in the country and by consistently producing successful NBA talent.

And then there are the games, the undeniable backbone of the rivalry. A Cardinals or Golden Eagles fan can describe nearly every recent contest the two have played with a single name: Deane, Wardle, Myles, Hutchins, Gaines, Garcia, Smith, Knowles. It's a testament to just how competitive the two programs were before the madness of conference realignment ripped them apart.

Before that happened here are the 10 most memorable games the two rivals played.

10. February 28, 2003: Marquette 78, Louisville 73

A month after a dramatic win in Milwaukee, the Cardinals lost a 19-point lead at home, a shot at the Conference USA title, and the heart and soul of their team all in one night. Louisville led 46–35 at the break, but Cardinals killer Dwyane Wade hit 8 of 11 shots and scored 19 points in the second half to lead the Golden Eagles all the way back and secure Conference USA Player of the Year honors. The game had been billed as a showdown between Wade and U of L star Reece Gaines, but Gaines was flustered all night. He finished with just 12 points on 4 of 11 shooting, and forced an awkward jumper in the last minute that missed badly and allowed Travis Diener to sink two game clinching free-throws on the other end.

But the biggest loss of the evening for the Cardinals didn't stem from the final score. After collecting one of his seven offensive rebounds on the night, junior center Ellis Myles went up for a follow but landed awkwardly and immediately went down to the ground clutching his knee and screaming in agony. An angry Marquette coach Tom Crean accused Myles of faking, when in fact the big man had torn his patellar tendon and would be forced to miss the rest of the season as well as the entire 2003–2004 season. (The two made amends before the 2005 edition of the rivalry, but Louisville fans would never be as forgiving of Crean.) Wade would go on to lead Marquette to the Final Four, while fourth-seeded Louisville would be upset by Butler in the Round of 32.

9. March 2, 2006: Louisville 67, Marquette 60 (OT)

Desperately needing a win to ensure a spot in the upcoming Big East Tournament, the underachieving Louisville Cardinals overcame a questionable no-call on what had appeared to be an obvious foul and an overtime-inducing buzzer beater to outlast MU 67–60 in the second-to-last regular-season contest for both teams.

The Cardinals had numerous chances to end the game in regulation but went 0-for-6 from the free throw line in the final minutes and allowed Marquette to close the second half on an 11–2 run. Up 58–55 with five seconds left, all freshman Chad Millard had to do was sink one shot from the free throw line to end the game, but he couldn't get the job done. Following Millard's second miss, it appeared that Brandon Jenkins had his jersey blatantly pulled from the back by Steve Novak, but the referee standing right in front of the play didn't blow his whistle and the Golden Eagles had one last shot. Freshman Dominic James took the ball and streaked down the right side of the court before unleashing a running 25-footer that found the net and sent the game into overtime. Taquan Dean, playing on Senior Night, took over in the extra period, hitting a huge three and knocking down a pair of free throws that put the game out of reach. Terrence Williams then capped off the night with an electrifying windmill dunk.

8. February 24, 2001: Louisville 77, Marquette 74 (3 OT)

Louisville finally got back at Marquette guard Brian Wardle by ruining his Senior Night with a 77–74 victory in triple overtime. Despite the loss Wardle scored 24 points and set a school record by playing all 52 minutes of the thriller. Marques Maybin led Louisville with 22, and Eric Brown chipped in 15. The meeting would be the last between the two in the Denny Crum era, as the Hall of Fame coach would retire two weeks later after the Cardinals were bounced from the Conference USA Tournament by UAB.

7. March 6, 2004: Marquette 81, Louisville 80

Down 80–78 with less than three seconds left, Louisville's Alhaji Mohammed became confused about who he was supposed to be guarding as the Cards prepared to defend a Marquette out-of-bounds play from underneath the goal. The recipient of this good fortune for the Golden Eagles was freshman Dameon Mason, who was standing all by himself in the left corner. Trigger man Scott Merritt found Mason, who drilled the baseline jumper and was fouled by Mohammed, attempting to make amends for his error. After a timeout Mason calmly sank the free throw, and Louisville threw the ball away to ensure yet another loss for the slumping 24th-ranked Cardinals.

It was a quick reversal of fortune since it seemed as if Louisville had caught a massive break moments earlier when Travis Diener was whistled for his fifth foul, but replay proved that it was actually Carlton Christian who was the guilty party. The Golden Eagles' Brandon Bell then came down and took a wild three-pointer that bounced hard off the backboard but went off the hands of Francisco Garcia to give MU its final shot.

The drama only increased after the final buzzer, when the Golden Eagles staff found multiple copies of a *Milwaukee Journal-Sentinel* article in the Louisville locker room which had been doctored to include a quote from Tom Crean calling the Cardinals one of C-USA's "lesser teams." Crean called the motivational ploy "low and ridiculous," while Pitino said it was a joke he had no prior knowledge of. The win was also notable because it was Crean's 100th at Marquette.

6. February 17, 2005: Louisville 64, Marquette 61

If Marquette fans thought a 47-point beatdown earlier in the season was brutal, they had no idea what was in store for them a month later. Fighting to keep their fading NCAA Tournament hopes alive, the Golden Eagles hit just one field goal in the final 10 minutes and blew an 11-point second-half lead to the 12th-ranked Cardinals. The final blow came at the hands of junior Francisco Garcia, who drilled a deep three-pointer from the left wing with 2.6 seconds remaining to give U of L its final margin of victory. Travis Diener's running three at the buzzer fell short, and MU's tourney hopes were dashed.

5. February 28, 1996: Marquette 80, Louisville 79 (2 OT)

After a pair of successful free throws gave Louisville a two-point lead, red-hot Aaron Hutchins took the ball up the court, faked a drive, stepped back, and drilled a deep trey with three seconds left to give Marquette a huge win. ESPN declared the double overtime classic the best game of the 1995–96 season. The Golden Eagles would follow the victory up with wins against conference leader Cincinnati and a win at Memphis that snapped the Tigers' 45-game home winning streak. Marquette would go on to earn a four seed and lose to fifth-seeded Arkansas in the second round of the NCAA Tournament, while sixth-seeded Louisville advanced to the Sweet 16 before being bounced by Tim Duncan and Wake Forest.

4. February 17, 2007: Louisville 61, Marquette 59

After a disappointing start, a young U of L team coming off of a signature 66–53 win on the road against Pittsburgh was looking for revenge against a Marquette squad that had already beaten them by nine earlier in the season at Freedom Hall. It didn't look like it was going to happen after freshman guard Edgar Sosa fouled Dominic James, who sank one of two free throws to give the Golden Eagles a 59–58 advantage with 5.5 seconds to play.

With no timeouts remaining, Sosa took the inbounds pass and drove the ball across half-court before finding fellow freshman guard Jerry Smith—a Wisconsin native who had been offered a scholarship by Marquette when he was in the eighth grade—who drilled a deep game-winning three just before the buzzer. The shot was sweet vindication for Smith, who many believed was denied that state's Mr. Basketball award the year before because of his decision not to attend an in-state school. "This is the best homecoming that he could ever imagine, hitting the game-winning shot in his hometown," Sosa said after the game. "Everyone's loving him right now."

Louisville's emerging freshmen proved to be the difference on a night when David Padgett got into foul trouble and Terrence Williams failed to score. Sosa led Louisville with 15 points, Derrick Caracter added 14, and Smith hit a trio of late three-pointers, including the game-winner.

3. Januray 15, 2011: Louisville 71, Marquette 70

Just three months into its existence, the KFC Yum! Center gained its first signature moment when Louisville pulled off the "Miracle on Main." Marquette dominated the game for significant stretches and led by 18 points with just 5:36 to play. But the Golden Eagles unraveled during the game's final five minutes, making just two field goals during that span and throwing away several chances to secure a key victory against the 17th-ranked Cardinals.

Preston Knowles took advantage. The senior captain hit four extremely difficult three-pointers in rapid succession to bring U of L to within one and then, with the defense focused solely on him, found a wide-open Kyle Kuric for the game-winning layup. "That's one of the top five comebacks," Rick

Pitino said. "They outplayed us for the first 34 minutes. I'm really proud of these guys. I'm shaking. It happened so fast."

2. January 3, 1998: Marquette 71, Louisville 70

It wasn't in the tournament, there wasn't a conference championship at stake, but ask any Cardinals fan to name their most painful Louisville losses of all time, and you're likely to hear this game earn a mention. After a missed Nate Johnson free throw kept Louisville's lead at 70–68, MU's Jarrod Lovette grabbed the rebound and gave the ball to guard Marcus West, who quickly pushed the ball up to the other end of the floor. With time winding down, West passed to Lovette at the top of the key and he found freshman Brian Wardle on the left wing, who drilled the game-winning three at the buzzer.

Marquette head coach Mike Deane, who was wearing sunglasses, then proceeded to dance around the court and appeared to give the middle finger (this is still hotly debated) to the home crowd. Outraged Louisville fans hurled drinks at Deane, who continued to dance and taunt the crowd. Cruelly, days later it was actually Denny Crum, who had complained after the game about a horrible late goaltending call on Nate Johnson, who was reprimanded by the league office.

1. February 15, 2003: Louisville 73, Marquette 70

Coming off of a 59–58 loss to St. Louis, Reece Gaines and No. 2 Louisville broke the hearts of a record crowd at the Bradley Center that saw No. 11 Marquette's home winning streak snapped at 28. With the Cardinals leading 70–67, Marquette point guard Travis Diener came off of a screen and stroked a three-pointer to tie the game with 15.3 seconds to go. Before Marquette fans even had a chance to stop high fiving, Gaines had brought the ball down the floor and pulled up from well beyond the three-point line to deliver a dagger with six seconds remaining. Diener missed a desperation three at the buzzer. "I knew that was the best shot I was going to get because I couldn't move to the basket," Gaines said. "They were going to trap me and [force me] to pass it to somebody else."

Gaines finished with 20 points, including 4 of 6 from three-point range, and Taquan Dean added 18 points for the Cardinals, who pulled off the most memorable win of Rick Pitino's second season with Louisville.

78 "Louie" the Cardinal Bird

Louisville's Cardinals mascot dates all the way back to 1913, when the wife of liberal arts dean John Patterson suggested that U of L adopt Kentucky's state bird as its official mascot, as well as the bird's red and black coloring for its official school colors. Patterson made it happen, and the Louisville Cardinals were born. Despite taking the name, U of L didn't have an official mascot until 1952, when cheerleader T. Lee Adams donned a cloth Cardinal head that brought the school's nickname to life.

Like most mascots the Cardinal Bird, who would later officially become known as "Louie," has changed a number of times throughout the decades. For most of that period, however, his most consistent and distinguishable trait has remained his fierce and menacing teeth. And while some have noted that actual cardinal birds don't have teeth, Louie has never allowed this fact to keep him from flashing his pearly whites at opposing benches during games.

Louie is recognized as a part of the U of L Spirit Group and is a member of Louisville's national powerhouse cheerleading team. He has also been known to show up from time to time at the birthday parties and weddings of Cardinals fans in the city of Louisville. In 2004 Louie was honored with the National Cheerleaders Association's Most Collegiate Mascot Award.

79 The National Dominance of the U of L Spirit Groups

The most dominant athletic group at the University of Louisville can be seen performing on football fields in the fall and on basketball courts in the winter, but they don't play either sport. Since their inception the Louisville dance team—known as "the Ladybirds"—has claimed 15 national championships. The U of L cheerleaders have been equally dominant, claiming a whopping 39 NCAA Collegiate National Championships. Of those titles 16 have come in the Large Coed division, 13 have come in the All-Girl, and 10 have come in the Small Coed.

"I believe in accountability," said U of L spirit coordinator Todd Sharp in a 2016 interview with *Extol Magazine.* "If a girl does not look her best or perform her best, we all lose. There is no justice like team justice. I tell my team and their families in the very beginning, 'This will be the hardest thing you have ever done. This experience on my team will be physically, mentally, emotionally and financially hard. I have zero tolerance for fighting—this goes for parents, too. The tail will not wag the dog. This team is not a democracy; it's a dictatorship.' I want girls on my teams that have the passion, raw talent, and desire to be there."

Sharp's drive has paid off in the form of Louisville earning an established reputation for being America's preeminent college cheerleading and dance program. That status was further cemented in 2013, when the character of Santana on the popular Fox show *Glee* received a scholarship to U of L and it was referred to as "the top cheerleading college in the country." What could be a better endorsement than that?

80 Louisville's 1948 NAIB Tournament Title

In 1937, a small group of prominent basketball figures including the sport's architect, Dr. James Naismith, created the National Association Intercollegiate Basketball Championship. The goal of the six-day, single elimination tournament was to create a way to crown a national basketball champion for small colleges and universities. The tournament's creation predates the birth of the NCAA Tournament by two years, and the National Invitational Tournament by one.

After the success of its initial tournament, the NAIB (now NAIA) elected to expand its tournament to 32 teams in 1938. A decade after that, the tournament became the first major national college basketball tournament to integrate.

Led by Jack Coleman and his 12.1 points per game, Peck Hickman's 1947–48 Louisville Cardinals had enjoyed a terrific 24–5 regular season before accepting an invitation to participate in the 1948 NAIB tournament. U of L had participated in postseason tournaments for the Kentucky Intercollegiate Athletic Conference and the Southern Intercollegiate Athletic Association in the past, but the NAIB would be its first shot at a true national crown. Led by the play of Coleman and second-leading scorer Deward "Dee" Compton, Louisville began a memorable run at the six-day tournament in Kansas City. The Cardinals nipped South Dakota State by three in the first round and took care of Emporia State (82–66) and Beloit (85–76) to advance to the semifinals, where they pulled off an exhilarating come-from-behind 56–49 win against Xavier.

Hickman wasn't the only one impressed by his team's play. Kansas City mayor William E. Kemp was so enamored with Louisville's style and toughness that he felt the need to send a telegraph to the mayor of Louisville following the Cardinals' triumph against Xavier.

The telegraph read:

To Honorable Charles Farnsley, Mayor of Louisville, and the People of Louisville:

The University of Louisville basketball team has endeared itself to Kansas City's people by its splendid play and courage in this tournament. Three times the Louisvillians have come from behind to win. After each of its games, Louisville has continued to build up more and more good friends here. Its fighting spirit in coming from behind after a slow start has made it one of the outstanding stories in the 10-year history of our tournament, which draws from all over the nation.

No matter what the outcome, the Louisville team already has done much to represent the people of Louisville as great and friendly competitors, and sincere and courageous sportsmen.

Signed,

William E. Kemp, Mayor of Kansas City

Awaiting Louisville in the NAIB championship game was mighty Indiana State, owners of a 27–6 record. The Sycamores were coached by none other than John Wooden (who, unbeknownst to anyone at the time, was about to coach his final game before leaving for UCLA and starting the greatest dynasty college basketball would ever see). Wooden's team had actually been invited to the tournament a year prior in 1947, but he had turned down the invitation, citing the NAIB's policy banning African American players. That ban would have kept one his players,

Clarence Walker, from participating. In what was described in *The Courier-Journal* the next day as "the biggest thing to ever happen to the University of Louisville in athletics," the Cardinals found a way to take down Indiana State 82–70 despite both Compton and Coleman fouling out of the game.

For the rest of his career, the 1948 NAIB championship game would exist as the only championship game a Wooden-coached team ever lost. It also laid the foundation for Louisville to go on to become the only basketball program in history to win national championships in both the NAIB (NAIA) and NCAA.

81 Never Wrong Poncho Wright

Despite possessing an extreme level of athleticism and a knack for scoring that earned him the nickname "Instant Offense," David "Poncho" Wright often found himself overshadowed when he was on the court with some of the other great Louisville basketball players of the late '70s and early '80s. But off the court? The Indianapolis native took a backseat to no one. Wright's inability to grasp Denny Crum's defensive philosophy had frustrated U of L coaches since his arrival on campus in the fall of 1979. His infectious and boisterous personality, however, had made him both a fan and locker room favorite. He also proved to be something of a prophet.

Before the start of the 1979–80 championship season, Louisville had played a public intrasquad scrimmage game in front of about 2,500 fans at Charlestown High School. Wright, then an unknown sophomore who had just joined the team, wasted no time making a first impression. He buried 10 of 14 field goal attempts, the majority of them coming from extremely deep.

His most notable impact that day, however, came after the scrimmage's final whistle. When he noticed Billy Reed, the legendary columnist for *The Courier-Journal*, sitting down for a postgame interview with teammate Wiley Brown, Wright couldn't help but walk over and interrupt. "Tell him, Wiley," Wright started out. "Tell him we're going to 'Nap! Nooooooooo stoppin'! Tell 'em all that. Tell [Purdue center] Joe Barry Carroll, tell [Ohio State center] Herb Williams, tell 'em all. The 'Ville is goin' all the way."

But what about Louisville's recent history of losing close games at the end of the season? The same recent history had earned them then-derogatory nickname of "Cardiac Cards." "Ain't no more 'Cardiac Cards,'" Wright said. "Forget that. We don't choke, we swallow. We gonna swallow everybody. Nooooooo stoppin'! Tell 'em all that Poncho and Wiley and Scooter all said so."

Then came a beautiful crescendo. Wright strung all his thoughts together and blurted out seven words that at the time made no sense to Reed or even to Brown. "The 'Ville is going to the 'Nap." When asked to elaborate (Reed would go on to refer to Wright's vernacular as "Panchoese"), Wright explained that the 'Ville was the way he referred to Louisville, and the 'Nap was what he called his hometown of Indianapolis, which just so happened to be hosting the 1980 Final Four. Reed shared this thought and all Wright's others in his column the next morning, and fans of every team in the area took notice. "I vaguely remember saying it," Wright said in the book *Tales from the 1980 Louisville Cardinals*. "I hadn't played with these guys the year before and remember thinking how tough, how dominating we looked. It just came out like that. Some people were like, "Yeah, they're going to the 'Nap all right—they're going to *take* a nap.' And I thought, 'Well, we'll see.'"

While Wright struggled with defense throughout his freshman season, his pure outside shot was on full display on multiple occasions—as was his personality. After the team's Midwest Regional

Final victory against LSU, Wright commandeered the public-address system on the team's charter flight home and announced "this is your zone-buster speaking."

Ultimately, Louisville's season ended exactly where Wright had predicted it would. The Cardinals defeated Iowa and UCLA inside Market Square Arena in Indianapolis to claim their first national title, and Wright claimed a status of basketball prophet—a distinction that he would hold on to forever. While his teammates would sign autographs for fans after that season with their names and numbers, Wright always felt the need to include his full title: "Never Wrong Poncho Wright."

82 Paul Rogers, "the Voice of the Cardinals"

Louisville native Paul Rogers had no idea that his first job would wind up being his only one. In 1973 Rogers was a recent graduate of the University of Kentucky with a degree in telecommunications who was simply looking to get the next phase of his life started. When the University of Louisville offered him a job covering the Cardinals for both WHAS radio and television, he jumped at the opportunity.

The man who extended Rogers his first job offer was Cawood Ledford, the legendary voice of the Kentucky Wildcats who balanced that gig with a management position at WHAS. "I had learned so much from Cawood before I ever knew him just from listening to him," Rogers said in a 2013 podcast interview with TheCrunchZone.com. "I had sent him a couple of my tapes in college, and he'd been kind enough to critique them. WHAS had an opening in the summer of 1973, and I sent in an application, but really didn't think anything of it. A few days later, Cawood called me, and I'll never forget it, he said, 'Boy, you have really improved.' He asked me to come down and see him the next day and immediately he started talking about all the things we were going to do."

Rogers' impact on the city of Louisville over the course of the next half century would stretch well beyond just U of L athletics. He would go on to call numerous races at Churchill Downs, including the local radio broadcasts of the Kentucky Derby and the Breeders Cup. Rogers also worked the Kentucky State Tournament for boys basketball and would later work NCAA Tournament games for CBS Radio.

Still, most in the Louisville area recognize Rogers' dulcet tone as the voice of the Louisville Cardinals. He began serving as the full-time play-by-play man for both the U of L football and men's basketball teams in the early '90s and has been a staple of every Cardinals fan's life ever since. "I just can't seem to get a promotion," Rogers joked when he was inducted into the Kentucky Athletic Hall of Fame in 2014. "How can you be promoted when you start at the top? This is what I always wanted to do—only it's worked out even better than I could have imagined. I'm often asked which sport do I like best. And truthfully, the answer is whichever one is in season."

Among his many accomplishments, Rogers was named the Kentucky Sportscaster of the Year in 1995, 1998, 2002, and 2013. Although the accolades are nice, it's the connection that the voice of Louisville sports has with listeners he's never met that he says makes his job so special. "It's been a long, great ride," he mused. "Who could ask for anything more?"

83 Pitino-Speak

There are those who dabble in hyperbole, and then there is Rick Pitino. Every Louisville fan has their own favorite branch of "Pitino-Speak," the head coach's very own language in which all listeners are aware of the fact that the words being uttered are only partly true.

One popular subset of this phenomenon is Pitino's recurring need to refer to whichever team Louisville faces in its opening game of the NCAA Tournament as the "toughest first-round opponent" of his coaching career. It's a March tradition that Cardinals fans have grown to look forward to nearly as much as Selection Sunday itself.

Here's a rundown of some of the greatest pre-tournament Pitino-Speak hits. They are taken from his pregame press conference in each season.

2005

The Team: No. 13 Louisiana-Lafayette

The Quote: "They don't have just one guy that you have to concern yourself with. Their point guard [Florida transfer Orien Greene] is terrific, and he's 6'5". Their center [Chris Cameron] is a big-time threat at 6'11", 270, and they've got scoring at the wings [Dwayne Mitchell and Brian Hamilton]. So this is the toughest first-round matchup I've ever had as a coach. But I'd probably rather have it that way because we play better against better talent anyway."

The Result: Louisville 68, Louisiana-Lafayette 62

2007

The Team: No. 11 Stanford

The Quote: "You're talking about a team that beat UCLA, beat Oregon by 20, beat Cal by 30. This is the toughest first-round opponent I've ever had as a head coach."

The Result: Louisville 78, Stanford 58

2008

The Team: No. 14 Boise State

The Quote: "They're a veteran ballclub, the toughest first-round matchup I've had since I've been coaching."

The Result: Louisville 79, Boise State 61

2010

The Team: No. 8 California

The Quote: "They're a top 20 team, they're a dominant team. We realize we're facing one of the more underrated teams in the country. It's the toughest first-round opponent one of my teams has ever faced."

The Result: California 77, Louisville 62

2012

The Team: No. 13 seed Davidson

The Quote: "This is the toughest first-round game I've had as a basketball coach. Davidson is very, very good. Everyone on their team can shoot it from the outside, and that makes them very difficult to prepare for."

The Result: Louisville 69, Davidson 62

84 Chris Redman

Kentucky isn't exactly known nationally as a hotbed for blue chip high school football talent. There are exceptions to this fact, and then there are extreme exceptions. Chris Redman was always going to be an extreme exception.

Redman was already being discussed as a potential future NFL quarterback before he ever took a snap for his coach and father, Bob Redman, at Louisville's Male High School. Once his high school career began, the notion that Redman would one day be shaking hands with the NFL commissioner only grew. His youth legend hit its peak during his high school senior season of 1994, when he threw for 3,752 yards and a then–national record 57 touchdowns. After the season, Redman was named the Parade National Player of the Year.

With the fact well known that both Redman's father and grandfather had played football at Louisville, it was of little surprise when Chris officially pledged allegiance to his hometown school in the fall of 1994. What was a surprise was the news just a few months later that U of L head coach Howard Schnellenberger, who was frustrated by the administration's decision to join the newly formed Conference USA, was leaving Louisville in order to become the next head coach at Oklahoma.

While suiting up for the Cardinals had always been the vision stuck in Redman's childhood head, in more recent years, the allure of taking his talents to U of L had been to be the man at the center of Schnellenberger's pass-friendly pro-style offense. Out of respect for his former employer, Schnellenberger did not recruit Redman after he took the job at Oklahoma. He did, however, bring recruiting coordinator Gary Nord, a longtime friend of the Redman family, with him to Norman. All of this led Redman to officially de-commit from Louisville in late December 1994. "It was tough," Redman recalled. "I had always dreamed of playing for Louisville and I had always thought that I was going to play for Louisville. Coach Cooper was a defensive-minded coach, and I was a little nervous about going to a school with a defensive-minded head coach. It was tough."

Initially it was Illinois that appeared to be the surprise benefactor of Louisville's coaching turnover. Redman committed to the Illini based mostly on the recruiting efforts of offensive coordinator Greg Landry but was then stunned to learn that Landry had been fired the day after Redman had signed his letter of commitment. Though Illinois coach Lou Tepper denied that he had intentionally tried to deceive Redman about Landry's future with the program, the NCAA stepped in and decided to void the letter of commitment based on the situation's peculiar circumstances.

In the spring of 1995, Redman took official visits to Tennessee and Auburn before announcing on March 21 that he planned to follow Schnellenberger to Oklahoma. Months later, however, concerns over Oklahoma's apparent logjam at quarterback and the distance between the school and his home led Redman to once again back out of a commitment. That summer, he came full circle and signed on to play football for new head coach Ron Cooper at Louisville.

After redshirting the 1995 season, Redman saw action in 10 games as a redshirt freshman in 1996 and emerged as the team's starting quarterback in the final five. After throwing for more than 1,700 yards, Redman picked up Conference USA All-Freshman honors and also established himself as the future of the Louisville football program. Records began to fall a year later, as Redman shattered single-season school passing marks in attempts (445), completions (261), yards (3,079), and total offense (2,958) during his sophomore season. Unfortunately, those numbers weren't enough to avoid a 1–10 season for Louisville that would result in Cooper's ouster.

Under the guidance of a new offensive-minded staff led by head coach John L. Smith and offensive coordinator Bobby Petrino, Redman continued his assault on the U of L record books in 1998. Despite missing one of his team's 11 games with a knee injury, the gunslinger set new Conference USA and Louisville single-season records for attempts (473), completions (309), yards (4,042), and touchdowns (29). This time the records came hand in hand with team success, as Louisville went 7–4 and earned a bid to its first bowl game in five years. "At that time, that was a really big deal," Redman said. "We got off to a rough start that season, but then things just started and clicking, and by the end of the year, we had the No. 1 offense in the entire country. That was an exciting year. We scored a ton of points. I remember dancing on the field after the Army game when we found out that we were going to a bowl game. It was the Motor City Bowl, but at that time it felt like the Super Bowl."

The good vibes carried over into 1999, when the Cards again went bowling after Redman completed 317 of 489 passes for 3,647 yards and 29 touchdowns. During the year Redman became the first quarterback in Division I-A history to complete more than 1,000 passes in his career. After the season he was named both the Conference USA Player of the Year and the recipient of the Johnny Unitas Golden Arm Award, which is given each year to the nation's top senior quarterback.

Redman ended his college career as the NCAA Division I-A career leader in both completions (1,031) and attempts (1,679). At that time his 12,541 career passing yards ranked third behind Brigham Young's Ty Detmer (15,031 yards) and Louisiana Tech's Tim Rattay (12,746). His jersey was honored by U of L in 2000.

85 The 2001 Liberty Bowl

By 2001 Louisville football coach John L. Smith had established a reputation for getting the Cardinals into the postseason. The only problem was that he'd also established a reputation for not being able to win once he got there. In three seasons under Smith, U of L had played in three bowl games—and had lost all three.

That narrative was shattered in Smith's fourth season, when Louisville captured its second consecutive Conference USA title and earned a return trip to the Liberty Bowl to square off against Mountain West champion BYU. The Cougars had begun their season 12–0 and had campaigned hard for a spot in a BCS game before falling to Hawaii in their regular-season finale.

Before an announced crowd of 58,968 in frigid Memphis, the 23rd-ranked Cardinals pasted the 19th-ranked Cougars in a rare postseason meeting between two nationally ranked conference champions. U of L quarterback Dave Ragone was named the game's MVP after tossing for 228 yards and three touchdowns. The victory improved Louisville to 11–2 on the season and also established a new program record for single-season victories. "What I've always said about this team is we might not have the most talent, but we have the most heart and we play together," Ragone said during the postgame press conference. "This is one of the best Louisville teams to come through here."

The game had been billed as a showdown between two of the nation's top offenses, but due in large part to the well-below-freezing temperatures, Louisville and BYU combined for just 562 yards. That was fine with the Cardinals defense, which held its opponents without a touchdown in the second half. "Louisville is a very good team," BYU head coach Gary Crowton said afterward. "We knew coming in they would play hard, play tough, and present one of the toughest games for us this season. They have an excellent coaching staff and did a better job of preparing for this game than we did. I thought we did a good job of preparing. We had some great practices, but they were a little better than we were today."

The postseason victory was Louisville's first since knocking off Michigan State in the 1993 Liberty Bowl.

86 Denny Crum Court

During a pregame ceremony before Louisville took on Georgetown in February 2007, the court inside Freedom Hall was officially branded "Denny Crum Court." It was a proper and necessary dedication to the man who had taken the Cardinals from solid program to national powerhouse. "For three decades, U of L Basketball was Denny Crum," said U of L athletic director Tom Jurich when the dedication was first announced. "It's a fitting tribute to honor him with this unique distinction for his success and years of hard work in guiding our men's basketball program consistently on a national level. We had envisioned honoring him within the new arena, but Rick Pitino and I were talking and thought 'Why wait?' Let's not wait any longer in getting his name on the court in Freedom Hall, where he coached for 30 years."

It was a sentiment echoed by Crum's successor. "Denny Crum *is* Louisville basketball," Pitino said. "He's built an unbelievable tradition, and I am very honored to carry on his tradition. Denny Crum Court will forever symbolize excellence, and symbolize someone who built this great tradition here."

Louisville dropped a 73–65 decision to Big East-leading Georgetown on that night, but that was an afterthought to the multitude of former players who had showed up to join in the celebration of their old head coach. "There's a time and place for

The unveiling of Denny Crum Court was a fitting tribute to a man who won 675 games and two national titles at Louisville.

everything, and this is the perfect time," Darrell Griffith, Crum's most famous player, told *The Courier-Journal.* "I'm elated. Coach gave so much of his life to this program. I always hoped they would do this. All his former players did."

When Louisville basketball made the move from Freedom Hall to the KFC Yum! Center, Denny Crum Court moved with it. The name is announced before the start of every game, and more often than not, Crum is in attendance to hear it.

87 Louisville's Second Bowl Appearance Ends in a Tie

Nearly 13 years after their debut postseason performance, the Louisville Cardinals parlayed a Missouri Valley Conference championship into a Pasadena Bowl appearance on December 19, 1970, at the Rose Bowl. U of L's opponent, the Long Beach State 49ers, proved to be a worthy adversary—some might say an equally worthy adversary.

Lee Corso's Cards led for the vast majority of the game, riding a strong rushing performance by quarterback John Madeya and a tremendous defensive effort from defensive captain Paul Mattingly. Mattingly was ultimately named the bowl's Defensive Player of the Game after recording a game-high 17 tackles and blocking a 32-yard field goal attempt in the fourth quarter.

A strange play near the end of the game seemed to secure victory for Louisville. Madeya threw a screen pass to tailback Tom Jesukaitis, who then sprinted toward the sideline before throwing another pass to a wide-open Cookie Brinkman for a touchdown. Only one forward pass per play was permitted at the time, however, and after what was reported by the Associated Press to be a "long and heated" 15 minute discussion, the touchdown was called back, and the Cardinals were penalized five yards. The penalty took U of L out of field goal range, and the game ended in a 24–24 tie. The bowl appearance remains the only one in the history of the Long Beach State football program.

Directly reflecting their head coach's laid-back mentality, Louisville took full advantage of its time in California. Brinkman's interview with *The Courier-Journal* interview produced quotes that would be the lead topic of every sports radio show in America if they had been made today. "Near the end of the season, everybody had long hair and mustaches," Brinkman said. "We were a pretty nasty-looking crew. We were loose away from the field, but a pretty close bunch, and when it came time to play, we were ready. Coach told us we were going out there to have fun. We did. There was one bed check at midnight the night before the game. The rest of the time we were on our own. No telling when some of the guys got in. We'd go to Hollywood, down on Sunset Strip, and we got to like a place called the Moustache [Café], a good delicatessen with good beer. We never practiced in pads. The day before the game we showed up, and it was kind of evident we were not in shape to do anything. Coach Corso took one look at us and said, 'You guys go back inside.' And we did."

The exploits of the team were especially frustrating for the players of Big Ten champion Ohio State, which was also in town to play in the Rose Bowl. Many of the Buckeyes players had grown up with players who were suiting up for the Cardinals and wished they could partake in some of their friends' off-the-field fun. "[The Buckeyes] had a 9:00 PM curfew every night," Brinkman said. "They practiced twice a day and they hit. At night they'd see us running around loose. They were mad as heck."

88 The 2013 Dream That Did Not Die

When it finally happened, I didn't cry. I didn't take off my pants and run out onto the court. My heart didn't automatically stop beating. I didn't do any of the things I always speculated I would if Louisville ever won a national championship in basketball.

It's not that the moment wasn't overwhelming. It was. It's just that there was too much going on to really think about all the implications. I wanted to get a good glimpse of the celebration on the court, I wanted to hug my friends and family, I wanted to hear what Rick Pitino had to say when he was given the mic. The enormity of *oh my goodness, that thing I've always dreamt about happening just happened* never really gets a chance to seep in.

The only time I got that hold it in, you're in public feeling in my upper chest was that night during the starting lineup festivities. It was the one chance my brain had to ponder the possibility before the game started, and I took full advantage. I thought about the hundreds of games I'd watched on the couch with my father, the trips to Freedom Hall and the KFC Yum! Center I'd made with friends and family, and the viewing parties at my house or friends' houses on special occasions.

Since I was probably nine years old, there hasn't been a Louisville basketball game that has passed without me either watching it live, following along online, or finding out the final score as quickly afterward as I could. All that was done with the hope that one day I'd be lucky enough to see April 8, 2013, live and in person.

I thought about all the random knowledge, the obscure facts, and the crazy memories of Louisville basketball that I'd collected over the years. I thought about refusing to come inside when U of L was making a dramatic comeback against Tulsa in the 1996 NCAA Tournament because I thought it'd jinx them. I thought about listening to Brian Kiser's game-winning three against UCLA in the car with my brother Oliver while we were at the Shelby Trails Park for one of my sister's shows. I thought about the dueling C-A-R-D-S and C-A-T-S cheers we had at Sacred Heart's junior-senior prom on the night before Louisville was stunned by Butler. I thought about how comforting it was to know that I wasn't alone in this madness.

The older you get as a Louisville fan, the more aware you become that there are plenty of others who share your obsession. When I meet a new U of L fan, I'm still amazed by just how similar our feelings and memories are. We remember things other fan bases would have forgotten mere months after they happened: the Damian Dantzler/Alvin Sims over-the-head save/dunk against Texas in 1997, Joseph N'Sima's free throw style (as well as the right way to spell his name), Diego Guevara's trademark move after making a shot. The list goes on and on. Everybody loves company, and Cardinals fans are blessed with some of the best company possible.

I thought about all the times during the spring and summer months in my early twenties when I'd had too much to drink and tried (unsuccessfully) to convince my friends to walk home from the bar because it was a chance to "experience the city." Everyone wants to get away when they're younger, but I think I realized sooner than most just how special my hometown is. Living elsewhere only reinforces it.

Louisville takes all the things I've enjoyed about other areas of the country—the charm of the South, the kindness of the Midwest, the outside-the-box thinking of the North—and makes them its own. The result is, to my mind at least, the perfect place to grow up, work, make friends, fall in love, start a family, or do anything else you think makes life worth living. I've met dozens of people who have come to Louisville from other parts of the world and fallen head-over-heels for it. More than a handful of them have used the same phrase: "It gets in your blood." That's not a coincidence.

I thought about how perfectly this particular team served as an extension of the city it represented. I thought about how fantastic it would be for them to be the ones to give the city its first championship of the 21st century. Kevin Ware's injury allowed the nation to get a taste of the character and the togetherness that we'd been privy to for months. From Gorgui Dieng's unrivaled likability, to Russ Smith's personality, to Peyton Siva's leadership, to Luke Hancock's ability to overcome adversity, and on and on. There hasn't been a U of L team in my lifetime more worthy of representing a generation.

When talking to friends, family, strangers, and anyone else willing to listen on April 8, 2013, the word that kept coming up was "forever." That's probably the best part of any realized dream: you get it forever. The team, the players, your own personal stories…all of it is forever.

Since starting Card Chronicle back in 2007, I've written a post every year on the day after Louisville is eliminated from the NCAA Tournament titled "The Worst Day of the Year." It's hyperbole only in the sense that there's no way for me to know what awful things are going to happen on other days. The truth is that, as far as guaranteed depressing occurrences are concerned, being faced directly with the knowledge that it'll be another 12 months before the dream has a chance to be realized has always ranked right at the top (or the bottom) of every Mike Rutherford calendar year. It's something I don't really get over, or allow myself to get over, until the Kentucky Derby rolls around in May.

Of course, there was no worst day of 2013 because the dream did not die that year. Realized dreams come along so rarely in life that they demand to be absorbed, celebrated, and soaked in as much as possible. The good thing is that you always get plenty of time to make that happen, because realized dreams are forever.

Bill Olsen

Had Bill Olsen not been serving as Louisville's athletic director in the 1980s, Lamar Jackson may have never won U of L's first Heisman Trophy in 2016. The dots between those two points become a bit easier to connect when you realize that Olsen's efforts may have been the only thing that kept Cardinals football existing at a Division I-A level.

With Louisville football struggling to both win games and draw major attendance numbers in the 1980s, the U of L board of trustees consistently pushed to pump the program down to the Division II level. In the eyes of the board, the basketball program was so overwhelmingly successful and so much more popular than its gridiron counterpart that the move would hardly be a blip on the city's radar. But Olsen understood that regardless of success, football is the engine that fuels college athletics. As a result, he refused to back down. "I knew what we needed to become a self-sufficient athletic department," Olsen said in a 1998 interview. "I had some ideas about us turning the corner in football."

Shortly after convincing the U of L board to back down from its proposition for good, Olsen was able to shut up everyone for good by landing one of the biggest hires in Cardinals athletic history. In 1985 he convinced Howard Schnellenberger, who was less than two years removed from winning a national championship at Miami, to become the new head football coach at Louisville. Five years later Louisville was kicking off the 1990s with a 10-win season and a 1991 New Year's Day Fiesta Bowl trouncing of Alabama.

Olsen's stance set the stage for the construction of a new football stadium, as well as the once-unthinkable success that coaches like Charlie Strong and Bobby Petrino would enjoy years later.

During his 17-year stint as U of L athletic director from 1980 to 1997, Olsen oversaw the high point of Louisville basketball, but perhaps just as importantly, he prevented Louisville football from hitting an irreversible low.

90 Anyone, Anywhere, Anytime

The party line of "big-time college football is played on Saturday and Saturday only" is one that has been used liberally by the sport's elite powers for years. Blue-blood programs from the SEC and the Big 12 that have rewarded generations of fans with success at the highest-level consistently turn up their nose at the mere thought of a weekend tailgate being snatched away in favor of a few extra eyes on television. It's a stance that Louisville football never had the luxury of taking.

When Tom Jurich took over as Louisville's athletic director in 1997, the program had just endured a 1–10 season and was at risk of being kicked out of Conference USA. The good news for Jurich was that he had a new head coach in John L. Smith and a new offensive coordinator in Bobby Petrino who he knew at the very least were going to make the team more enjoyable to follow because of its offensive output. He knew he would have a product that was much superior than what it had been. Now he just had to figure out a way to make the rest of the country see it. (Jurich would eventually go to ESPN, the entity who controls that sort of thing.) U of L football wasn't in a position to call any significant shots, so Jurich played the best hand he had available to him. "Louisville came to us and said, 'We'll play anyone, anywhere, anytime,'" former ESPN

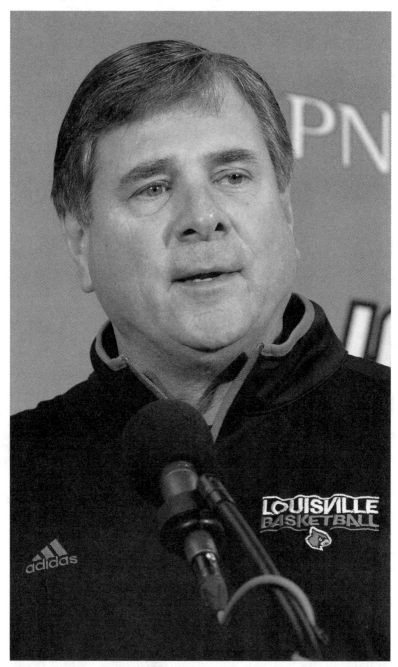

Perhaps more than any other individual, Tom Jurich is most responsible for Louisville's ascendance as a national athletic power.

head of programming and production Mark Shapiro told *The New York Times* in 2013. "It was a programmer's dream. We already had NFL on Sunday nights, NHL and MLB on multiple nights, Thursday night college football. We were all filled up. So I said, 'How about Tuesday nights?' They seized it, and over time their results have been spectacular."

Just as Jurich had suspected, Louisville football began lighting up the scoreboard on a weekly basis. And just as he had hoped, a viewing audience that would have flipped right past the Cardinals on a jammed Saturday began to appreciate the U of L team it was now regularly seeing play only-show-in-town games on weekday nights.

In 2001, Louisville appeared on ESPN or ESPN2 five times. A year later it was six games, including a Tuesday night game, three Thursday games, and a late Saturday night game. "We owe them so, so much," Jurich said of ESPN. "They were willing to take a chance on us. We became America's team."

Thanks to the added exposure, Louisville was also able to start landing a better breed of recruits. Quarterback Stefan LeFors, the 2003 Conference USA Player of the Year, admitted after he arrived at U of L that he knew nothing about the program before it started putting up absurd numbers on unordinary nights. He also said those games were the only reason he chose to come play for the Cardinals.

With the addition of players such as LeFors, Louisville was able to reach the postseason in every year from 1997 to 2006. It was also able to go from a struggling program in a struggling conference to one that made the jump to the Big East in 2005 and then the ACC in 2014.

91 The Louisville-Memphis Rivalry

It was a feud that was eventually ruined by the greed of conference realignment, but for a time, the basketball rivalry between Louisville and Memphis burned as brightly as any in the country.

How bad was the blood between the two programs? So bad that during one game in the 1980s at Memphis' Mid-South Coliseum, an angry Tigers fan sent a switchblade sailing from the stands onto the court as a warning to the visiting team. Memphis (then Memphis State) was also known to place a caged tiger right outside the Louisville locker room. It also had its pep band play extra close to the visiting bench when the Cardinals were in town.

As for the actual on-court action, Louisville and Memphis enjoyed so much success when they played in the same conference that they met three times in the same season on 13 separate occasions. The Tigers beat the Cardinals for the Metro Tournament title in 1982 and '87, and Louisville beat Memphis to return the favor with Milt Wagner's late free throws in 1986 and then again in '88.

The final meeting between the two teams as conference foes took place in 2005 in the championship game of the Conference USA tournament. Playing in front of its home crowd, the Tigers had to claim C-USA's automatic bid if they wanted to make an appearance in the NCAA Tournament. Louisville, meanwhile, was ranked in the nation's top five and was simply playing for an improved seed and bragging rights. With Louisville leading by two and just seconds remaining, Memphis freshman guard Darius Washington raced up the court with the intention of creating the next great milestone in the rivalry's history. He would succeed—just not in the manner he had envisioned.

Washington attempted a wild three-point shot and was fouled by U of L's Francisco Garcia with no time remaining on the clock. The call meant that Washington would stroll to the line by himself for three shots that would end regulation one of three ways. Make one, your season's over. Make two, you go to overtime. Make all three, you're conference champions and you're going to the big dance.

The freshman calmly sank the first shot, then looked over to then–Memphis head coach John Calipari and boldly proclaimed, "It's over." He missed the next two and caught a glimpse of the Louisville players celebrating their championship before he collapsed to the court in agony. The Cardinals left for the Big East that season, taking with them the final right hook in a rivalry in which blows had been exchanged for decades.

92 Rick Pitino's Championship Tattoo

On the evening of February 9, 2013, Rick Pitino walked into the losing team's locker room knowing his players were in desperate need of a pick-me-up. The Cardinals had just cemented their spot on the wrong side of history, losing 104–101 in five overtimes at Notre Dame in what was the longest regular-season game in the history of the Big East Conference. To make matters worse, U of L had appeared to be in complete control for the bulk of regulation and then also had opportunities to pull out the victory in the final seconds of each of the first three overtime periods.

Pitino didn't think the situation called for some sort of advice that could be utilized down the road. Instead, he needed to tell his guys what was about to happen down the road. In a tempered but direct manner, Pitino told his Cardinals that they were going to finish the regular season with seven straight wins, including a revenge victory against Notre Dame on U of L's Senior Day. He then said the team was going to go to Madison Square Garden and win the Big East Tournament in its final year of participation. Next up would be the NCAA Tournament, where the Cards were going to be a top seed that reeled off six consecutive victories to claim their first national championship in nearly three decades. In all? Pitino told his team that they were about to win 16 straight games.

When the spiel was over, Pitino started to walk out of the locker room to take care of his media responsibilities. Before he could make it out the door, his senior point guard and captain, Peyton Siva, had a request. The fully inked native of Seattle was buying what his coach was selling, but he also wanted to sweeten the pot. If Louisville won 16 straight, Pitino had to get a tattoo—something he had told his players that they needed fewer of—commemorating the championship forever. Perhaps not fully believing that his team was capable of bringing to life the vision he'd just laid out, Pitino agreed.

Two months later, Rick Pitino was at Tattoo Salvation in Louisville getting a permanent reminder of his second national championship on the upper-left portion of his back. The image was Louisville's trademark "L" and "NCAA Champions" complete with the year the title was won as well as the team's record. "The championship meant a lot to me," Pitino said after making good on his promise. "It'll last forever because it's not going away on my back. It was a lot of fun."

93 Charlie Strong

When Charlie Strong was hired by University of Louisville athletic director Tom Jurich on December 9, 2009, he was taking over a program that needed to dig itself out of a huge hole. The Cardinals had been to nine straight bowl games and finished in the nation's top 10 twice between 1998 and 2006. Then Bobby Petrino left to become the head coach of the Atlanta Falcons, and Steve Kragthorpe began a three-year stint during which Louisville would fail to play in a single bowl game.

For Strong, the day was the realization of a moment he had started to think might never come. Despite the fact that he had long established himself as one of the top defensive coordinators in the entire country, Strong had consistently found himself passed over when it came to head coaching vacancies. There were various theories about why. Some said Strong didn't interview well. Others said the issue lay with the fact that he was applying for jobs in the Deep South, and he was a black man with a white wife.

Regardless of why it took so long, when the moment finally came for Charlie Strong to give his first address as the head coach of a football program, he was noticeably overcome with emotion. "This is a very big day for me and my family," Strong said while fighting through tears. "Because you just never knew if it would happen."

What happened next for Strong was more immediate than anyone saw coming. Despite being picked to finish dead last in the Big East before the start of the season, Strong led Louisville to a surprising 7–6 season and capped it off with a win against Southern Mississippi in the Beef 'O'Brady's Bowl. The bowl appearance and win were the Cardinals' first since their Orange Bowl triumph against Wake Forest in Petrino's final season.

A year later Louisville was again picked to finish last in the Big East. Again, the Cardinals drastically exceeded expectations, winning a share of the conference's regular-season title and earning a bid to the Belk Bowl in Charlotte.

While Louisville enjoyed more success than expected early on with former two-star recruits and walk-ons, Strong and his staff were busy laying a foundation for the future on the recruiting trail. They landed a number of high-profile players from the state of Florida, including Miami Northwestern quarterback Teddy Bridgewater, and put together a 2011 recruiting class that would eventually send seven players to the NFL, including three who were first-round draft picks.

With Strong's initial success came the predictable wave of job offers. When Tennessee reportedly came calling after the 2011 season, there was plenty of speculation that Strong had significant interest in making a move back to the conference where he'd spent so much time as a coordinator. He ultimately chose to stick with U of L, saying later in a WHAS radio interview that he had always remembered the words of former Louisville coach John L. Smith, who had fallen on hard times after leaving U of L for seemingly greener pastures. "I remember having a conversation with Coach Smith when I found out that Tom [Jurich] was considering me, and he told me that leaving Louisville was the biggest mistake he ever made," Strong said. "He told me, 'If you get that job, don't ever leave.'"

Strong would eventually go against that advice but not before leading Louisville to 11 wins and a stunning Sugar Bowl victory against Florida in 2012 and 12 wins and a Russell Athletic Bowl victory against Miami in the season after that. Shortly after the Miami win, Strong revealed to the world that he was leaving Louisville to take over at Texas.

Even though the way his departure went down didn't sit particularly well with some of his coworkers and a portion of the Louisville fan base, Strong left U of L having done the program a huge favor. At a time when it seemed uncertain that the Cardinals could ever play their way back into a national title chase, Strong proved it was indeed possible. He also proved that the program was in perfectly fine shape to answer the phone if a conference like the ACC came calling. These were all things that were far from guaranteed on the day Strong accepted the job.

94 Louisville's 1956 NIT Title

In 1956 the NCAA Tournament handed out one invitation per conference. Teams could finish at the top of the standings in some of the toughest conferences in the country, but if they had one bad night and got picked off in their league tournament, their chance to play for a national title was gone.

The biggest beneficiary of this already outdated philosophy was the National Invitational Tournament, which gladly scooped up the overwhelmingly successful teams that weren't able to serve as their conference's single representative in the NCAAs. That being the case, there were years when conference tournaments had been especially nutty, when the field of teams participating in the NIT was actually superior to the NCAA Tournament lineup.

This wasn't an issue for Louisville, which was smack in the middle of a 15-year period under Peck Hickman when the program wasn't affiliated with any conference. The 1955–56 Cardinals had gone 23–3 in the regular season and were ranked No. 6 in the country when tournament time rolled around. Believing that the

NIT possessed a superior group of teams that year and also wanting his team to play at Madison Square Garden, Hickman elected to accept a bid to the tournament when one was sent his way.

Even after notching double-digit victories against Duquesne (84–72) and St. Joseph's (89–79), Louisville walked into its NIT championship matchup against No. 3 Dayton as an underdog. Incredibly, despite having been narrowly beaten by U of L twice during the regular season, the Flyers had been deemed as the No. 1 seed in the NIT. They were also a team that was playing in the tournament's championship game for the fourth time in five years.

Playing in a game that millions watched on national television, Louisville scored what was at that time easily the biggest win in program history, claiming the NIT title with a 93–80 besting of Dayton. The star of stars was a predictable one, as Cardinals All-American Charlie Tyra led all scorers with 27 points. Following the game, he was honored as the tournament's MVP.

Ken Lolla and the Rise of Louisville Soccer

In addition to getting together with family, gearing up for the Louisville-Kentucky basketball game and watching the Cardinals football team play in a bowl game, a recent holiday tradition in the Derby City has become watching Ken Lolla's U of L men's soccer team chase a national title.

Under Lolla, the Louisville program has gone from one which had never qualified for an NCAA Tournament to one which played in the national championship game in 2010 and advanced to the Round of 16 in four of the six seasons after that. That level of success resulted in the idea for and the ultimate creation of Dr. Mark &

Cindy Lynn Stadium. The stadium was opened in 2014 and features chairback seating for 2,400 fans. The $18.5 million project features an overall seating capacity for more than 5,300 and also includes a 15,500–square-foot training center. "It is the best soccer stadium in the country," Lolla said at the stadium's opening. "We'll attract the best [players] and [expand our] fan base because of this. This will help in the development of the soccer community."

On August 29, 2014, Lolla's team officially opened Lynn Stadium with a 1–0 upset of second-ranked Maryland. The victory would prove to be a sign of things to come, as Louisville would go 10–6–1 against ranked foes during its first three seasons in games at its new stadium.

Under Coach Lolla's watch, Louisville has also been extremely successful when it comes to sending players into professional soccer, specifically Major League Soccer. Including the 2012 draft, Louisville has produced five first-round selections in the MLS SuperDraft, including Andrew Farrell as the No. 1 overall pick in 2013. The Cardinals have also had two or more selections in the first two rounds of the SuperDraft four times, and that was highlighted by a school-record four selections in 2012. Overall, 13 players from the University of Louisville have been chosen in the MLS SuperDraft since 2012.

Perhaps more impressive than any of the records or championships is the fact that Lolla has taken a team that the majority of people in the city of Louisville didn't know existed and turned it into one that regularly plays in front of crowds of several thousands. "Whenever we have big crowds, it's a massive advantage for us," Lolla said before his team's 2016 NCAA Tournament match against UCLA. "The energy and the positive atmosphere are a huge lift for our guys, and our best moments have always come when we've had good crowds. It's the best stadium in the NCAA, and to be able to showcase that on the national stage is awesome. More importantly, it's our home."

96 The Shot Heard 'Round the Commonwealth

Edgar Sosa's up-and-down four-year career frustrated both Louisville basketball fans and Rick Pitino to no end. Still, it was one of those ups on January 4, 2009, that solidified Sosa's spot as a rivalry immortal. After a bizarre sequence of events led Louisville to go from seemingly having a rivalry win against Kentucky in hand to in a tie game with just seconds to play, Sosa found himself with the ball in his hands and a chance to be a hero. Two years earlier, as a freshman, he had been a similar spot and came up empty. A pair of clanked free-throws and a missed three-pointer at the buzzer in U of L's second round NCAA Tournament loss to Texas A&M had haunted the enigmatic point guard ever since.

This time, the past didn't prevent Sosa from trying to play hero in another big-time situation. In fact, he didn't even want any help. When fellow guard Will Scott came over to lend a hand with a high screen, Sosa waved him off. With the clock dwindling closer and closer to zero, the U of L point guard squared Kentucky floor general Michael Porter and prepared to make his move—except when he started, he noticed that Porter was already on his heels. Instinctively, Sosa did what he'd always been taught to do in that situation: pull up. Only this time he was doing it from 26 feet deep and with the fate of the nation's most contentious rivalry hanging in the balance. "Man, he pulled up from deep," Porter said after the game. "I didn't think there was a chance in heck he'd make it. We knew he wasn't one of their better three-point shooters percentage-wise, but he's a good player. Good players make big shots."

Sosa made the biggest one. When his bomb ripped through the net with barely any time left on the clock, it was just the second field goal Louisville had made in the final 9:04 of a game it felt like it should have won by a much greater margin than a miracle three-pointer. If it had, though, then one of the rivalry's most iconic moments never would have taken place. "As the time has passed, I'm coming to realize how big that shot was," Sosa told *The Courier-Journal* in the days leading up to the next year's matchup against Kentucky. "Years from now, I think that shot's going to mean even more to me."

97 Sing Along to "My Old Kentucky Home"

You know they sing it before every Kentucky Derby, but the U of L band and cheerleaders also come together for a rendition after every Cardinals sporting event. Win or lose, you might as well sing along. Here is the modern version of the full lyrics to "My Old Kentucky Home," originally published in 1853 as "My Old Kentucky Home, Good-Night" and written by Stephen Collins Foster.

> *The sun shines bright in the old Kentucky home.*
> *'Tis summer, the people are gay,*
> *The corn top's ripe and the meadow's in the bloom*
> *While the birds make music all the day.*
>
> *The young folks roll on the little cabin floor,*
> *All merry, all happy, and bright.*
> *By 'n by hard times comes a-knocking at the door,*
> *Then my old Kentucky home, good night.*
>
> *(Chorus) Weep no more my lady,*
> *Oh, weep no more today!*

We will sing one song
For my old Kentucky home,
For the old Kentucky home far away.

They hunt no more for the 'possum and the coon,
On the meadow, the hill and the shore,
They sing no more by the glimmer of the moon,
On the bench by the old cabin door.

The day goes by like a shadow o'er the heart,
With sorrow where all was delight.
The time has come when the people have to part,
Then my old Kentucky home, good night!
(Chorus)

The head must bow and the back will have to bend,
Wherever the people may go.
A few more days and the trouble all will end,
In the field where the sugar-canes grow.

A few more days for to tote the weary load,
No matter 'twill never be light.
A few more days till we totter on the road,
Then my old Kentucky home, good-night!

(Chorus)

98 Preston Knowles and "Louisville First"

The 2010–11 Louisville Cardinals and their star guard are a combination destined to be increasingly overlooked as time passes. That's both a shame and a disservice to the history of the program. If Preston Knowles never came to U of L and if his senior team never dramatically overachieved, there is a very real chance that Rick Pitino would have called it a career in 2011, and the hugely successful seasons that followed would have never taken place.

In a day and age where everyone with an above-average ability to put a ball inside a hoop is reminded of how special they are at least a hundred thousand times before they graduate high school, Pitino is a harsh dose of reality. At some point in the middle of his tenure at Louisville, the man who redefined modern full-court pressure and who took advantage of the three-point shot like no one before him became old school. Pitino has never made any bones about the fact that if you were going to come play basketball for him, you were going to be broken down a bit. You were going to work harder than you were used to, you were going to be criticized more than you were used to, and perhaps most shockingly to an 18-year-old bedecked in Adidas garb, you were not going to play as often or score nearly as much as you're used to. Previous accolades and potential future earnings have zero bearing on these facts.

It's no a coincidence that Louisville's attrition rate during the Pitino era doesn't exactly sparkle. Many times a player arrived at U of L with high hopes of being the next Cardinals star only to decide months (or maybe years) later that all that wasn't for him. If he felt that way, more times than not Pitino was in agreement.

Though he came to Louisville as a two-star recruit with no other major scholarship offers, Knowles is not an exception to this rule. The native of Winchester, Kentucky, arrived at U of L hungry to prove himself worthy of a scholarship that many had criticized at the time it had been offered. He also arrived with a reputation for being volatile and difficult to coach. To the surprise of no one, Knowles often found himself in Pitino's doghouse early on in his Cardinals career. He was reprimanded for a pair of off-the-court incidents and consistently criticized for his decision-making on it.

Through it all, Knowles still managed to become a fan favorite. His dogged commitment to defense demanded court time despite the slew of talented upperclassmen on Louisville's roster. A high-rising jump shot that found the bottom of the net more consistently than any scout had predicted didn't hurt either.

Like a fraternity member applauding a successful pledge, Pitino likes to play up seniors who have successfully traversed the first few years of his boot camp. His criticisms of Knowles dissolved into statements like "I wish I could coach 12 Preston Knowles," and "Preston Knowles will never have senioritis. He truly plays for Louisville. He's not concerned about his future."

U of L fans and players alike took the turnabout in stride. It wasn't that the words of praise weren't genuine. It was just that Knowles' criticisms had been so obviously overblown. Knowles had always been a team-first guy, the one guy on the court who you always knew would give maximum effort every single possession.

With the last vestiges of his highly successful 2007–08 and 2008–09 teams gone and with a top five recruiting class waiting in the wings, Pitino tried to temper expectations for the team that would be sandwiched in between the two eras. He dubbed the season "a bridge year" at his preseason conference and warned that while fans would love the effort with which his team would play they might not love the win total at the end of the season.

Though Knowles had come a long way in a short time when it came to putting aside his stubbornness, this was one instance where he would again ignore words of his head coach. Rejecting the notion of a bridge year, Knowles seamlessly made the transition from career role player to unquestioned star. He led the team in scoring (14.6 points per game), ranked second in assists (3.1 assists per game), and was always the guy with the ball in his hands at the end of a close game. The star turn resulted in Louisville massively overachieving to the tune of 25 wins, a third-place finish in a Big East that sent a record 11 teams to the NCAA Tournament, and a runner-up finish in the league's postseason tournament.

It also resulted in Knowles becoming one of the more beloved Cardinals players in recent memory. Following a victory against Providence on his Senior Night, Knowles summed up his college motto after being asked if he would have liked to have scored more in his last game at the KFC Yum! Center. "As long as we win, I couldn't care less," Knowles said. "My average can go down to four points and zero rebounds. As long as we win, I don't care."

In the end, the unpredictably perfect season came to an unpredictably imperfect end. In the second half of Louisville's NCAA Tournament opener against Morehead State, Knowles broke his left foot. It was an injury that would delay his professional career by a year and also set the stage for the fourth-seeded Cardinals to be stunned on a three-pointer in the game's final seconds.

Although the injury, the lack of a postseason run, and the high level of success that came in the next two seasons may forever cloud what Knowles and the 2010–11 team were able to accomplish, there's one person who will never forget. "That Preston Knowles team really inspired me to keep coaching," Pitino said. "I had an offer to work in television at the time and I really thought that might be it for me in coaching. Those kids and the kids that came after them really reinvigorated me. They wanted to be coached.

And when that's the case, you can't wait to get to work in the morning."

In addition to keeping him from an early retirement, Knowles also provided Pitino with a teaching example he could use for the rest of his career: the two-star recruit who worked to become an All-Big East performer. The former problem child who put his ego aside for the betterment of the team and who inspired his teammates to do the same. The player who coined the motto of "Louisville First."

99 Attend a Louisville Baseball Game at Jim Patterson Stadium

Even if Louisville didn't field a baseball team that is perennially ranked among the nation's elite, catching one of their games at Jim Patterson Stadium during the spring would still be a worthwhile endeavor. The fact that the Cardinals are always one of the best teams in the country is certainly an added bonus.

Since Jim Patterson Stadium opened in 2005, it has provided the U of L baseball program with one of the best home-field advantages in college baseball. The stadium had an initial seating capacity of 2,500 before it underwent an expansion project prior to the 2013 season to increase its capacity to more than 4,000 while maintaining Jim Patterson Stadium as one of the nation's best college ballparks.

Before 2018 what had separated Jim Patterson from the homes of most of the country's other elite college baseball programs was that admission—with the exception of postseason play and one or two regular-season games—was free. That was the way the donor, Jim Patterson, initially intended the stadium to exist, and despite the program's rise to prominence, that was the way it remained for more than a decade.

Along with 3,000 chairback seats, Jim Patterson has a tiered turf berm in left field as well as additional bleachers to accommodate overflow seating. There is also a playground area behind the center field wall that's a perfect distraction for children of all ages who might need a bit more persistent stimulation than the game on the field can provide. The stadium also features a number of different promotions throughout the season, and typically provides dollar beers and dollar hot dogs for patrons who attend Friday night games.

In its first decade of existence, the stadium hosted six NCAA Regionals (2009, 2010, 2013, 2014, 2015, and 2016) and four NCAA Super Regionals (2007, 2014, 2015, and 2016).

100 Snow Days with Everyone's Favorite Walk-On

Whenever Louisville is crippled by a sudden accumulation of snow in the months of January or February, my mind immediately shifts to 1998 and the greatest snow day I ever experienced.

I was a "shoot first, shoot second, pass third" guard on a seventh grade basketball team that had just begun what would eventually become a run to the city championship game. Every practice counted at this most paramount of times, which meant my 13-year-old brothers and I couldn't allow the mere cancellation of school to keep us off the court. There was just one problem. The snow day had also postponed the science fair (no, I wouldn't place), which meant all the tables littered with trifold poster board would have to remain untouched in the school gym. We were actors without a stage, men without a country, city-runners-up-to-be without a gym.

Thankfully, reprieve came in the form of a team dad who happened to work at the University of Louisville. He told us we could use the Cardinals basketball team's practice gym later that day. At this point in my life, I had only attended a handful of games inside Freedom Hall, so being on the Louisville campus, walking into the team facility, and seeing all the framed pictures and banners was almost certainly more special than I could detail here.

We were the only ones using the gym, which made us all (regardless of red vs. blue rooting interests) feel like a big-time college basketball team for that fleeting hour. We bricked layups on goals offset by the Final Four banners behind them. We excitedly threw the ball away when trapped near midcourt on top of the Cardinals logo. We airballed three-pointers from the same spot that DeJuan Wheat had probably sunk a thousand of them. It was magical.

We had been at it for about 45 minutes or so when a figure, who just about every kid my age in the city of Louisville could recognize, walked into the building. It was Troy Jackson, the 400-pound younger brother of NBA player Mark Jackson. Troy was in his second season with the Cardinals. Despite the fact that he rarely saw the court, Jackson's size, infectious personality, and affinity for theatrics whenever he did get into a game had made him a fan favorite from the day he arrived on campus.

Practice stopped when the big man walked into the gym, and only a shrill whistle blow and some shouts of encouragement could snap us out of the daze. Jackson began to run laps around the gym while we all pretended like we didn't notice and weren't trying to impress him. A short while later, Jackson opted to cut his workout short in favor of seeing if he could get some runs in with us. While there wasn't a 13-year-old on the squad with the inside presence necessary to deal with this type of pickup, we all decided it was okay.

Jackson scrimmaged with us for a few minutes, and it was wonderful. At one point I attempted to wow him with my trademark move of the period: a completely unnecessary NBA-style three-pointer with no defender in my general area. It missed badly, and Jackson corralled the rebound himself, which was cool enough.

Our allotted time in the gym came to a crushing end, and Jackson parted ways by imploring all of us to make it out to the game the next day and support the squad. It was his last season at Louisville, but Jackson would go on to make a name for himself in the basketball world through the AND1 Mixtape Tour, where he performed under the name "Escalade" from 2002 until his untimely death in 2011. He was only 38.

The next day Louisville would lose at home to South Florida, another brutal defeat in a dismal season, in which the Cardinals would experience 20 of them. Still, the clearest memory I took away from that season wasn't one of the many negatives; it was the unbridled joy of playing basketball on a snow day against an actual Cardinals basketball player inside the actual Cardinals practice gym. A larger-than-life experience with a larger-than-life man inside a larger-than-life place.

Acknowledgments

Ten years ago a bored college kid opened up a blogger account and started writing words about Louisville sports because he thought it might be a fun way to pass the time. I never imagined at that time that such a simple act might result in a brand new career path and, eventually, a real book with my name on the front cover. There are far too many people to thank for the sequence of events that has led me from that point to this one, but a handful demand special mention here.

I am eternally grateful to Jeff Fedotin, Josh Williams, Adam Motin, and everyone else at Triumph Books for thinking of me for this project and giving me the opportunity to try and write a book for the first time. I am even more grateful for the unflinching patience they exhibited in the months that transpired after they initially reached out.

Everyone within the University of Louisville athletic department has been so helpful both during the writing of this book and throughout my time covering the Cardinals. A special thanks to athletic director Tom Jurich and SID Kenny Klein for their continued support and their perpetually open door.

It is an honor to have Hall of Fame head coach Rick Pitino write the foreword for this book. I spent far too much of my childhood daydreaming about what it might be like to watch Louisville recapture its former glory and play in the Final Four and win a national title. He made those dreams of mine and an entire generation of Cardinals fans become a reality. I've never expressed my gratitude for that to him personally, so I'll do it here. Thank you.

These words would not have been published without the efforts of all those who read and responded to my work on Card

Chronicle, SB Nation, and wherever else they have appeared over the years. All of you who followed the silly but unforgettable sagas of Chicken Knowles, Bryce Cotton, and everything else, you guys made this happen.

A lot of people think they have the best friends and family in the world. I am one of them.

Thank you to my parents, who have never wavered in their support of anything and everything I have ever attempted to do. To my sister and my brothers who are always available for conversation and who made every stage of growing up so fun. To my grandmother, who I think has been the biggest fan of my writing since before I could even hold a pencil. To all my aunts, uncles, in-laws, and nephews for their encouragement over the years. Even my nephew Charlie, who brutally told me that he liked NPR more than my radio show when he was only eight years old. And to my friends, especially the "U of L Guys" text group, for always being around to bounce ideas off of or to share a laugh with.

Lastly, thank you to my wife, Mary. Your love and support are the best and most treasured gifts I have ever received. If you hadn't stepped up and been an absolute star when this opportunity presented itself, then there is quite literally no way this could have happened. I love you always.

Sources

Books

Einhorn, Eddie. *How March Became Madness: How the NCAA Tournament Became the Greatest Sporting Event in America.* Chicago: Triumph Books, 2006.

Hager, Tom. *The Ultimate Book of March Madness: The Players, Games, and Cinderellas that Captured a Nation.* Minneapolis: MVP Books, 2012.

Sahadi, Lou. *Johnny Unitas: America's Quarterback.* Chicago: Triumph Books, 2004.

Terhune, Jim. *Tales from the 1980 Louisville Cardinals.* Champaign: Sports Publishing L.L.C., 2004.

Thompson, Darcy et al. *I Said Bang! A History of the Dirt Bowl, the Crown Jewel of the Most Basketball-Obsessed City in America.* Louisville: Louisville Story Program, 2016.

Towle, Mike. *Johnny Unitas: Mr. Quarterback.* Nashville: Cumberland House Publishing, 2003.

Newspapers

Chicago Tribune
The Kansas City Star
Lexington Herald-Leader
Los Angeles Daily News
Los Angeles Times
The Louisville Cardinal
The Louisville Courier-Journal
Louisville Eccentric Observer (L.E.O.)
The New York Times
New York Daily News
The Oklahoman

The Tampa Tribune
USA TODAY
The Washington Post

Magazines
Louisville Magazine
Sports Illustrated
The Sporting News
Time

Websites
CardChronicle.com
CBSSports.com
TheCrunchZone.com
CSTV.com
ESPN.com
GoCards.com
Louisville.edu
ThePlayersTribune.com
UofLCardGame.com
WindyCityGridiron.com
Yahoo.com

Personal Interviews
Tom Jurich
Rick Pitino
Denny Crum
Bobby Petrino
Howard Schnellenberger
Jeff Walz
Darrell Griffith
Wiley Brown
Chris Redman

Robbie Valentine
Milt Wagner
Paul Rogers
Terry Meiners
John Ramsey
Marques Maybin
Robby Wine
Eric Wood

Miscellaneous
The Associated Press
Basketball and Beyond SiriusXM Radio
Louisville Basketball Media Guide, 2016–17
Louisville Football Media Guide, 2016
Phi Slama Jama ESPN 30 for 30
Year of the Cardinal ESPN special
The Rivalry: Red v. Blue